AMBEDKAR
As Critic of Hindu Religion

Ambedkar
As critic of Hindu Religion

Lalit K. Sahay

MOHIT PUBLICATIONS
New Delhi - 110002 (India)

Published 2020

ISBN : 978-81-7445-527-7

Published by :
MOHIT PUBLICATIONS
4675/21, Ansari Road, Daryaganj-110002
Phone : 23255141; Fax. : 23284126

PRINTED IN INDIA

Published by Sangita Goel for Mohit Publications, New Delhi-02, Typeset by Abhijeet Typesetters and Printed at Nav Prabhat Printing Press Delhi.

Preface

What is the Hinduism? This is a question which arises in its logical sequence. But apart from its logical sequence its importance is such that it can never be omitted from consideration. Without it no one can understand the aims and ideals of Hinduism. It is obvious that such a study must be preceded by a certain amount of what may be called clearing of the ground and defining of the terms involved. At the outset it may be asked what does this proposed title comprehend? Is this title of the Philosophy of Hinduism of the same nature as that of the Philosophy of Religion? One does not have a clear idea of what is meant by Philosophy of Religion. This is probably due to two facts. In the first place while religion is something definite, there is nothing definite as to what is to be included in the term philosophy. In the second place Philosophy and Religion have been adversaries if not actual antagonists as may be seen from the story of the philosopher and the theologian. According to the story, the two were engaged in disputation and the theologian accused the philosopher that he was "like a blind man in a dark room, looking for a black cat which was not there". In reply the philosopher charged the theologian saying that "he was like a blind man in the dark room, looking for a black cat which was not there but he declared to have found there".

India's Constitution does not give a definition of the term Hindu, but it does define to whom the "Hindu Law" applies. It has to do this because in spite of its pretence to secularism, the Indian Constitution allows Muslims, Christians and Parsis a separate Personal Law. In a way, this separate treatment of different communities merely continues the communal autonomy of castes and sects accepted in pre-modern Hindu states, but it exposes the credibility deficit of Indian secularism. Dr. Bhimrao Ambedkar first introduced the Hindu Code Bill in 1951, Sikh spokesman Sardar Hukum Singh regarded the Bill as "a dubious attempt on the part of the Hindus to absorb the Sikhs". Dr. Ambedkar replied: "The application of the Hindu Code to Sikhs, Buddhists and Jains was a historical development and it would be too late, sociologically, to object to it. When the Buddha differed from the Vedic Brahmins, he did so only in matters of creed, but left the Hindu legal framework intact. He did not propound a separate law for his followers. The same was the case with Mahavir and the ten Sikh gurus. The Privy Council had as early as 1830 laid down that the Sikhs were governed by the Hindu law."

Inequality is the soul of Hinduism. The morality of Hinduism is only social. It is unmoral and inhuman to say the least. What is unmoral and inhuman easily becomes immoral, inhuman and infamous. This is what Hinduism has become. Those who doubt this or deny this proposition should examine the social composition of the Hindu Society and ponder over the condition of some of the elements in it. Among the Hindu social reformers there is a moderate section. This section holds that untouchability is separate from the caste system. Following this ideology they hold that it is possible to remove untouchability without attacking the caste system.

—*Author*

Contents

1 Introduction to Hinduism

INTRODUCTION

Hinduism, commonly called Sanatana Dharma by Hindus, is the oldest major world religion still practised today and first among Dharma faiths. Hinduism is characterized by a diverse array of belief systems, practices and scriptures. It has its origin in ancient Vedic culture at least as far back as 2000 BC. It is the third largest religion with approximately 890 million followers worldwide, 96% of whom live in the Indian subcontinent. Perhaps the Hindu spirit, inspired by no one man or woman in particular, is best captured in a line from the ancient Rig Veda, the "oldest religious scripture in the world.":

"Truth is One, though the Sages know it as Many." The Rig Veda (Book I, Hymn CLXIV, Verse 46)

Essentially, any kind of spiritual practice followed with faith, love and persistence will lead to the same ultimate state of self-realization. Thus, Hindu thought distinguishes itself by strongly encouraging tolerance for different beliefs since temporal systems cannot claim sole understanding of the one transcendental Truth. To the Hindu, this idea has been an active force in defining the 'Eternal Dharma.' It has been for Hinduism what the infinite Divine Self of Advaita is to existence, remaining forever unchanged and self-luminous, central and pervasive, in spite of all the chaos and flux around it. In general, Hindu views are broad and range from monism, dualism, pantheism, panentheism, alternatively called monistic theism by some scholars, and strict monotheism, but are not polytheistic as outsiders perceive the religion to be. Hinduism has often been confused to be polytheistic as many of

Hinduism's adherents are monists, and view multiple manifestations of the one God or source of being.

Hindu monists see one unity, with the personal Gods, different aspects of only One Supreme Being, like a single beam of light separated into colours by a prism, and are valid to worship. Some of the Hindu aspects of God include Devi, Vishnu, Ganesha, and Shiva. One of the most prominent Hindu monists is the great saint, Ramakrishna whose preferred form of God is Devi and reiterated traditional Hindu beliefs, that aver devotees can invoke God, in whatever form a devotee prefers, (or as monists prefer to call, Ishta Devata, *i.e.*, the preferred form of God) and ask for God's grace in order to attain Moksha, end of the cycle of rebirth. However, like Judaeo-Christian religions which believe in angels, Hindus also believe in less powerful entities, such as devas. Contemporary Hinduism is now divided into four major divisions:

- Vaishnavism,
- Shaivism,
- Shaktism,
- and Smartism.

Just as Jews, Christians, and Muslims all believe in the same one God but differ in their conceptions of Him, Hindus all believe in one God but differ in their conceptions. The two primary form of differences are between the two monotheistic religions of Vaishnavism which conceives God as Vishnu and Shaivism, which conceives God as Shiva. Other minor forms are aspects of Vishnu or Shiva.

A BRIEF OVERVIEW

Hinduism rests on the spiritual bedrock of the Vedas, hence Veda Dharma, and their mystic issue, the Upanishads, as well as the teachings of many great Hindu gurus through the ages. Many streams of thought flow from the six Vedic/Hindu schools, Bhakti sects and Tantra Agamic schools into the one ocean of Hinduism, the first of the Dharma religions. The great debate between followers among the major Hindu philosophical school, Vedanta, from followers of Advaita philosophy on one hand and the strict theistic schools such as those of Ramanuja and Madhva on the other, focused on the true nature of Brahman, on whether Brahman was essentially attributeless or with attributes, *i.e.*, a personal Supreme Being.

The Eternal Way

"The Eternal Way", or the "Perennial Philosophy/Harmony/Faith", is the one name that has represented Hinduism for many thousands of years. According to Hindus, it speaks to the idea that certain spiritual principles hold eternally true, transcending man-made constructs, representing a pure science of consciousness. But this consciousness is not merely that of the body or mind and intellect, but of a supramental soul-state that exists within and beyond our existence, the unsullied Self of all. Religion to the Hindu is the native search for the divine within the Self, the search to find the One truth that in actuality never was lost. Truth sought with faith shall yield itself in blissful luminescence no matter the race or creed professed. Indeed, all existence, from vegetation and beasts to mankind, are subjects and objects of the eternal Dharma.

This inherent faith, therefore, is also known as Arya/Noble Dharma, Veda/Knowledge Dharma, Yoga/Union Dharma, Hindu Dharma or, simply, the Dharma. What can be said to be common to all Hindus is belief in Dharma, reincarnation, karma, and moksha (liberation) of every soul through a variety of moral, action-based, and meditative yogas. Still more fundamental principles include ahimsa (non-violence), the primacy of the Guru, the Divine Word of Aum and the power of mantras, love of Truth in many manifestations as Gods and Goddessess, and an understanding that the essential spark of the Divine (Atman/Brahman) is in every human and living being, thus allowing for many spiritual paths leading to the One Unitary Truth. An example of the pervasiveness of this paramount truth-seeking spirituality in daily life is the bindi (seen left), which is a common marker for Hindu women. It symbolizes the need to cultivate supramental consciousness, which is achieved by opening the mystic "third eye."

Hindus across the board stress meditative insight, an intuition beyond the mind and body, a trait that is often associated with the ascetic god Shiva. Men, too, will bear on their foreheads the equivalent tilak mark, usually on religious occasions, its shape often representing particular devotion to a certain main deity: a 'U' shape stands for Vishnu, a group of three horizantal lines for Shiva. It is not uncommon for some to meld both in an amalgam marker signifying Hari-Hara (Vishnu-Shiva indissoluble).

The Four Major Sects of Hinduism

Contemporary Hinduism is traditionally divided into four major divisions: Shaivism, Shaktism, Vaishnavism, and Smartism. Hinduism is a very rich and complex religion. Each of its four sects shares rituals, beliefs, traditions and gods with one another, but each sect has a different philosophy on how to achieve life's ultimate goal (moksha, liberation) and on their views of the Gods. Each sect fundamentally believes in different methods of self-realization and in different aspects of the One Supreme God. However, each sect respects and accepts all others, and conflict of any kind is rare. Some sects of Hinduism believe in a monotheistic ideal of Vishnu (often as Krishna), Shiva, or Devi; this view does not exclude other gods, as they are understood to be aspects of the chosen ideal (*e.g.*, to many devotees of Krishna, Shiva is seen as having sprung from Krishna's creative force). Often, the monad Brahman is seen as the one source, with all other gods emanating therefrom. Thus, with all Hindus, there is a strong belief in all paths being true religions that lead to one God or source, whatever one chooses to call the ultimate truth.

Shaktism

Shaktism is a denomination of Hinduism that worships Shakti, the Divine Mother, in all of her forms whilst not rejecting the importance of masculine and neuter divinity. Shaktism as we know it today developed between the 4th and the 7th centuries CE in India. It was during this development that the many religious texts, known as the Tantras, were written. One may consider themselves a Shakta (a devotee of Shakti), a Shaiva (a devotee of Shiva), and a Vaishnava (a devotee of Vishnu) all at the same time. This form of Hinduism, known as is strongly associated with Vedanta, Samkhya and Tantra Hindu philosophies and is ultimately monist, though there is a rich tradition of Bhakti yoga associated with it.

The feminine energy (Shakti) is considered to be the motive force behind all action and existence in the phenomenal cosmos in Hinduism. The cosmos itself is Brahman, the concept of the unchanging, infinite, immanent and transcendent reality that is the Divine Ground of all being, the "world soul". Masculine potentiality is actualized by feminine dynamism, embodied in multitudinous goddesses who are ultimately reconciled in one. The keystone text is the Devi Mahatmya which combines earlier Vedic theologies, emergent Upanishadic philosophies and developing tantric cultures in a laudatory exegesis of Shakti religion. Demons of ego, ignorance and desire bind the soul in maya (illusion) (also alternately ethereal or embodied) and it is Mother Maya, shakti, herself, who can free the bonded individual. The immanent Mother, Devi, is for this reason focused on with intensity, love, and self-dissolving concentration in an effort to focus the shakta (as a Shakti worshipper is sometimes known) on the true reality underlying time, space and causation, thus freeing one from karmic cyclism. A common hymn describing the 1000 names of Devi is the Lalitha sahasranama.

Shaivism

Also known as Shaivism, Shaivism is a branch of Hinduism that worships Shiva as the Supreme God. Followers of Shaivism are called Shaivites. Shaivism is a monotheistic faith. Shaivites believe that there is only one God, who simultaneously permeates all creation and exists beyond it, being both immanent and transcendent. The concept is in contrast with many Semitic religious traditions, where God is seen as transcendent only. As all other Hindu denominations, Shaivism acknowledges the existence of many lower Gods under the Supreme One. These Gods are encompassed by Him, seen as either as manifestations of the Supreme Being or as powerful entities who are permeated by Him, as is all Creation. This type of Monotheism is called Panentheism or Monistic Theism. Shaivism is a very deep, devotional and mystical sect of Hinduism.

It is considered the oldest of the Hindu denominations, with a long lineage of sages and saints who have outlaid practices and paths aimed at self-realization and the ultimate goal of moksha, liberation. As a very broad religion, Shaivism encompasses philosophical systems, devotional rituals, legends, mysticism and varied yogic practices. It has both monistic and dualistic traditions. Shaivites believe God transcends form, and devotees often worship Shiva in the form of a lingam, symbolizing all universe. God Shiva is also revered in Shaivism as the anthropomorphic manifestation of Shiva Nataraja. Originated in India, Shaivism has appeal all over India and is particularly strong in South India (especially, Tamil Nadu) and the island of Sri Lanka.

Some traditions credit the spreading of Shaivism into southern India by the great sage, Agastya, who is said to brought Vedic traditions as well as the Tamil language. There can be found almost innumerable Saivite temples and shrines, with many shrines accompanied as well by murtis dedicated to Ganesha, Lord of the Ganas, followers of Shiva, and son of Shiva and Shakti. Benares is considered the holiest city of all Hindus and Shaivites. A very revered Saivite temple is the ancient Chidambaram, in South India. One of the most famous hymns to Shiva in the Vedas is Shri Rudram. The foremost Saivite Vedic Mantra is Aum Namah Shivaya. Major theological schools of Shaivism include Kashmir Shaivism, Shaiva Siddhanta and Virashaivism.

Smartism

Smartism is a denomination of the religion of Hinduism and is closely affiliated with the Advaita tradition. Smartism is monist in theological belief. Smartas (followers of Smartism) accept and worship all major forms of God, (Ganesha, Shiva, Shakti, Vishnu, Surya and Skanda). Following a meditative, philosophical path, the denomination is generally considered to be liberal and non-sectarian. In Smartism, devotees pray to whatever form of God a devotee prefers, (or as monists prefer to call, Ishta Devata, *i.e.,* the preferred form of God) and ask for God's grace in order to achieve Moksha, end of the cycle of rebirth.

Notably, Shakti is worshipped to reach Shiva, whom for Shaktas is the impersonal Absolute. Additionally, Shaivites and Vaishnavites often regard Surya as an aspect of Shiva and Vishnu, respectively. For example, the sun is called Surya Narayana by Vaishnavites. In Saivite theology, the sun is said to be one of eight forms of Shiva, the Astamurti. Additionally, Ganesha and Skanda for them, would be aspects of Shiva and Shakti. Hence, it appears to be the case that most Hindus worship Saguna Brahman as Vishnu or Shiva.

Vaishnavism

Vaishnavism is the branch of Hinduism in which Vishnu or one of his avatars (*i.e.*, incarnations) is worshipped as the supreme God and is a monotheistic faith. Major branches of Vaishnavism include Srivaishnavism, (espoused by Ramanuja) who advocated Vishishtadvaita, Dvaita (espoused by Shri Madhvacharya) and Gaudiya Vaishnavism (espoused by Shri Chaitanya Mahaprabhu adhered by ISKCON).

The distinction between this branch and others is made by those who study religion. However it may not always be clear to practising Hindus who often take freely from the practices of the different branches. It is likely that a majority (75-80%) of today's Hindus would consider themselves Vaishnava, if pressed to make a distinction. Of the remainder, most would probably consider themselves Shaivites. Vishnu and Shiva are sometimes visualized as a single divinity named Harihara.

Hinduism Origins, Nomenclature and Society

In a 1966 ruling, the Supreme Court of India defined the Hindu faith as follows for legal purposes:

- Acceptance by all systems of Hindu philosophy of the belief in rebirth and pre-existence.
- Spirit of tolerance and willingness to understand and appreciate the opponent's point of view based on the realization that truth is manysided.
- Acceptance of the Vedas with reverence as the highest authority in religious and philosophic matters and acceptance with reverence of Vedas by Hindu thinkers and philosophers as the sole foundation of Hindu philosophy.
- Acceptance of great world rhythm—vast periods of creation, maintenance and dissolution follow each other in endless succession—by all six systems of Hindu philosophy.

- Recognition of the fact that the means or ways to salvation are many.
- Realization of the truth that numbers of Gods to be worshipped may be large, yet there are Hindus who do not believe in the worshipping of idols.

DHARMA IN ORTHODOX HINDU CASTE SOCIETY

According to one view, the Caste system shows how strongly many have felt about each person following his or her dharma, or destined path. A perversion, according to many Hindus, of dharma's true meaning, caste still plays a significant role in Hindu society; however, post Independence, caste is rapidly losing favour in India and caste-based discrimination has been illegitimised. The British Raj and the subsequent governments have used the caste based politics effectively to divide and conquer for their own personal political gains.

The Vedas do not condone discrimination of any sort. The four 'varna's (literally, 'colour') or castes, were based upon the duties to society and worked together towards the welfare of the society. They had equal standing in the society. However over a period of time this division of labour was misunderstood and exploited. This became more ingrained over centuries until social mobility all but became a thing of the past. In spite of centuries of numerous reform movements, notably within Vedanta, bhakti yoga and Hindu streams of Tantra, and reformers, with recent stalwarts like Swami Vivekananda and Mahatma Gandhi, caste is so deeply ensconced in the Indian consciousness that even Christian converts have been known to separate church meetings for different castes. A number of Muslim communities have retained caste practices as well. What was first an injunction to living one's dharma in surrender to God became an oppressive mandate to surrender to Man. See caste for more.

THE SIX VEDIC SCHOOLS OF THOUGHT

Six Schools: The six Astika or orthodox (accepting the authority of the Vedas) schools of Hindu philosophy are Nyaya, Vaisheshika, Samkhya, Yoga, Purva Mimamsa (also called just 'Mimamsa'), and Uttara Mimamsa (also called 'Vedanta'). The non-Vedic schools are called Nastika, or heterodox, and refer to Buddhism, Jainism and Lokayata. The schools that continue to affect Hinduism today are Purva Mimamsa, Yoga, and Vedanta. See Hindu philosophy for a discussion of the historical significance of Samkhya, Nyaya, and Vaisheshika.

Purva Mimamsa: The main objective of the Purva ("earlier") Mimamsa school was to establish the authority of the Vedas. Consequently this school's most valuable contribution to Hinduism was its formulation of the rules of Vedic interpretation. Its adherents believed that revelation must be proved by reasoning, that it should not be accepted blindly as dogma. This empirical and eminently sensible manner of religious application is key to the Sanatana/Hindu Dharma and was especially championed by rationalists like Adi Shankara and Swami Vivekananda. For greater depth, please see Purva Mimamsa.

Yoga: Sadhus (Hindu ascetic) are often seen meditating in padmasana (lotus pose). The Yoga system is generally considered to have arisen from the Samkhya philosophy. The yoga referred to here, however, is specifically Raja Yoga (or meditational union). It is based on the sage Patanjali's extremely influential text entitled the Yoga Sutra, which is essentially a compilation and systematization of meditational Yoga philosophy that came before. Upanishads and Bhagwad Gita are also indispensable literature in the study of Yoga. The most significant difference from Samkhya is that the Yoga school not only incorporates the concept of Ishvara (a personal God) into its metaphysical worldview but also that it holds Ishvara as the ideal upon which to meditate. This is because Ishvara is the only aspect of purusha (the infinite Divine Ground) that has not become entangled with prakrti (the temporal creative forces). It also utilizes the Brahman/Atman terminology and concepts that are found in depth in the Upanishads, adopting Vedantic monist concepts. Realization of the goal of Yoga is known as moksha or samadhi. It, like the Upanishads, seeks realization of the Atman as being nothing other than the infinite Brahman through ethical (mind), physical (body) and meditational (soul) practices of one-pointedness on the 'one supreme truth.'

Uttara Mimamsa: The Three Schools of Vedanta: The Uttara ("later") Mimamsa school is perhaps one of the cornerstone movements of Hinduism and certainly was responsible for a new wave of philosophical and meditative inquiry, renewal of faith, and cultural reform. Primarily associated with the Upanishads and their commentary by Badarayana, the Vedanta Sutras, Vedanta thought split into three groups, initiated by the thinking and writing of Adi Shankara. Most Hindu thought today in some way relates to changes affected by Vedantic thought, which focused on meditation, morality and centeredness on the one Self rather than on rituals and societal distinctions like caste. The great debate between followers among the major Hindu philosophical school, Vedanta, from followers of Advaita philosophy on one hand and the strict theistic schools such as those of Ramanuja and Madhva on the other, focused on the true nature of Brahman, on whether Brahman was essentially attributeless or with attributes, *i.e.*, a personal Supreme Being.

PURE MONISM: ADVAITA

Advaita literally means "not two"; thus this is what we refer to as a monistic (or non-dualistic) system, which emphasises oneness. Its consolidator was Shankara (788?-820?). Shankara expounded his theories largely based on previous teachings of the Upanishads and his own guru Govinda Bhagwadpada. By analysis of experiential consciousness, he exposed the relative nature of the world and established the non-dual reality of Brahman in which Atman (the individual soul) and Brahman (the ultimate reality) are identified absolutely. It is not merely philosophy, but a conscious system of applied ethics and meditation, all geared towards attaining peace and understanding of truth. Adi Shankara denounced caste and meaningless ritual as foolish, and in his own charismatic manner, exhorted the true devotee to meditate on God's love and apprehend truth. To Advaitists (nondualists) Ultimate Truth is best expressed as Nirguna Brahman, or God without form, or God without personal attributes; indeed, some might go so far as to say it is not 'God' but something beyond.

However, even that definition can be limiting. Nirguna Brahman can never be described as that as It transcends all definitions. All personal forms of God such as Vishnu or Shiva are different aspects of God in personal form or God with attributes,

Saguna Brahman. God's energy is personified as Devi, the Divine Mother. For Vaishnvaites who follow Ramanuja's philosophy, Devi is Lakshmi, who is the Mother of all and who pleads with Vishnu for mankind who is entrenched in sin. For Shaivites, Devi is Parvati. For Shaktas, who worship Devi, Devi is the personal form of God to attain the impersonal Absolute, God, *i.e.*, Shiva. For them, Shiva is personified as God without attributes.

QUALIFIED MONISM: VISHISTADVAITA

Ramanuja (1040-1137) was the foremost proponent of the concept of Sriman Narayana as the supreme Brahman. He taught that Ultimate reality had three aspects: Isvara (Vishnu), chit (soul) and achit (matter). Vishnu is the only independent reality, while souls and matter are dependent on God for their existence. Because of this qualification of Ultimate reality, Ramanuja's system is known as qualified non-dualism.

Tantrism

According tŏ the most famous Western Tantrik scholar, Sir John Woodroffe (pseudonym Arthur Avalon): "The Indian Tantras, which are numerous, constitute the Scripture (Shastra) of the Kaliyuga, and as such are the voluminous source of present and practical orthodox 'Hinduism'. The Tantra Shastra is, in fact, and whatever be its historical origin, a development of the Vaidika Karmakanda, promulgated to meet the needs of that age. Shiva says: 'For the benefit of men of the Kali age, men bereft of energy and dependent for existence on the food they eat, the Kaula doctrine, O auspicious one! is given'. To the Tantra we must therefore look if we would understand aright both ritual, yoga, and sadhana of all kinds, as also the general principles of which these practices are but the objective expression." The word "tantra" means "treatise" or "continuum", and is applied to a variety of mystical, occult, medical and scientific works as well as to those which we would now regard as "tantric". Most tantras were written in the late middle ages and sprang from Hindu cosmology and Yoga.

Origins: The earliest evidence for certain (minor) elements of Hinduism date back as far as the late neolithic to the early Harappan period (ca. 5500–2600 BC). The beliefs and practices of the pre-classical era (ca. 1500-500 BC) are called the "Vedic religion". The oldest text of Hinduism is the Rigveda, which is dated to between 1700–1100 BC based on linguistic and philological evidence.

Dualism: Dvaita

Like Ramanuja, Madhva (1199-1278) identified God with Vishnu, but his view of reality was purely dualistic in that he understood a fundamental differentiation between the ultimate Godhead and the individual soul, and the system is therefore called Dvaita (dualistic) Vedanta.

Alternative Cultures of Worship

The Bhakti schools-The Bhakti (Devotional) school takes its name from the Hindu term that signifies a blissful, selfless and overwhelming love of God as the beloved Father, Mother, Child, or whatever relationship finds appeal in the devotee's heart. The philosophy of Bhakti seeks to tap into the universal divinity through personal form, which explains the proliferation of so many Gods and Goddesses in India, often reflecting the singular inclinations of small regions or groups of people. Seen as a form of Yoga, or union, it seeks to dissolve the ego in God, since consciousness of the body and limited mind as self is seen to be a divisive factor in spiritual realization. Essentially, it is God who effects all change, who is the source of all works, who acts through the devotee as love and light. 'Sins' and evildoings of the devotee are said to fall away of their own accord, the devotee shriven, limitedness even transcended, through the love of God. The Bhakti movements rejuvenated Hinduism through their intense expression of faith and their responsiveness to the emotional and philosophical needs of India.

They can rightly be said to have affected the greatest wave of change in Hindu prayer and ritual since ancient times. The most popular means of expressing love for God in the Hindu tradition has been through puja, or ritual devotion, frequently using the aid of a murti (statue) in conjunction with the singing or chanting of meditational prayer in the form of mantras. Devotional songs called bhajans (written primarily from the 14th-17th centuries), kirtan (praise), and arti (a filtered down form of

Vedic fire ritual) are sometimes sung in conjunction with performance of puja. This rather organic system of devotion attempts to aid the individual in connecting with God through symbolic medium.

It is said, however, that the bhakta, through a growing connection with God, is eventually able to eschew all external form and is immersed entirely in the bliss of undifferentiated Love in Truth. Shri Ganesha is the son of Shiva and Parvati; beloved by many Hindus, he is widely worshipped as Vignesh, the remover of obstacles. Altogether, bhakti resulted in a mass of devotional literature, music and art that has enriched the world and given India renewed spiritual impetus, one eschewing unnecessary ritual and artificial social boundaries.

The Age of Mahajanapadas

During the Iron Age in India, several schools of thought arose and developed in Hindu philosophy including Samkhya, Yoga, Nyaya, Vaisheshika, Purva-Mimamsa and Vedanta. Three key revolutions underpinned the nascence of a new epoch in Hindu thought. These were the spiritual upheaval initiated by the Upanishads, and the arrival of Mahavira (founder of Jainism) and the Buddha (founder of Buddhism). Charvaka, the leader of an atheistic materialist school, also came to the fore in North India in the sixth century BC. The Upanishads, Mahavira and Buddha taught that to achieve moksha or nirvana, one did not have to accept the authority of the Vedas or the caste system; the Buddha went a step further and claimed that the existence of a Self/soul or God was unnecessary. In this intellectual ferment, many Hindus became Buddhists and Jains while others were influenced by their teachings. The arrival of new philosophies substantially changed the religion during the Maurya and Gupta periods.

Islam and Bhakti

From the last twelfth century successive waves of armies from Muslim kingdoms invaded and to varying degrees, gained control over North India. During this period Buddhism declined rapidly, and many Hindus converted to Islam. Some Muslim rulers such as Aurangzeb destroyed Hindu temples and otherwise persecuted non-Muslims, while others, such as Akbar, were more tolerant.

Hinduism underwent profound changes due in large part to the influence of the prominent teachers Ramanuja, Madhva, and Chaitanya. Followers of the Bhakti movement moved away from the abstract concept of Brahman, which the philosopher Adi Shankara consolidated a few centuries before, to a focus on the more accessible avataras, especially Krishna and Rama. A new attitude toward God—emotional, passionate love—replaced the old approaches of sacrificial rite and meditation on the formless Brahman.

Epic and Puranic Periods

The epic poems Ramayana and Mahabharata were composed roughly from 400 BC to 200 CE but were transmitted orally for hundreds of years prior to this period. The Ramayana and Mahabharata contain secular and mythological stories of the rulers and wars of ancient India as well as on the avatars Rama and Krishna respectively. They are interspersed with treatises on various Hindu philosophical concepts. These include the nature of the atma, karma, dharma, moksha, and the organisation of society and government. The later Puranas recount tales about devas and devis, their interactions with humans and their battles against demons.

Indology and Reform Movements

The 19th and 20th centuries saw an unprecedented interaction between Hindu and European thought (in the form of Abrahamic religions and Western Philosophy). This intercultural correspondence catalyzed developments in Indology, formations of new schools of Hindu thought, the global spread of Hinduism and changes within Hindu society. Meanwhile, traditional systems of Hinduism witnessed revivals and new developments that flourished independently. Indology as an academic discipline of studying Indian culture from a European perspective was established in the 19th century, led by Max Muller and John Woodroffe. They brought much of the Vedic, Puranic and Tantric literature and philosophy to Europe and the United States.

At the same time, societies such as the Brahmo Samaj and the Theosophical Society attempted to reconcile and fuse Abrahamic and Dharmic philosophies, endeavouring to institute societal reform. This period also saw the emergence of movements which, while sometimes highly innovative, were rooted in indigenous tradition, sometimes based on the personalities and teachings of individuals, as with Shri Ramakrishna and Ramana Maharshi. Prominent Hindu philosophers, including Sri Aurobindo and Swami Prabhupada (founder of ISKCON) translated, reformulated and presented Hinduism's foundational texts for contemporary audiences in new iterations, attracting followers and attention in India and abroad. Others such as Swami Vivekananda, Paramahansa Yogananda, B.K.S. Iyengar and Swami Rama have been instrumental in raising the profiles of traditional Yoga and Vedanta in the West. In the Indian subcontinent, Hinduism is still practised by the majority of India's inhabitants although the number in the areas of modern Pakistan and Bangladesh have dwindled after the Partition of India. Hinduism is the official religion in Nepal, which is the world's only Hindu state.

The Vedic Period

Sacred Mount Kailash in Tibet is regarded as the spiritual abode of Shiva. Modern Hinduism grew out of the Vedas. The earliest of these, the *Rigveda,* centres on worship of deities such as *Indra, Varuna* and *Agni,* and on the *Soma* ritual. They performed fire-sacrifices, called *yajna* and chanted Vedic mantras but did not build temples or icons. Buddhist and Jain texts claim that animals were sacrificed in larger *yajnas.* The oldest Vedic traditions exhibit strong similarities to Zoroastrianism and with other Indo-European religions.

HINDUISM IN THE MEDIEVAL AGES

Bhakti Movement

Bhakti movements are Hindu religious movements in which the main spiritual practice is the *fostering of loving devotion to God,* called bhakti. They are monotheistic movements generally devoted to worship of Shiva or Vishnu or Shakti. The first documented bhakti movement was founded by Karaikkal-ammaiyar. She wrote poems in Tamil about her love for Shiva and probably lived around the 6th century CE. The twelve Alvars who were Vaishnavite devotees and the sixty-three Nayanars who were

Shaivite devotees nurtured the incipient bhakti movement in Tamil Nadu. They constitute South India's 75 Apostles of Bhakti. During the 12th century CE, the bhakti movement took the form of the Virashaiva movement from Karnataka state inspired by Basavanna, a great Hindu reformer who created the sect of Lingayats or Shiva *bhaktas*. During this time, a unique and native form of Kannada literature-poetry called Vachanas was born. The last Hindu empire of India-The Maratha Empire in 1760. During the 14th-17th century, the Bhakti movement called the haridasa movement was propagated in Kannada language by great saints of Karnataka like Purandaradasa, Kanakadasa, Vyasatirtha, guru Raghavendra Swami of Mantralaya, Gopaladasa, Vijayadasa, Jagannathadasa, Narahari tirtha, Sri Kamalesha Vitthala and others. During this time, the teachings of Madhvacharya were propagated through out south India, sowing the seeds of carnatic music and instilling a strong Hindu sentiment at a time when north India was ruled by Muslim Empires.

Muslim Invasion

Muslim rulers began to extend their rule across Hindu populated lands in the 8th century CE and Islam began to spread across the Indian-subcontinent over several centuries. Most converts were from Hinduism or Buddhism; the two dominant local religions. The prime drivers attributed to the conversions are: duress by the invaders, political expediency, oppressive legal/legislative climate against Hindus and Buddhists, oppressive caste structure in Hindu society at the time, jizya, Sufi missionaries, intermarriage and immigration from other Islamic lands. Many of the new Muslim rulers looked down upon Hindu Iconodulistic religious practices, and were to various degrees iconoclastic. In times of conflict they also took the liberty to sack Hindu temples, which were repositaries of significant wealth. In addition, Hindus who were converted to Islam were called "Ajlaf" (the low-born) over the so-called "Arab-descended Ashraf" and subjected to the Caste system among South Asian Muslims

The Reign of Shivaji

The Hindu Marathas long had lived in the Desh region around Satara, in the western portion of the Deccan plateau, where the plateau meets the eastern slopes of the Western Ghats mountains. They had resisted incursions into the region by the Muslim Mughal rulers of northern India. Under their leader Shivaji, the Maratha freed themselves from the Muslim sultans of Bijapur to the southeast, and became much more aggressive and began to frequently raid Mughal territory, sacking the Mughal port of Surat in 1664. Shivaji was proclaimed Emperor in 1674. The Maratha had spread and conquered much of central India by Shivaji's death in 1680.

Modern Hinduism

Modern Hinduism is the reflection of continuity and progressive changes that occurred in various traditions and institutions of Hinduism during the 19th and 20th centuries. This continuity and adaptation to modern ideas is still a continuing process. Modern Hinduism has as its values rational thought, modern education and the ideals of humanism, rationalism and religious universalism. This has meant combating the conservative and obscurantist elements, imbibing modernity, modern education compared to classical Sanskritic education system, and countering Christian missionary criticism. The positive consequences of modernity in Hinduism is most visible in the status of women and the dalits. Also, ritualism has declined.

Reform Movements

Brahmo Samaj is a social and religious movement founded in Kolkata, India in 1828 by Raja Ram Mohan Roy. He was influenced by western thought and was one of the first Indians to visit Europe. He died in Bristol, England. The Brahmo Samaj movement thereafter resulted in the Brahmo religion in 1850 founded by Debendranath Tagore better known as the father of Rabindranath Tagore. Arya Samaj (*Aryan Society* or *Society of Nobles*) is a Hindu reform movement in India that was founded by Swami Dayananda in 1875. He was a sannyasin (renouncer) who believed in the infallible authority of the Vedas. Dayananda advocated the doctrine of karma and reincarnation, and emphasised the ideals of brahmacharya (chastity) and sanyasa (renunciation). Sri Ramakrishna and his pupil Swami Vivekananda led a reform in Hinduism in late 19th century. Their ideals and sayings have inspired numerous Indians as well as non-Indians, Hindus as well as non-Hindus. Among the prominent figures whose ideals were very much influenced by them were Rabindranath Tagore, Gandhi, Subhaṣ Bose, Satyendranath Bose, Meghnad Saha, and Sister Nivedita.

Converts

Though Hindus have never proselytized, modernity has led to an infusion of newer ideas into the Hindu religion, thereby making it more open, so that we find many non-Asians taking on Hinduism. This is particularly interesting because there is no large-scale proselytising effort in Hinduism. An important aspect of 20th-century Hinduism has been its spread among non-Indians, who have accepted the religion voluntarily. This perhaps began with the sojourn of Vivekananda to the World Parliament of Religions in Chicago in 1893, where he made a huge impact on the people. He founded the Ramakrishna Mission, which today operates temples, ashrams, charitable hospitals, and schools worldwide. In our times, Transcendental Meditation has become popular. And the International Society for Krishna Consciousness, inspired by the Vaishnavite strand of Bhakti, has established centres around the world. Of late, Pandurang Shastri Athavale a social reformer, philosopher, and spiritual teacher from the Western Indian state of Maharashtra, Guru of Swadhyay Movement, is also a modern spiritual teacher of Hinduism. The new Hindu communities in Java tend to be concentrated around recently built temples (*pura*) or around archaeological temple sites (*chandi*) which are being reclaimed as places of Hindu worship.

An important new Hindu temple in eastern Java is Pura Mandaragiri Sumeru Agung, located on the slope of Mt. Semeru, Java's highest mountain. Mass conversions have also occurred in the region around Pura Agung Blambangan, another new temple, built on a site with minor archaeological remnants attributed to the kingdom of Blambangan, the last Hindu polity on Java, and Pura Loka Moksha Jayabaya (in the village of Menang near Kediri), where the Hindu king and prophet Jayabaya is said to have achieved spiritual liberation (*moksha*). Another site is the new Pura Pucak Raung in East Java, which is mentioned in Balinese literature as the place from where Maharishi Markandeya took Hinduism to Bali in the fifth century CE. Hinduism in general does not encourage converting. This largely explains why there has never been any missionary activities in Hinduism. It is the belief of Hinduism that each person chooses their own path to reach god. You are never encouraged to stray from the path that you have chosen. Each religion is just a path to god. Converting to another religion takes you to an entirely new path, which in Hinduism is seen as unnecessary.

Shuddhi Movement

Started by Arya Samaj in early 20th century to bring back to Hinduism people converted to Islam and Christianity. Dayananda claimed to be rejecting all non-Vedic beliefs altogether. Hence the Arya Samaj unequivocally condemned idolatry, animal sacrifices, ancestor worship, pilgrimages, priestcraft, offerings made in temples, the caste system, untouchability and child marriages, on the grounds that all these lacked Vedic sanction. It aimed to be a universal church based on the authority of the Vedas. Dayananda stated that he wanted to make the whole world Aryanae. That is, he wanted to develop *missionary* Hinduism based on the universality of the Vedas. To this end the Arya Samaj set up schools and missionary organisations, extending its activities outside India. It now has branches around the world.

It has a disproportional amount of adherents among people of Indian ancestry in Suriname and the Netherlands, in comparison with India. Hinduism is a way of life, an Indian tradition that encompasses several religious beliefs, cultural practices and ideologies. The exact date of Hinduism's origin is not known, though estimates vary from 3200 BC to 2500 BC. It is the world's oldest major religion. It is also the third largest religion with a following of approximately a 1.2 billion people. The Indian subcontinent is home to 98% of this populace. The Himalayan kingdom of Nepal is the only nation which has Hinduism for its state religion. The term Hindu itself derives from the name of the Sindhu river. Hinduism comes under a branch of religions known as the Dharmic religions. The Dharmic religions are less prone to dogma and offer generic universal truths. Such universal truths serve as general guidelines for their follower's philosophies and actions. They remain open to interpretation, adaptation and enrichment at any date and in any age. This core makes Hinduism flexible in accommodating even contradictory opinions seamlessly within its fabric. Hinduism provides several paths to the common goal of divine bliss.

The choice of a particular path is left to the ability, discretion and temperament of the follower. Experience of the divine supreme knowledge, known as moksha, is the core concept of Hinduism. Hinduism teaches its followers the ability to differentiate between the pure actions of virtue and the wrongful actions of evil. The concept of karma lays forth free-willed human actions and how such actions can lead both to moksha and to the cycles of birth and death. The soul is ever thirsty for this divine knowledge and it accumulates knowledge through all human experiences. Virtuous actions take the soul closer to the divine supreme, Brahman. Realization and experience of the divine bliss makes all the soul's desires redundant, including the desire for another worldly-experience-giving cycle of birth. Evil hinders recognition of the Brahman and misleads the Atman (soul) to seek knowledge through experiences in various forms of worldly life. All human actions leave their imprint on the soul. They affect and even decide the form and circumstances of life sought by the soul in its next cycle of birth.

2 Ambedkar on Tyranny of Hindus

BALAIS REFUSE COMPLIANCE

The Balais refused to comply; and the Hindu element proceeded against them. Balais were not allowed to get water from the village wells, they were not allowed to let their cattle graze. Balais were prohibited from passing through land owned by a Hindu; so that if the field of a Balai was surrounded by fields owned by Hindus, the Balai could have no access to his own field. The Hindus also led their cattle to graze down the fields of Balais. The Balais submitted petitions to the Darbar against these persecutions; but as they could get no timely relief, and the operation continued, hundreds of Balais, with their wives and children, were obliged to abandon their homes in which their ancestors lived for generations and migrate to adjoining States, *viz.*, to villages in Dhar, Dewas, Bhopal, Gwalior and other States.

RULES FOR BALAIS

Mode of Life Laid Down: "Last May (1927) High Caste Hindus, *viz.* Kalotas, Rajputs and Brahmins, including the patels and putwaris of villages Kanaria, Bicholee Hafsi, Mardana and of about 15 other villages in the Indore District, informed the Balais of their respective village that if they wished to live among them, they must conform to the following rules: (1) Balais must not wear gold lace bordered pugrees; (2) they must not wear dhoties with coloured or fancy borders; (3) they must convey intimation of the death of any Hindu to relatives of the deceased—no matter how far away these relatives might be living; (4) in all Hindu marriages, the Balais must play music before the processions, and during the marriage; (5) the Balai women must not wear gold or silver ornaments; they must not wear fancy gowns, or jackets; (6) Balai women must attend all cases of confinement of Hindu women; (7) the Balais must render services without demanding remuneration, and must accept whatever a Hindu is pleased to give; (8) if the Balais do not agree to abide by these terms, they must clear out of the villages.

COMPULSORY AGREEMENT

Only a few days ago the Hindus of Reoti village, barely seven miles to north of Indore City, ordered the Balais to sign a stamped agreement in accordance with the rules framed against the Balais by the Hindus of other villages. The Balais refused to comply. It is alleged that some of them were beaten by the Hindus; and one Balai was fastened to a post, and was told that he would be let go on agreeing to sign the agreement. He signed the agreement and was released. Some Balais from this village ran up to the Prime Minister the next day, *i.e.* on the 20th December, and made a complaint about the ill treatment they received from the Hindu villagers of Reoti. They were sent to the Subha of the district. This officer, with the help of the police, made inquiries at the village, and recommended that action be taken against the Hindus under section 342 and 147 and against the Balais under section 147, Indian Penal Code.

BALAIS LEAVE VILLAGES

Caste Tyranny

Ignorance of Law a Handicap: "There has been no improvement in the treatment of the Balais by the Hindu residents of certain villages. Balais, it has already been reported, have been ill treated by the higher caste Hindus. From the Dopalpur Pargana alone, Indore District, a large number of Balais have had to leave their homes and find shelter in adjoining States. The villages from which Balais have been forced to clear out are Badoli, Ahirkharal, Piploda, Morkhers, Pamalpur, Karoda, Chatwada, Newri, Pan, Sanauda, Ajnoti, Khatedi and Sanavada. Pamalpur village has been altogether deserted and not a Balai man, woman or child is to be found there. Nanda Balai a resident of one of the above villages, it is alleged, was severely beaten by the Hindus of the village. In one village, the report goes, the Hindus burnt down all the dwellings of the Balais but the offenders have not yet been traced.

"Balais are ignorant village folk, who are ignorant of legal procedure and think that if a petition is sent to the Sirkar all that is required will be done for them. They have not the knowledge; or the means and practices, to pursue a complaint to its end; and, as they, it is said in some cases, failed to attend or produce witnesses in support of their allegations, the magistrate had no alternative but to dismiss their complaint." Looked at from the point of view of Dharma and Adharma, can it be doubted that underneath the lawlessness and ruthlessness of the Hindus in suppressing the revolt of the untouchables, they are actuated by what they think a noble purpose of preventing an outrage upon their Dharma? It may well be asked how much of this Dharma of Manu now remains? It must be admitted that as law in the sense of rules which a Court of Judicature is bound to observe in deciding disputes, the Dharma of Manu has ceased to have any operative force-except in matters such as marriage succession etc. matters which affect only the individual.

As Law governing social conduct and civic rights it is inoperative. But if it has gone out as law, it remains as custom. Custom is no small a thing as compared to Law. It is true that law is enforced by the state through its police power; custom, unless it is valid it is not. But in practice this difference is of no consequence. Custom is enforced by people far more effectively than law is by the state. This is because the compelling force of an organized people is far greater than the compelling force of the state. Not only has there been no detriment to its enforceability on account of its having ceased to be law in the technical sense but there are circumstances which are sufficient to prevent any loss of efficacy to this Dharma of Manu. Of these circumstances the first is the force of custom. There exists in every social group certain (habits) not only to acting, but of feeling and believing, of valuing, of approving and disapproving which embody the mental habitudes of the group. Every new comer whether he comes in the group by birth or adoption is introduced into this social medium.

In every group there goes on the process of persistently forcing these mental habitudes of the group upon the attention of each new member of the group. Thereby the group carries on the socialization of the individual of the shaping of the mental and practical habits of the new comer. Being dependent upon the group he can no more repudiate the mental habitudes of the group than he can the condition and regulation of his physical environment. Indeed, so dependent the individual is on the group that he readily falls in line and allows the current ways of esteeming and behaving prevailing in the community, to become a standing habit of his own mind. This socializing process of the individual by the group has been graphically described by Grote.

He says: "This aggregate of beliefs and predispositions to believe, ethical, Religious, Aesthetical, and Social respecting what is true, or false, probable or improbable, just or unjust, holy or unholy, honourable or base, respectable or contemptible, pure or impure, beautiful or ugly, decent or indecent, obligatory to do, or obligatory to avoid, respecting the status and relations of each individual in the society, respecting even the admissible fashions of amusement and recreation—this is an established fact and condition of things, the real origin of which for the most part unknown, but which each new member of the group is born to and finds subsisting..... It becomes a part of each person's nature, a standing habit of mind, or fixed set of mental tendencies, according to which particular experience is interpreted and particular persons appreciated..... The community hate, despise or deride any individual member who proclaims his dissent from their social creed..... Their hatred manifests itself in different ways..... At the very best by exclusion from that amount of forbearance, good will and estimation without which the life of an individual becomes insupportable."

But what is it that helps to bring about this result? Grote has himself answered this question. His answer is that, this is due to—"Nomos (Law and Custom), King of all "(which Herodotus cites from Pindar) exercises plenary power, spiritual and temporal, over individual minds, moulding the emotions as well as the intellect, according to the local type.... and reigning under the appearance of habitual, self suggested tendencies. What all this comes to is that, when in any community, the ways of acting, feeling, believing, or valuing or of approving and disapproving have become crystallised into customs and traditions, they do not need any sanction of law for their enforcement. The amplitude of plenary powers which the group can always generate by mass action is always ready to see that they are not broken. The same thing applies to the Dharma laid down by Manu.

This Dharma of Manu, by reason of the governing force which it has had for centuries, has become an integral and vital part of the customs and traditions of the Hindus. It has become ingrained and has given colour to their life blood. As law it controlled the actions of the Hindus. Though now a custom, it does not do less. It moulds the character and determines the outlook of generation after generation. The second thing which prevents the Dharma of Manu from fading away is that the law does not prevent its propagation. This is a circumstance which does not seem to be present to the minds of many people. It is said that one of the blessings of the British Rule is that Manusmriti has ceased to be the law of the land. That the Courts are not required to enforce the provisions contained in Manusmriti as rules of law is undoubtedly a great blessing—which might not be sufficiently appreciated except by those who were crushed beneath the weight of this "infamous" thing. It is as great a blessing to the untouchables as the Reformation was to the peoples of Europe.

At the same time it must be remembered that the Reformation would not have been a permanent gain if it had been followed by what is called the Protestant Revolution. The essential features of the Protestant Revolution as I understand them are:

(1) That the state is supreme and the Church is subordinate to the state.

(2) The doctrine to be preached must be approved by the state.

(3) The clergy shall be servants of the state and shall be liable to punishment not only for offences against the general law of the land but also liable for offences involving moral turpitude and for preaching doctrines not approved of by the state. I am personally a believer in the "Established Church". It is a system which gives safety and security

against wrong and pernicious doctrines preached by any body and every body as doctrines of religion. I know there are people who are opposed to the system of an "Established Church". But whether the system of an "Established Church" is good or bad, the fact remains that there is no legal prohibition against the propagation of the Dharma laid down by Manu. The courts do not recognize it as law. But the law does not treat it as contrary to law. Indeed every village every day. When Pandits are preaching it to parents and parents preach it to their children, how can Manusmriti fade away? Its lessons are reinforced every day and no body is allowed to forget that untouchability is a part of their Dharma.

This daily propagation of the Dharma of Manu has infected the minds of all men and women young and old. Nay, it has even infected the minds of the judges. There is a case reported from Calcutta. A certain Dome (untouchable) by name Nobin Dome was prosecuted for theft of a goat. He was found to be not guilty. He filed a complaint for defamation against the complaint. The magistrate dismissed the complaint on the ground that as he was low caste man he had no reputation. The High Court had to intervene and direct the Magistrate that he was wrong in his view and that under the Penal Code all persons were equal.

But the question remains, how did the Magistrate get the idea that an untouchable had no reputation? Surely from the teaching of the Manusmriti. The Dharma of Manu had never been a mere past. It is as present as though it were enacted today. It bids fair to continue to have its sway in the future. The only question is whether its sway will be for a time or forever.

UNDER THE PROVIDENCE OF MR. GANDHI

(1) His work through the Congress

1. A Strange Welcome.
2. The Great Repudiation.
3. A Charge Sheet.
4. The Basis of the Charge Sheet.
5. The Tragedy of Gandhi.

6. His Legacy to India and the Untouchables.

On the 28th December, 1931, Mr. Gandhi returned to India from London where he had gone as a delegate to attend the second Session of the Indian Round Table Conference. At the Round Table Conference, Mr. Gandhi had been an utter, ignominious failure both as a personality and as a politician. I know that my opinion will not be accepted by the Hindus. But the unfortunate part is that my opinion in this respect coincides with the opinion of Mr. Gandhi's best friend. I will cite the opinions of two. This is what Mr. Ewer, who was closely associated with Mr. Gandhi during the Round Table Conference, wrote about the role Mr. Gandhi played at the Round Table Conference in London. "Gandhi in the St. James Palace has not fulfilled the unwise expectation of those who saw him bestriding the Conference like a colossus........... He was out of his elements."

"His first speech, with its sentimental appeal, its over-stressing of humility, its reiteration of single-minded concern for the dumb suffering millions, was a failure. No one questioned its sincerity. But somehow it rang false. It was the right thing, perhaps, but it was in the wrong place. Nor were his later interventions on the whole more successful. A rather querulous complaint that the British Government had not produced a plan for the new Indian Constitution shocked some of Gandhi's colleagues, who had hardly expected to see the representative of the National Congress appealing to British Ministers for guidance and initiative. The protest against the pegging of the rupee to the pound was astonishingly ineffective. The contributions to the discussions on franchise and kindred matters were of little importance. Behind the scenes he was active enough in the Hindu-Moslem negotiations, but here, too, results were intangible. Not for a moment did Gandhi take the lead or materially influence the course of committee work. He sat there, sometimes speaking, sometimes silent, while the work went on, much as it would have gone on without him."

This is what Bolton has to say about Mr. Gandhi's achievement at the Round Table Conference. How did Mr. Gandhi fare as a statesman and a politician? At the close of the first session of the Round Table Conference there were three questions which had not been settled. The question of minorities, the question of the Federal structure and the question of the status of India in the Empire, were the three outstanding problems, which were the subject matter of controversy. Their solution demanded great statesmanship. Many said that these questions were not settled because the wisdom and authority of the Congress was not represented at the Round Table Conference.

At the second session, Mr. Gandhi came and made good the deficiency. Did Mr. Gandhi settle any of these unsettled problems? I think it is not unfair to say that Mr. Gandhi created fresh disunity in the Conference. He began the childish game of ridiculing every Indian delegate. He questioned their honesty, he questioned their representative character. He taunted the liberals as armchair politicians and as leaders without any followers. To the Muslims he said that he represented the Muslim masses better than they did. He claimed that the Depressed Class delegates did not represent the Depressed Classes and that he did. This was the refrain which he repeated *ad nauseum at* the end of every speech. The non-Congress delegates deserve the thanks of all honest people for their having tolerated this nonsense and arrogance of Mr. Gandhi and collaborated with him to save him and to save the country from his mistake.

Apart from this discourtesy to fellow-delegates, did Mr. Gandhi stand up for the cause he came to champion? He did not. His conduct of affairs was ignominious. Instead of standing up and fighting he began to yield on issues on which he ought never to have ceased fire. He yielded to the Princes and agreed that their representatives in the Federal legislature should be nominated by them and not elected, as demanded by their subjects. He yielded to the conservatives and consented to be content with provincial autonomy and not to insist upon central responsibility for which many lakhs of Indians went to gaol. The only people to whom he would not yield were the minorities — the only party to whom he could have yielded with honour to himself and advantage to the country.

Nothing has helped so much to shatter the prestige of Mr. Gandhi as going to the Round Table Conference. The spectacle of Mr. Gandhi at the Round Table Conference must have been painful to many of his friends. He was not fitted to play the role he undertook to play. No country has ever sent a delegate to take part in the framing of the constitution who was so completely unequipped in training and in study. Gandhi went to the Round Table Conference with a song of the saint Narsi Mehta on his tongue. It would have been better for him and better for his country if he had taken in his arm pit a volume on comparative constitutional law. Devoid of any knowledge of the subject he was called upon to deal with, he was quite powerless to destroy the proposals put forth by the British or to meet them with his alternatives. No wonder Mr. Gandhi, taken out of the circle of his devotees and placed among politicians, was at sea. At every turn he bungled and finding that he could not even muddle through, he gave up the game and returned to India. How was Mr. Gandhi received when he landed on the Indian soil?

It may sound strange to outsiders and to those who are not the devotees of Mr. Gandhi but it is a fact that when the *S. S. Pilsner* of the Lloyd Triestino entered the harbour of Bombay at 8 a.m. in the morning of the 28th December 1931 there came to receive him an enthusiastic crowd of men, women and children who had assembled at the Pier in tens of thousands to greet him, to welcome him back and to have his *Durshan*. The following extracts from the *Times of India* and the *Evening News* of Bombay will serve to give a vivid idea of the grandeur of this reception. The Pilsner was escorted into the harbour by Desh Sevikas (women volunteers of the Congress) in saffron coloured sarees who went out in launches some distance from the pier.

The Congress Committee had asked the Bombay Flying Club to fly an Aeroplane or two over the Pilsner and drop garlands as she came along side the pier, but the Flying Club, sanely preferring to keep out of politics, refused to grant the Congress demand. The spacious Central Hall at Ballard Pier was decorated with festoons and Congress flags and a large dais was put up at the centre with chairs placed on all sides for representatives of various organisations, local and upcountry, who were given passes for admission. Both the approaches to the reception hall from the wharf and from the city were lined by Desh Sevikas waving national flags and the duty of guarding the dais and of regulating and directing the assembly inside the hall was also entrusted to the women volunteers.

Mr. Gandhi reached the dais escorted by the Congress leaders and received an ovation. Hardly had he stepped on the dais when he began to be flooded with telegraph messages (presumably of welcome) which arrived one after another. Standing on the dais he was garlanded in turn by representatives of the public bodies who had assembled and whose names were called out from a long printed list of which copies were previously distributed. The proceedings inside the reception hall terminated with the garlanding. A procession was then formed in four, in place of the carriage which was intended to be the conveyance for Mr. Gandhi.

He was seated in a gaily decorated motor car, with Mr. Vallabhbhai Patel to his left and Mr. Vitthalbhai Patel to his right and Mr. K. F. Nariman, President of the Bombay Provincial Congress Committee, on the front seat. Preceded by a pilot car and followed by others containing the Congress Working Committee members, the procession passed through the Ballard Pier Road, Hornby Road and Kalbadevi which had been decorated by the citizens at the instance of the Congress Committee and lined on either side by cheering crowds, five to ten deep till the party reached *"Mani Bhuvan,* Gamdevi". At no stage of this welcome did Mr. Gandhi open his lips to acknowledge it. This man of vows was under his Sunday vow of silence which had not run out till then and nor did he think that etiquette, good manners or respect for those who had assembled required that he should terminate his vow earlier. The official historian of the Congress describes' this reception given to Mr. Gandhi in the following terms: "There were gathered in Bombay representatives of all parts and Provinces in India to accord a fitting welcome to the Tribune of the people. Gandhi greeted the friends that went on board the steamer to welcome him, patting many, thumping a few and pulling the venerable Abbas Tyabji by his beard. There was a formal welcome in one of the Halls of Customs House and then a procession in the streets of Bombay which kings might envy in their own country".

On reading this account one is reminded of the Irish Sein Fein Delegates who in 1921, just 10 years before, had gone to London at the invitation of Mr. Lloyd George for the settlement of the Irish Home Rule question. As is well known the Irish Delegates secured from the British Cabinet a treaty which was signed on the 8th December 1921. The Treaty was subsequently submitted for approval to the Dail, the Parliament of the Sein Fein Party which met from 14th December 1921 to 7th January 1922. On the 7th January a division was taken. There were 64 votes for ratifying the treaty and 57 against. And what was the reception given to the Irish delegates who secured this treaty? Arthur Griffith— who was the head of the Irish Delegation and Michael Collins who was his most prominent colleague, were both of them shot by the anti-treaty Sein Feiners, the former on the 12th and the latter on the 22nd August 1922. The reason for sending them to such cruel death was that the treaty which they signed did not secure the inclusion of Ulster and a republic for Ireland. It is true the treaty did not grant this. But if it is remembered that negotiations were opened on the express understanding on the part of both sides that these two questions were outside the scope of negotiations it will be granted that if the treaty did not include these it was no fault of the Irish Delegates. The fury and ferocity of the anti treaty Sein Feiners against the Irish Delegates had no moral foundation and the fate that befell Arthur Griffith and Michael Collins can by no stretch of imagination be said to be one which they deserved.

Be that as it may, this welcome to Mr. Gandhi will be regarded as a very strange event. Both went to win Swaraj, Griffith and Collins for Ireland, Gandhi for India, Griffith and Collins succeeded, almost triumphed; Gandhi failed and returned with nothing but defeat and humiliation. Yet Collins and Griffith were shot and Gandhi was given a reception which kings could have envied!! What a glaring and a cruel contrast between the fate that awaited Collins and Griffith and the reception arranged for Gandhi? Are the Indian Patriots different from the Irish Patriots? Did the masses render this welcome out of blind devotion or were they kept in darkness of the failure of Mr. Gandhi by a mercenary Press? This is more than I can answer. While this great welcome was being accorded to Mr. Gandhi the Untouchables of Bombay had come to the Pier to repudiate. Mr. Gandhi. Referring to this demonstration, the newspaper reports said: "Just outside the gate of Ballard Pier, the scene was most exciting. On one side were drawn up Depressed Class volunteers in uniform, weaving black flags to the accompaniment of derisive shouts against Mr. Gandhi and laudatory cries in praise of their leader, while on the other side Congress followers kept up a din of counter shouts."

This Untouchable demonstration included men and women. The demonstrators numbered thousands, all waving Black Flags as a mark of repudiation of Mr. Gandhi. They were a determined crowd and, despite intimidation by the superior forces of the Congress assembled there to welcome Mr. Gandhi, were bent on showing that they repudiated Mr. Gandhi. This led to a clash and blood was split. There were forty casualties on each side. For the first time Mr. Gandhi was made aware that there could be black flags even against him.

This must have come to him as a shock. When he was asked about it later in the day, he said he was not angry, the Untouchables being the flesh of his flesh and bone of his bone. This is of course the Mahatmaic way of concealing the truth. One would not mind this convenient and conventional lie if there were behind it a realization that the crowd could not always be trusted to be loyal to its hero. Congressmen in India sadly lack the realism of a man like Cromwell.

It is related that when Cromwell returned after a great battle, an enormous crowd came out to greet him. A friend sought to impress upon him the immensity of the crowd. But Cromwell dismissed the subject with the leconic remark, "Oh yes, I know many more will come to see me hanged."! No Congress leader feels the realism of Cromwell. Either he believes that the day will never come when he will be hanged or he believes that the Indian crowd will never become a thinking crowd. That part of the Indian crowd does think was shown by the representatives of the Untouchables who assembled on the 28th to greet Mr. Gandhi with black flags.

Why did the Untouchables repudiate Mr. Gandhi? The answer to this question will be found in a statement issued by the organizers of these demonstrations which was printed and circulated on that day. The following are extracts from it. "Our Charge sheet against

Gandhiji and Congress", "Enough of patronising attitude and lip sympathy. We ask for justice and fair play."

1. In spite of the fact that the removal of untouchability has been included in the constructive programme of the Congress, practically nothing has so far been done by that body to achieve that object, and in our fights against untouchability at Mahad and Nasik most of the local Congress leaders have been our bitter opponents.
2. The attitude of Gandhiji at the Round Table Conference in London with regard to the demands of the Depressed Classes as put forward by their accredited and trusted leader Dr. Ambedkar, was most unreasonable, obstinate and inexplicable.
3. Gandhiji was prepared to concede on behalf of the Congress the special claims of the Mohamedans and the Sikhs including their demand for separate representation on "historic grounds", but he was not willing even to concede reserved seats in general electorates to the Depressed Classes, although he knew, or should have known, what sort of treatment they would get, should they be thrown upon at the mercy on caste Hindus.
4. Gandhiji has said in opposing the claims of the Depressed Classes for separate representation that he does not want the Hindu Community to be subjected to vivisection or dissection. But the Congress is now dissecting the community of Untouchables by playing one section against another. Gandhiji and the Congress are not playing the fair game. Open enemies are far better than treacherous friends.
5. Attempts are being made to show that Gandhiji and the Congress alone represent the Depressed Classes by presenting addresses through a handful of hirelings and dupes. Is it not our duty to demonstrate the fact by coming out in thousands and proclaiming the truth? This is our charge sheet against Gandhiji and the Congress.

Let those who are not blind hero worshippers and blind partisans judge and give their verdict. Is this charge sheet true? Mr. Gandhi is known to the world not merely as the Political leader of India, but also as the Champion of the Untouchables. It is perhaps true that the outside world takes more interest in Mr. Gandhi because he is the champion of the Untouchables than because he is a political leader. For instance the Manchester Guardian very recently devoted an editorial to the work of Mr. Gandhi for the Untouchables. In the face of this, the charge appears to be quite unfounded.

For, has not Mr. Gandhi made the Congress pledge itself to remove untouchability? The Congress before it came into the hands of Mr. Gandhi had refused to allow any social problem to be placed before it for consideration. A clear cut distinction was made between political and social question, and scrupulous attempt was made to confine the deliberations and activities of the Congress to purely political questions. The old Congress refused to take notice of the Untouchables. It was with great difficulty that the Congress in 1917 for the first time allowed the question of the Untouchables to be placed before it and condescended to pass the following resolution: "The Congress urges upon the people of India the necessity, justice and righteousness of removing all disabilities imposed by custom upon the Depressed Classes, the disabilities being of a most vexatious and oppresssive character, subjecting those classes to considerable hardship and inconvenience." The Congress fell onto the hands of Mr. Gandhi in 1920 and the Congress at its ordinary session held at Nagpur passed the following resolution:

INTERCOMMUNAL UNITY

"Finally, in order that the Khilafat and the Punjab wrongs may be redressed and Swarajya established within one year, this Congress urges upon all public bodies, whether affiliated to the Congress or otherwise, to devote their exclusive attention to the promotion of non-violence and non-cooperation with the Government and, inasmuch as the movement of non-cooperation can only succeed by complete cooperation amongst the people themselves, this Congress calls upon public associations to advance Hindu-Muslim unity and the Hindu delegates of this Congress

> *call upon the leading Hindus to settle all disputes between Brahmins and Non-Brahmins, wherever they may be existing, and to make a special effort to rid Hinduism of the reproach of untouchability, and respectfully urges the religious heads to help the growing desire to reform Hinduism in the matter of its treatment of the suppressed classes."*

Again did not Mr. Gandhi make the removal of untouchability a condition precedent for achieving Swaraj? In the *Young India* of December 29, 1920, Mr. Gandhi wrote: "Non-cooperation against the Government means cooperation among the governed, and if Hindus do not remove the sin of untouchability, there will be no Swaraj in one year or one hundred years...."

Writing again on the conditions of Swaraj in the issue of *Young India* for February 23, 1921, he said: "Swaraj is easy of attainment before October next if certain simple conditions can be fulfilled. I ventured to mention one year in September last because I knew that the conditions were incredibly simple and I felt that the atmosphere in the country was responsive. The past five months experience has confirmed me in the opinion. I am convinced that the country has never been so ready for establishing Swaraj as now." "But what is necessary for us as accurately as possible to know the conditions. One supreme indispensible condition is the continuance of non-violence."

"The next condition is...... establishing a Congress Agency in every village." "There are certain things that are applicable to all. The potent thing is Swadeshi. Every home must have the spinning wheel and every village can organize.... and become self supporting." "Every man and woman can give some money—be it even a pice—to the Tilak Swaraja Fund. And we need have no anxiety about financing the movement." "We can do nothing without Hindu-Moslem unity and without killing the snake of untouchability." "Have we honest, earnest, industrious, patriotic workers for this very simple programme? If we have, Swaraj will be established in India before next October." What more did the Untouchables want? Here is Mr. Gandhi who had held himself out as the friend of the Untouchables.

He prides himself on being their servant. He claims and fought for being accepted as their representative. Why should the Untouchables show such a lack of confidence in Mr. Gandhi? On the basis of words, the charge perhaps appears unfounded. But does it appear equally unfounded if we have regard to deeds? Let me examine Mr. Gandhi's deeds. The work which is claimed by Mr. Gandhi and his friends to have been done by him and the Congress for the Untouchables falls into two periods, the period which precedes the Poona Pact and the period which follows the Poona Pact. The first period may be called the period of the Bardoli Programme. The second period may be called the period of the Harijan Sevak Sangh.

First Period

To begin with the Bardoli Programme period. The Bardoli Programme or what is called the Constructive Programme of the Congress was the direct outcome of the new line of action adopted by the Congress in securing the political demands of the country. At the session of the Congress held at Nagpur in 1920 the Congress declared: Whereas the people of India are now determined to establish Swaraj; and Whereas all methods adopted by the people of India prior to the last special session of the Indian National Congress have failed to secure due recognition of their rights and liberties; Now this Congress while reaffirming the resolution on nonviolent non-cooperation passed at the Special Session of the Congress at Calcutta declares that the entire or any part or parts of the scheme of non-violent non-cooperation, with the renunciation of voluntary association with the present Government at one end and the refusal to pay taxes at the other, should be put in force at a time to be determined by either the Indian National Congress or the All India Congress Committee and in the meanwhile to prepare the Country for it.

At the session of the Congress held at Ahmedabad in 1921 it was declared that: "This Congress is further of opinion that Civil Disobedience is the only civilized and effective substitute for an armed rebellion.... and therefore advises all Congress Workers and others.... to organize individual civil disobedience and mass civil disobedience"..... It is to give effect to this policy of non-cooperation and civil disobedience and to prepare the people to take part in them that the Working Committee of the Congress met at Bardoli in February 1922 and drew up the following programme of action. "The Working Committee advises all Congress organisations to be engaged in the following activities:

(1) To enlist at least one crore of members of the Congress.

(2) To popularise the spinning wheel and to organise the manufacture of hand-spun and handwoven khaddar.

(3) To organise national schools.

(4) To organise the Depressed Classes for a better life, to improve their social, mental and moral condition to induce them to send their children to national schools and to provide for them the ordinary facilities which the other citizens enjoy.

(5) To organise the temperance campaign amongst the people addicted to the drink habit by house-to-house visits and to rely more upon appeal to the drinker in his home than upon picketing.

(6) To organise village and town Panchayats for the private settlement of all disputes, reliance being placed solely upon the force of public opinion and the truthfulness of Panchayat decisions to ensure obedience to them.

(7) In order to promote and emphasize unity among all classes and races and mutual goodwill, the establishment of which is the aim of the movement of non-cooperation, to organise a social service department that will render help to all, irrespective of differences, in times of illness or accident.

(8) To continue the Tilak Memorial Swaraj Fund collections and call upon every Congressman or Congress sympathiser to pay at least a one-hundredth part of his annual income for 1921. Every province to send every month twenty-five per cent of its income from the Tilak Memorial Swaraj Fund to the All-India Congress Committee.

The above resolution shall be brought before the forthcoming session of the All-India Congress Committee for revision if necessary." This programme was placed before the All-India Congress Committee at its meeting at Delhi on 20th February 1922 and was confirmed by the same. The programme is a very extensive programme and I am not concerned with what happened to the whole of it, how it was received and how it was worked out. I am concerned with only one item and that which relates to the Depressed Classes. After it was confirmed by the All-India Congress Committee, the Working Committee met at Lucknow in June 1922 and passed the following resolution.

"This Committee hereby appoints a committee consisting of Swami Shraddhanandji, Mrs. Sarojini Naidu and Messrs. I. K. Yajnik and G. B. Deshpande to formulate a scheme embodying practical measures to be adopted for bettering the condition of the so-called Untouchables throughout the country and to place it for consideration before the next meeting of this Committee, the amount to be raised for the scheme to be Rs. 2 lacs for the present." This resolution was placed before the All-India Congress Committee at its meeting in Lucknow in June 1922. It accepted the resolution with the amendent that "the amount to be raised for the scheme should be 5 lacs for the present", instead of 2 lacks as put forth in the resolution of the Working Committee. How did this programme fare, what practical measures did the Committee suggest and how far were these measures given effect to? These questions one must ask in order to assess the work of Mr. Gandhi and the Congress for the Untouchables. It seems that before the resolution appointing the Committee was adopted by the Working Committee, one of its Members Swami Shradhanand tendered his resignation of the membership of the Committee. For one finds that at the very sitting at which the Working Committee passed this resolution, another resolution to the following effect was passed by the Working Committee: "Read letter from Swami Shradhanandji, dated 8th June 1922 for an advance for drawing up a scheme for depressed classes work. Resolved that Mr. Gangadharrao B. Deshpande be appointed convener of the sub-committee appointed for the purpose and he be requested to convene a meeting at an early date, and that Swami Shradhanand's letter be referred to the sub-committee."

The Working Committee met again in July 1922 in Bombay and passed the following Resolution: "That the General Secretary be asked to request Swami Shradhanand to reconsider his resignation and withdraw it and a sum of Rs. 500/-be remitted to the Convener, Shri G. B. Deshpende, for the contingent expenses of the Depressed Classes Sub-Committee." The year 1922 thus passed away without anything being done to further that item of the Bardoli Programme which related to the Depressed Classes. The year 1923 came on.

The Working Committee met at Gaya in January 1923 and passed the following resolution: "With reference to Swami Shraddhanand's resignation, resolved that the remaining members of the Depressed Classes Subcommittee do form the Committee and Mr. Yajnik be the convener." The All-India Congress Committee met in Feb. 1923 at Bombay and seeing that nothing was done as yet, recorded the following resolution: "Resolved that the question of the condition of the Untouchables be referred to the Working Committee for necessary action." What did the Working Committee do then? It met at Poona on the 17th April 1923 and resolved as follows: "Resolved that while some improvement has been effected in the treatment of the so-called Untouchables in response to the policy of the Congress this Committee is conscious that much work remains yet to be done in this respect and inasmuchas this question of untouchability concerns the Hindu community particularly, it requests the All-India Hindu Mahasabha also to take up this matter and to make strenuous efforts to remove this evil from amidst the Hindu community."

Thus came to an end the Constructive Programme undertaken by Mr. Gandhi and the Congress for the Untouchables. The Bardoli programme for the Untouchables was in no sense a revolutionary programme. It did attempt to abolish untouchability. It does not attempt to break up caste. There is no mention of intermarriage or interdinning. It accepts the principle of separate wells and separate schools for Untouchables. It was purely an ameliorative programme. And yet such a harmless programme the Congress failed to carry through. It must further be remembered that this was a time when the Congress was on the war path.

It was determined to fight British Imperialism and was most anxious to draw every community towards itself and make all disaffected towards the British. This was the time when the

Congress could have been expected to show to the Untouchables that the Congress stood for them and was prepared to serve them in the same way that it was prepared to serve the Musalmans. There could be no more propitious circumstance which could make the Hindus overcome their antipaty towards the Untouchables and undertake to serve. But even such propitious circumstance did not prove sufficient to energize Congressmen to do this small bit for the Untouchables. How hard must be the anti-social feelings of the Hindus against the Untouchables that even the highest bliss and the greatest stimulant, namely the prospect of winning Swaraj, were not sufficient to dissolve that spirit. The tragedy and the shamelessness of this failure by the Congress to carry through their programme for the Untouchables is aggravated by the way in which the matter was disposed of.

The work of the amelioration of the Untouchables could not have been left in worse hands. If there is any body which is quite unfit for addressing itself to the problem of the Untouchables, it is the Hindu Mahasabha. It is a militant Hindu organization. Its aim and object is to conserve in every way everything that is Hindu, religious and culture. It is not a social reform association. It is a purely political organization whose main object and aim is to combat the influence of the Muslims in Indian politics. Just to preserve its political strength it wants to maintain its social solidarity and its way to maintain social solidarity is not to talk about caste or untouchability. How such a body could have been selected by the Congress for carrying on the work of the Untouchables passes my comprehension. This shows that the Congress wanted somehow to get rid of an inconvenient problem and wash its hands of it. The Hindu Mahasabha, of course, did not come forth to undertake the work and the Congress had merely passed a pious resolution recommending the work to them without making any promise for financial provision.

So the project came to an inglorious and ignominious end. Yet there will not be wanting thousands of Congressmen who would not be ashamed to boast that the Congress has been fighting for the cause of the Untouchables and what is worse is that there will not be wanting hundreds of foreigners who are ready to believe it under the false propaganda carried on by men like Charles F.

Andrews, who is the friend of Mr. Gandhi and who thinks that to popularize Gandhi in the Western World is his real mission in life.'

It is not enough to know that the effort failed and had to be wound up. It is necessary to inquire why Swami Shradhanand resigned and refused to serve on the proposed Committee. There must be some good reason for it. For the Swami was the most enlightened Arya Samajist and very conscientiously believed in the removal of untouchability. On this point, the correspondence that passed between the Swami and the General Secretary to the All India Congress Committee throws a flood of light on the mentality of the Congressmen and I make no apology for reproducing below the whole of it.

3 The Hinduism's Philosophy

PHILOSOPHY OF HINDUISM

What is the philosophy of Hinduism? This is a question which arises in its logical sequence. But apart from its logical sequence its importance is such that it can never be omitted from consideration. Without it no one can understand the aims and ideals of Hinduism. It is obvious that such a study must be preceded by a certain amount of what may be called clearing of the ground and defining of the terms involved. At the outset it may be asked what does this proposed title comprehend? Is this title of the Philosophy of Hinduism of the same nature as that of the Philosophy of Religion? One does not have a clear idea of what is meant by Philosophy of Religion.

This is probably due to two facts. In the first place while religion is something definite, there is nothing definite as to what is to be included in the term philosophy. In the second place Philosophy and Religion have been adversaries if not actual antagonists as may be seen from the story of the philosopher and the theologian. According to the story, the two were engaged in disputation and the theologian accused the philosopher that he was "like a blind man in a dark room, looking for a black cat which was not there". In reply the philosopher charged the theologian saying that "he was like a blind man in the dark room, looking for a black cat which was not there but he declared to have found there".

Perhaps it is the unhappy choice of the title-Philosophy of Religion-which is responsible for causing confusion in the matter of the exact definition of its field. The nearest approach to an intelligible statement as to the exact subject matter of Philosophy of Religion can be perhaps in Prof. Pringle-Pattison who observes: "The facts with which a philosophy of religion has to deal are supplied by the history of religion, in the most comprehensive sense of that term. As Tiele puts it, "all religions of the civilised and uncivilised world, dead and living", is a 'historical and psychological phenomenon' in all its manifestations.

These facts, it should be noted, constitute the data of the philosophy of religion; they do not themselves constitute a 'philosophy' or, in Tiele's use of the term, a 'science' of religion. 'If, he says, I have minutely described all the religions in existence, their doctrines, myths and customs, the observances they inculcate, and the organisation of their adherents, tracing the different religions from their origin to their bloom and decay, I have merely. "A few words may be useful at the outset as an indication of what we commonly mean by the Philosophy of Religion. Plato described philosophy long ago as the synoptic view of things. That is to say, it is the attempt to see things together-to keep all the main features of the world in view, and to grasp them in their relation to one another as parts of one whole. Only thus can we acquire a sense of proportion and estimate aright the significance of any particular range of facts for our ultimate conclusions about the nature of the world-process and the world-ground.

Accordingly, the philosophy of any particular department of experience, the Philosophy of Religion, the Philosophy of Art, the Philosophy of Law, is to be taken as meaning an analysis and interpretation of the experience in question in its bearing upon our view of man and the world in which he lives. And when the facts upon which we concentrate are so universal, and in their nature so remarkable, as those disclosed by the history of religion-the philosophy of man's religious experience-cannot but exercise a determining influence upon our general philosophical conclusions. In fact with many writers the particular discussion tends to merge in the more general." Collected the materials with which the science of religion works'. 'The historical record, however complete, is not enough; pure history is not philosophy. To achieve a philosophy of religion we should be able to discover in the varied manifestations a common principle to whose roots in human nature we can point, whose evolution we can trace by intelligible-stages from lower to higher and more adequate forms, as well as its intimate relations with the other main factors in human civilisation".

Philosophy of Religion

If this is Philosophy of Religion it then it is merely a different name for that department of study, which is called comparative religion with the added aim of discovering a common principle in the varied manifestations of religion. Whatever be the scope and value of such a study, the title Philosophy of Religion to denote something quite different from the sense and aim given to it by Prof. Pringle-Pattison. It meant teachings as it did when people spoke of the philosophy of Socrates or the philosophy of Plato. In another sense it meant critical reason used in passing judgements upon things and events. Proceeding on this basis Philosophy of Religion is not a merely descriptive science. But should be regarded as being both descriptive as well as normative. In so far as it deals with the teachings of a Religion, Philosophy of Religion becomes a descriptive science.

A study of the Philosophy of Religion me involves the determination of three dimensions. They are like the unknown quantities contained as factors in a product. One must ascertain and define these dimensions of the Philosophy of Religion if an examination of it is to be fruitful. Of the three dimensions, Religion is the first. One must therefore define what he understands by religion in order to avoid argument being directed at cross-purposes. This is particularly necessary in the case of Religion for the reason that there is no agreement as to its exact definition. This is no place to enter upon an elaborate consideration of this question.

The word Religion is being used to mean Theology. This will perhaps be insufficient for the purposes of definition. For there are different kinds of Theologies. Historically there have been two Theologies spoken of from ancient times. Mythical theology and Civil theology. The Greeks who distinguished them gave each a definite content. By Mythical theology they meant the tales of gods and their doings told in or implied by current imaginative literature. Civil theology according to them consisted of the knowledge of the various feasts and fasts of the State Calendar and the ritual appropriate to them. Here it means theology natural theology which is-the doctrine of God and the divine, as an integral part of the theory of nature. As traditionally understood there are three thesis which 'natural theology' propounds. (1) That God exists and is the author of what we call nature or universe (2) That God controls all the events which make nature and (3) God exercises a government over mankind in accordance with his sovereign moral law. As Revealed Theology-spontaneous self disclosure of divine reality-which may be distinguished from Natural theology.

But this distinction does not really matter. For as has been pointed out that a revelation may either "leave the results won by Natural theology standing without modifications, merely supplementing them by further knowledge not attainable by unassisted human effort" or it "may transform Natural theology in such a way that all the truths of natural theology would acquire richer and deeper meaning when seen in the light of a true revelation." But the view that a genuine natural theology and a genuine revelation theology might stand in real contradiction may be safely excluded as not being possible. Taking the tnree thesis of theology namely: (1) the existence of God, (2) God's providential government of the universe and (3) God's moral government of mankind, Religion to mean the propounding of an ideal scheme of divine governance the aim and object of which is to make the social order in which men live a moral order. This is what one understand by Religion and this is the sense in which shall be used "The Term Religion".

The traditional usage of religion had grown up gradually in the course of many centuries, and reflected habits of thought, characteristic of very diverse stages of man's intellectual and moral development. No conception of the nature of the gods could possibly afford the clue to all parts of that motley complex of rites and ceremonies which the later paganism had received by inheritance, from a series of ancestors in every state of culture from pure savagery upwards. The record of the religious thought of mankind, as it is embodied in religious institutions, resembles the geological record of the history of the earth's crust; the new and the old are preserved side by side, or rather layer upon layer.

We have seen a religion growing up from stage to stage, from the simplest childish prayers to the highest metaphysical abstractions. In the majority of the hymns of the Veda we might recognise the childhood; in the Brahmanas and their sacrificial, domestic and moral ordinances the busy manhood; in the Upanishads the old age of the Vedic religion.

We could have well understood if, with the historical progress of the Indian mind, they had discarded the purely childish prayers as soon as they had arrived at the maturity of the Brahamans; and if, when the vanity of sacrifices and the real character of the old god's had once been recognised, they would have been superseded by the more exalted religion of the Upanishads. But it was not so. Every religious thought that had once found expression in India that had once been handed down as a sacred heirloom was preserved, and the thoughts of the three historical periods, the childhood, the manhood, and the old age of the Indian nation, were made to do permanent service in the three stages of the life of every individual. Thus alone can we explain how the same sacred code, the Veda, contains not only the records of different phases of religious thought, but of doctrines which we may call almost diametrically opposed to each other.

Fundamental Characteristic of Positive Religions

But this difficulty is not so great in the case of Religions which are positive religions. The fundamental characteristic of positive Religions, is that they have not grown up like primitive religions, under the action of unconscious forces operating silently from age to age, but trace their origin to the teaching of great religious innovators, who spoke as the organs of a divine revelation. Being the result of conscious formulations the philosophy of a religion which is positive is easy to find and easy to state. Hinduism like Judaism, Christianity and Islam is in the main a positive religion. One does not have to search for its scheme of divine governance. It is not like an unwritten constitution. On the Hindu scheme of divine governance is enshrined in a written constitution and any one who cares to know it will find it laid bare in that Sacred Book called the Manusmriti, a divine Code which lays down the rules which govern the religious, ritualistic and social life of the Hindus in minute detail and which must be regarded as the Bible of the Hindus and containing the philosophy of Hinduism.

The third dimension in the philosophy of religion is the criterion to be adopted for judging the value of the ideal scheme of divine governance for which a given Religion stands. Religion must be put on its trial. By what criterion shall it be judged? That leads to the definition of the norm. Of the three dimensions this third one is the most difficult one to be ascertained and defined. Unfortunately the question does not appear to have been tackled although much has been written on the philosophy of Religion and certainly no method has been found for satisfactorily dealing with the problem.

One is left to one's own method for determining the issue. It is safe to proceed on the view that to know the philosophy of any movement or any institution one must study the revolutions which the movement or the institution has undergone. Revolution is the mother of philosophy and if it is not the mother of philosophy it is a lamp which illuminates philosophy. Religion is no exception to this rule. Therefore it seems quite evident that the best method to ascertain the criterion by which to judge the philosophy of Religion is to study the Revolutions which religion has undergone. Students of History are familiar with one Religious Revolution. That Revolution was concerned with the sphere of Religion and the extent of its authority.

There was a time when Religion had covered the whole field of human knowledge and claimed infallibility for what it taught. It covered astronomy and taught a theory of the universe according to which the earth is at rest in the centre of the universe, while the sun, moon, planets and system of fixed stars revolve round it each in its own sphere. It included biology and geology and propounded the view that the growth of life on the earth had been created all at once and had contained from the time of creation onwards, all the heavenly bodies that it now contains and all kinds of animals of plants. It claimed medicine to be its province and taught that disease was either a divine visitation as punishment for sin or it was the work of demons and that it could be cured by the intervention of saints, either in person or through their holy relics; or by prayers or pilgrimages; or (when due to demons) by exorcism and by treatment which the demons (and the patient) found disgusting. It also claimed physiology and psychology to be its domain and taught that the body and soul were two distinct substances.

Domination of Religion

Bit by bit this vast Empire of Religion was destroyed. The Copernican Revolution freed astronomy from the domination of Religion. The Darwinian Revolution freed biology and geology from the trammels of Religion. The authority of theology in medicine is not yet completely destroyed. Its intervention in medical questions still continues. Opinion on such subjects as birth control, abortion and sterilisation of the defective are still influenced by theological dogmas. Psychology has not completely freed itself from its entanglements. None the less Darwinism was such a severe blow that the authority of theology was shattered all over to such an extent that it never afterwards made any serious effort to remain its lost empire. It is quite natural that this disruption of the Empire of Religion should be treated as a great Revolution. It is the result of the warfare which science waged against theology for 400 years, in which many pitched battles were fought between the two and the excitement caused by them was so great that nobody could fail to be impressed by the revolution that was blazing on.

There is no doubt that this religious revolution has been a great blessing. It has established freedom of thought. It has enabled society "to assume control of itself, making its own the world it once shared with superstition, facing undaunted the things of its former fears, and so carving out for itself, from the realm of mystery in which it lies, a sphere of unhampered action and a field of independent thought". The process of secularisation is not only welcomed by scientists for making civilisation-as distinguished from culture-possible, even Religious men and women have come to feel that much of what theology taught was unnecessary and a mere hindrance to the religious life and that this chopping of its wild growth was a welcome process. But for ascertaining the norm for judging the philosophy of Religion we must turn to another and a different kind of Revolution which Religion has undergone. That Revolution touches the nature and content of ruling conceptions of the relations of God to man, of Society to man and of man to man.

How great this revolution was can be seen from the differences which divide savage society from civilized society. Strange as it may seem no systematic study of this Religious Revolution has so far been made. None the less this Revolution is so great and so immense that it has brought about a complete transformation in the nature of Religion as it is taken to be by savage society and by civilised society although very few seem to be aware of it. To begin with the comparison between savage society and civilised society. In the religion of the savage one is struck by the presence of two things.

First is the performance of rites and ceremonies, the practice of magic or tabu and the worship of fetish or totem. The second thing that is noticeable is that the rites, ceremonies, magic, tabu, totem and fetish are conspicuous by their connection with certain occasions. These occasions are chiefly those, which represent the crises of human life. The events such as birth, the birth of the first born, attaining manhood, reaching puberty, marriage, sickness, death and war are the usual occasions which are marked out for the performance of rites and ceremonies, the use of magic and the worship of the totem. Students of the origin and history of Religion have sought to explain the origin and substance of religion by reference to either magic, tabu and totem and the rites and ceremonies connected therewith, and have deemed the occasions with which they are connected as of no account. Consequently we have theories explaining religion as having arisen in magic or as having arisen in fetishism. Nothing can be a greater error than this.

It is true that savage society practices magic, believes in tabu and worships the totem. But it is wrong to suppose that these constitute the religion or form the source of religion. To take such a view is to elevate what is incidental to the position of the principal. The principal thing in the Religion of the savage are the elemental facts of human existence such as life, death, birth, marriage etc. Magic, tabu, totem are things which are incidental. Magic, tabu, totem, fetish etc., are not the ends. They are only the means. The end is life and the preservation of life. Magic, tabu etc., are resorted to by the savage society not for their own sake but to conserve life and to exercise evil influences from doing harm to life. Thus understood the religion of the savage society was concerned with life and the preservation of life and it is these life processes which constitute the substance and source of the religion of the savage society.

So great was the concern of the savage society for life and the preservation of life that it made them the basis of its religion. So central were the life processes in the religion of the savage society that everything, which affected them, became part of its religion. The ceremonies of the savage society were not only concerned with the events of birth, attaining of manhood, puberty, marriage, sickness, death and war they were also concerned with food. Among pastoral peoples the flocks and herds are sacred.

Among agricultural peoples seedtime and harvest are marked by ceremonials performed with some reference to the growth and the preservation of the crops. Likewise drought, pestilence, and other strange, irregular phenomena of nature occasion the performance of ceremonials. Why should such occasions as harvest and famine be accompanied by religious ceremonies? Why is magic, tabu, totem be of such importance to the savage. The only answer is that they all affect the preservation of life. The process of life and its preservation form the main purpose. Life and preservation of life is the core and centre of the Religion of the savage society. As pointed out by Prof. Crawley the religion of the savage begins and ends with the affirmation and conservation of life.

In life and preservation of life consists the religion of the savage. What is however true of the religion of the savage is true of all religions wherever they are found for the simple reason that constitutes the essence of religion. It is true that in the present day society with its theological refinements this essence of religion has become hidden from view and is even forgotten. But that life and the preservation of life constitute the essence of religion even in the present day society is beyond question. This is well illustrated by Prof. Crowley. When speaking of the religious life of man in the present day society, he says how: "A man's religion does not enter into his professional or social hours, his scientific or artistic moments; practically its chief claims are settled on one day in the week from which ordinary worldly concerns are excluded. In fact, his life is in two parts; but the moiety with which religion is concerned is the elemental. Serious thinking on ultimate questions of life and death is, roughly speaking, the essence of his Sabbath; add to this the habit of prayer, giving the thanks at meals, and the subconscious feeling that birth and death, continuation and marriage are rightly solemnised by religion, while business and pleasure may possibly be consecrated, but only metaphorically or by an overflow of religious feeling." Comparing this description of the religious concerns of the man in the present day society with that of the savage, who can deny that the religion is essentially the same, both in theory and practice whether one speaks of the religion of the savage society or of the civilised society.

It is therefore clear that savage and civilised societies agree in one respect. In both the central interests of religion-namely in the life processes by which individuals are preserved and the race maintained-are the same. In this there is no real difference between the two. But they differ in two other important respects. In the first place in the religion of the savage society there is no trace of the idea of God. In the second place in the religion of the savage society there is no bond between morality and Religion. In the savage society there is religion without God. In the savage society there is morality but it is independent of Religion. How and when the idea of God became fused in Religion it is not possible to say.

It may be that the idea of God had its origin in the worship of the Great Man in Society, the Hero-giving rise to theism-with its faith in its living God. It may be that the idea of God came into existence as a result of the purely philosophical speculation upon the problem as to who created life-giving rise to Deism-with its belief in God as Architect of the Universe. In any case the idea of God is not integral to Religion. How it got fused into Religion it is difficult to explain. With regard to the relation between Religion and Morality this much may be safely said. Though the relation between God and Religion is not quite integral, the relation between Religion and morality is. Both religion and morality are connected with the same elemental facts of human existence-namely life, death, birth and marriage. Religion consecrates these life processes while morality furnishes rules for their preservation. Religion in consecrating the elemental facts and processes of life came to consecrate also the rules laid down by Society for their preservation. Looked at from this point it is easily explained why the bond between Religion and Morality took place. It was more intimate and more natural than the bond between Religion and God. But when exactly this fusion between Religion and Morality took place it is not easy to say. Be that as it may, the fact remains that the religion of the Civilised Society differs from that of the Savage Society into two important features. In civilised society God comes in the scheme of Religion. In civilised society morality becomes sanctified by Religion.

RELIGIOUS REVOLUTION

This is the first stage in the Religious Revolution. This Religious Revolution must not be supposed to have been ended here with the emergence of these two new features in the development of religion. The two ideas having become part of the constitution of the Religion of the Civilised Society have undergone further changes which have revolutionized their meaning and their moral significance. The second stage of the Religious Revolution marks a very radical change. The contrast is so big that civilized society has become split into two, antique society and modern society, so that instead of speaking of the religion of the civilised society it becomes necessary to speak of the religion of antique society as against the religion of modern society.

The religious revolution, which marks off antique society from modern society, is far greater than the religious revolution, which divides savage society from civilised society. Its dimensions will be obvious from the differences it has brought about in the conceptions regarding the relations between God, Society and Man. The first point of difference relates to the composition of society. Every human being, without choice on his own part, but simply in virtue of his birth and upbringing, becomes a member of what we call a natural society. He belongs that is to a certain family and a certain nation. This membership lays upon him definite obligations and duties which he is called upon to fulfil as a matter of course and on pain of social penalties and disabilities while at the same time it confers upon him certain social rights and advantages. In this respect the ancient and modern worlds are alike. But in the words of Prof. Smith: "Thus a man was born into a fixed relation to certain gods as surely as he was born into relation to his fellow men; and his religion, that is, the part of conduct which was determined by his relation to the gods, was simply one side of the general scheme of conduct prescribed for him by his position as a member of society. There was no separation between the spheres of religion and of ordinary life. Every social act had a reference to the gods as well as to men, for the social body was not made up of men only, but of gods and men."

"There is this important difference, that the tribal or national societies of the ancient world were not strictly natural in the modern sense of the word, for the gods had their part and place in them equally with men. The circle into which a man was born was not simply a group of kinsfolk and fellow citizens, but embraced also certain divine beings, the gods of the family and of the state, which to the ancient mind were as much a part of the particular community with which they stood connected as the human members of the social circle. The relation between the gods of antiquity and their worshippers was expressed in the language of human relationship, and this language was not taken in a figurative sense but with strict literally. If a god was spoken of as father and his worshippers as his offspring, the meaning was that the worshippers were literally of his stock, that he and they made up one natural family with reciprocal family duties to one another. Or, again, if the god was addressed as king, and worshippers called themselves his servants, they meant that the supreme guidance of the state was actually in his hands, and accordingly the organisation of the state included provision for consulting his will and obtaining his direction in all weighty matters, also provision for approaching him as king with due homage and tribute. Thus in ancient Society men and their Gods formed a social and political as well as a religious whole. Religion was founded on kinship between the God and his worshippers. Modern Society has eliminated God from its composition. It consists of men only. The second point of difference between antique and modern society relates to the bond between God and Society. In the antique world the various communities "believed in the existence of many Gods, for they accepted as real the Gods of their enemies as well as their own, but they did not worship the strange Gods from whom they had no favour to expect, and on whom their gifts and offerings would have been thrown away. Each group had its own God, or perhaps a God and Goddess, to whom the other Gods bore no relation whatever."

The God of the antique society was an exclusive God. God was owned by and bound to one singly community. This is largely to be accounted for by "the share taken by the Gods in the feuds and wars of their worshippers. The enemies of the God and the enemies of his people are identical; even in the Old Testament `the enemies of Jehovah' are originally nothing else than the enemies of Israel. In battle each God fights for his own people, and to his aid success is ascribed; Chemosh gives victory to Moab and Asshyr to Assyria; and often the divine image or symbol accompanies the host to battle. When the ark was brought into the camp of Israel, the Philistines said, "Gods are come into the camp; who can deliver us from their own practice, for when David defeated them at Baalperazirm, part of the booty consisted in their idols which had been carried into the field. When the Carthaginians, in their treaty with Phillip of Macedon, speak of "the Gods that take part in the campaign," they doubtless refer to the inmates of the sacred tent which was pitched in time of war beside the tent of the general, and before which prisoners were sacrificed after a victory. Similarly an Arabic poet says, "Yaguth went forth with us against Morad"; that is, the image of the God Yaguth was carried into the fray".

This fact had produced solidarity between God and the community. "Hence, on the principle of solidarity between Gods and their worshippers, the particularism characteristic of political society could not but reappear in the sphere of religion. In the same measure as the God of a clan or town had indisputable claim to the reverence and service of the community to which he belonged, he was necessarily an enemy to their enemies and a stranger to those to whom they were strangers". God had become attached to a community, and the community had become attached to their God.

God had become the God of the Community and the Community had become the chosen community of the God. This view had two consequences. Antique Society never came to conceive that God could be universal God, the God of all. Antique Society never could conceive that there was any such thing as humanity in general. The third point of difference between ancient and modern society, has reference to the conception of the fatherhood of God. In the antique Society God was the Father of his people but the basis of this conception of Fatherhood was deemed to be physical. "In heathen religions the Fatherhood of the Gods is physical fatherhood. Among the Greeks, for example, the idea that the Gods fashioned men out of clay, as potters fashion images, is relatively modern. The older conception is that the races of men have Gods for their ancestors, or are the children of the earth, the common mother of Gods and men, so that men are really of the stock or kin of the Gods. That the same conception was familiar to the older Semites appears from the Bible.

Jeremiah describes idolaters as saying to a stock, Thou art my father; and to a stone, Thou has brought me forth. In the ancient poem, Num. xxi. 29, The Moabites are called the sons and daughters of Chemosh, and at a much more recent date the prophet Malachi calls a heathen woman "the daughter of a strange God". These phrases are doubtless accommodations to the language, which the heathen neighbours of Israel used about themselves. In Syria and Palestine each clan, or even complex of clans forming a small independent people, traced back its origin to a great first father; and they indicate that, just as in Greece this father or progenitor of the race was commonly identified with the God of the race. With this it accords that in the judgment of most modern enquirers several names of deities appear in the old genealogies of nations in the Book of Genesis.

Edom, for example, the progenitor of the Edomites, was identified by the Hebrews with Esau the brother of Jacob, but to the heathen he was a God, as appears from the theophorous proper name Obededom, "worshipper of Edom", the extant fragments of Phoenician and Babylonian cosmogonies date from a time when tribal religion and the connection of individual Gods with particular kindreds was forgotten or had fallen into the background. But in a generalized form the notion that men are the offspring of the Gods still held its ground. In the Phoenician cosmogony of Philo Bablius it does so in a confused shape, due to the authors euhemerism, that is, to his theory that deities are nothing more than deified men who had been great benefactors to their species. Again, in the Chaldaean legend preserved by Berosus, the belief that men are of the blood of the Gods is expressed in a form too crude not to be very ancient; for animals as well as men are said to have been formed out of clay mingled with the blood of a decapitated deity."

This conception of blood kinship of Gods and men had one important consequence. To the antique world God was a human being and as such was not capable of absolute virtue and absolute goodness. God shared the physical nature of man and was afflicted with the passions infirmities and vices to which man was subject. The God of the antique world had all the wants and appetites of man and he often indulged in the vices in which many revelled. Worshipers had to implore God not to lead them into temptations. In modern Society the idea of divine fatherhood has become entirely dissociated from the physical basis of natural fatherhood. In its place man is conceived to be created in the image of God; he is not deemed to be begotten by God. This change in the conception of the fatherhood of God looked at from its moral aspect has made a tremendous difference in the nature of God as a Governor of the Universe. God with his physical basis was not capable of absolute good and absolute virtue. With God wanting in righteousness the universe could not insist on righteousness as an immutable principle. This dissociation of God from physical contact with man has made it possible for God to be conceived of as capable of absolute good and absolute virtue. The fourth point of difference relates to the part religion plays when a change of nationality takes place. In the antique world there could be no change of nationality unless it was accompanied by a change of Religion.

In the antique world, "It was impossible for an individual to change his religion without changing his nationality, and a whole community could hardly change its religion at all without being absorbed into another stock or nation. Religions like political ties were transmitted from father to son; for a man could not choose a new God at will; the Gods of his fathers were the only deities on whom he could count as friendly and ready to accept his homage, unless he forswore his own kindred and was received into a new circle of civil as well as religious life." How change of religion was a condition precedent to a Social fusion is well illustrated by the dialogue between Naomi and Ruth in the Old Testament. "Thy Sister" says Naomi to Ruth, "is gone back unto her people and unto her Gods"; and Ruth replies, "Thy people shall be my people and thy God my God." It is quite clear that in the ancient world a change of nationality involved a change of cult. Social fusion meant religious fusion.

MODERN SOCIETY ABANDONMENT OF RELIGION

In modern society abandonment of religion or acceptance of another is not necessary for social fusion. This is best illustrated by what is in modern terminology and naturalisation, whereby the citizen of one state abandons his citizenship of the state and becomes a citizen of new state. In this process of naturalisation religion has no place. One can have a social fusion which is another name for naturalisation without undergoing a religious fusion. To distinguish modern society from antique society it is not enough to say that Modern Society consists of men only. It must be added that it consists of men who are worshippers of different Gods.

The fifth point of difference relates to the necessity of knowledge as to the nature of God as part of religion. "From the antique point of view, indeed the question what the Gods are in themselves is not a religious but a speculative one; what is requisite to religion is a practical acquaintance with the rules on which the deity acts and on which he expects his worshippers to frame their conduct-what in Kings xvii. 26 is called the "manner" or rather the "customary law" (misphat) of the God of the land. This is true even of the religion of Israel. When the prophets speak of the knowledge of the laws and principles of His government in Israel, and a summary expression for religion as a whole is "the knowledge and fear of Jehovah," i.e. the knowledge of what Jehovah prescribes, combined with a reverent obedience. An extreme scepticism towards all religious speculation is recommended in the Book of Ecclesiastes as the proper attitude of piety, for no amount of discussion can carry a man beyond the plain rule, to "fear God and keep His Commandments". This counsel the author puts into the mouth of Solomon, and so represents it, not unjustly, as summing up the old view of religion, which in more modern days had unfortunately begun to be undermined."

The sixth point of difference relates to the place of belief in Religion. In ancient Society: "Ritual and practical usages were, strictly speaking, the sum total of ancient religions. Religion in primitive times was not a system of belief with practical applications; it was a body of fixed traditional practices, to which every member of society conformed as a matter of courage. Men would not be men if they agreed to do certain things without having a reason for their action; but in ancient religion the reason was not first formulated as a doctrine and then expressed in practice, but conversely, practice preceded doctrinal theory. Men form general rule of conduct before they begin to express general principles in words; political institutions are older than political theories and in like manner religious institutions are older than religious theories. This analogy is not arbitrarily chosen, for in fact the parallelism in ancient society between religious and political institutions is complete. In each sphere great importance was attached to form and precedent, but the explanation why the precedent was followed consisted merely of legend as to its first establishment. That the precedent, once established, was authoritative did not appear to require any proof. The rules of society were based on precedent, and the continued existence of the society was sufficient reason why a precedent once set should continue to be followed."

The seventh point of difference relates to the place of individual conviction in Religion. In ancient Society: "Religion was a part of the organized social life into which a man was born, and to which he conformed through life in the same unconscious way in which men fall into any habitual practice of the society in which they live. Men took the Gods and their worship for granted, just as they took the other usages of the state for granted, and if they reason or speculated about them, they did so on the presupposition that the traditional usages were fixed things, behind which their reasoning must not go, and which no reasoning could be allowed to overturn. To us modern's religion is above all a matter of individual conviction and reasoned belief, but to the ancients it was a part of the citizen's public life, reduced to fixed forms, which he was not bound to understand and was not at liberty to criticize or to neglect. Religious nonconformity was an offence against the state; for if sacred tradition was tampered with the bases of society were undermined, and the favour of the Gods was forfeited. But so long as the prescribed forms were duly observed, a man was recognized as truly pious, and no one asked how his religion was rooted in his heart or affected his reason. Like political duty, of which indeed it was a part, religion was entirely comprehended in the observance of certain fixed rules of outward conduct."

The eighth point of difference pertains to the relation of God to Society and man, of Society to Man in the matter of God's Providence. First as to the difference in the relation of God to Society. In this connection three points may be noted. The faith of the antique world "Sought nothing higher than a condition of physical bien ere.... The good things desired of the Gods were the blessings of earthly life, not spiritual but carnal things." What the antique societies asked and believed themselves to receive from their God lay mainly in the following things: "Abundant harvests, help against their enemies and counsel by oracles or soothsayers in matters of natural difficulty." In the antique world "Religion was not the affair of the individual but of the Community.... It was the community, and not the individual, that was sure of the permanent and the unfailing hand of the deity." Next as to the difference in the relation of God to man. "It was not the business of the Gods of heathenish to watch, by a series of special providence, over the welfare of every individual. It is true that individuals laid their private affairs before the Gods, and asked with prayers and views for strictly personal blessings. But they did this just as they might crave a personal boon from a king, or as a son craves a boon from a father, without expecting to get all that was asked. What the Gods might do in this way was done as a matter of personal favour, and was not part of their proper function as heads of the community." "The Gods watched over a man's civic life, they gave him his share in public benefits, the annual largess of the harvest and the vintage, national peace or victory over enemies, and so forth, but they were not sure helpers in every private need, and above all they would not help him in matters that were against the interests of the community as a whole. There was therefore a whole region of possible needs and desires for which religion could and would do nothing." Next the difference in the attitude of God and Society to man.

In the antique world Society was indifferent to individual welfare. God as no doubt bound to Society. But "the compact between the God and his worshippers was not held to pledge the deity to make the private cares of each member of the Community his own." "The benefits expected of God were of a public character affecting the whole community, especially fruitful seasons, increase of flocks of herds and success in war. So long as community flourished the fact that an individual was miserable reflected no discredit on divine providence." On the contrary the antique world looked upon the misery of a man as proof.

"That the sufferer was an evildoer, justly hateful to the Gods. Such a man was out of place among the happy and the prosperous crowd that assembled on feast days before the alter." It is in accordance with this view that the leper and the mourner were shut out from the exercise of religion as well as from the privileges of social life and their food was not brought into the house of God. As for conflict between individual and individual and between society and the individual God had no concern.

In the antique world: "It was not expected that God should always be busy righting human affairs. In ordinary matters it was men's business to help themselves and their own kins folk, though the sense that the God was always near, and could be called upon at need, was a moral force continually working in some degree for the maintenance of social righteousness and order. The strength of this moral force was indeed very uncertain, for it was always possible for the evildoer to flatter himself that his offence would be overlooked." In the antique world man did not ask God to be righteous to him. "Whether in civil or in profane matters, the habit of the old world was to think much of the community and little of the individual life, and no one felt this to be unjust even though it bore hardly on himself. The God was the God of the national or of the tribe, and he knew and cared for the individual only as a member of the community."

That was the attitude that man in the antique world took of his own private misfortune. Man came to rejoice before his God and "in rejoicing before his God man rejoiced with and for the welfare of his kindred, his neighbours and his country, and, in renewing by solemn act of worship the bond that united him to God, he also renewed the bonds of family, social and national obligation." Man in the antique world did not call upon his maker to be righteous to him. Such is this other Revolution in Religion.

There have thus been two Religious Revolutions. One was an external Revolution. The other was an internal Revolution. The External Revolution was concerned with the field within which the authority of Religion was to prevail. The Internal Revolution had to do with the changes in Religion as a scheme of divine Governance for human society. The External Revolution was not really a Religious Revolution at all. It was a revolt of science against the extra territorial jurisdiction assumed by Religion over a field which did not belong. The Internal Revolution was a real Revolution or may be compared to any other political Revolution, such as the French Revolution or the Russian Revolution. It involved a constitutional change. By this Revolution the Scheme of divine governance came to be altered, amended and reconstituted. How profound have been the changes which this internal Revolution, has made in the antique scheme of divine governance can be easily seen.

By this Revolution God has ceased to be a member of a community. Thereby he has become impartial. God has ceased to be the Father of Man in the physical sense of the word. He has become the creator of the Universe. The breaking of this blood bond has made it possible to hold that God is good. By this Revolution man has ceased to be a blind worshipper of God doing nothing but obeying his commands. Thereby man has become a responsible person required to justify his belief in God's commandments by his conviction. By this Revolution God has ceased to be merely the protector of Society and social interests in gross have ceased to be the centre of the divine Order. Society and man have changed places as centres of this divine order. It is man who has become the centre of it. All this analysis of the Revolution in the Ruling concepts of Religion as a scheme of divine governance had one purpose namely to discover the norm for evaluating the philosophy of a Religion. The impatient reader may not ask where are these norms and what are they? The reader may not have found the norms specified by their names in the foregoing discussion. But he could not have failed to notice that the whole of this Religious Revolution was raging around the norms for judging what is right and what is wrong. If he has not, let it be made explicit what has been implicit in the whole of this discussion. We began with the distinction between antique society and modern society as has been pointed out they differed in the type of divine governance they accepted as their Religious ideals.

Religious Ideal

At one end of the Revolution was the antique society with its Religious ideal in which the end was Society. At the other end of the Revolution is the modern Society with its Religious ideal in which the end is the individual. To put the same fact in terms of the norm it can be said that the norm or the criterion, for judging right and wrong in the Antique Society was utility while the norm or the criterion for judging right and wrong in the modern Society is Justice. The Religious Revolution was not thus a revolution in the religious organization of Society resulting in the shifting of the centre-from society to the individual-it was a revolution in the norms. Some may demur to the norms suggested. It may be that it is a new way of reaching them.

But there is no doubt that they are the real norms by which to judge the philosophy of religion. In the first place the norm must enable people to judge what is right and wrong in the conduct of men. In the second place the norm must be appropriate to current notion of what constitutes the moral good. From both these points of view they appear to be the true norms. They enable us to judge what is right and wrong. They are appropriate to the society which adopted them. Utility as a criterion was appropriate to the antique world in which society being the end, the moral good was held to be something which had social utility. Justice as a criterion became appropriate to the Modern World in which individual being the end, the moral good was held to be something which does justice to the individual.

There may be controversy as to which of the two norms is morally superior. But there can not be any serious controversy that these are not the norms. If it is said that these norms are not transcendental enough; the reply is that if a norm whereby one is to judge the philosophy of religion must be Godly, it must also be earthly. At any rate these are the norms propose to be adopt in examining the philosophy of Hinduism. This is a long detour. But it was a necessary preliminary to any inquiry into the main question. However, when one begins the inquiry one meets with an initial difficulty. The Hindu is not prepared to face the inquiry. He either argues that religion is of no importance or he takes shelter behind the view-fostered by the study of comparative Religion-that all religions are good. There is no doubt that both these views are mistaken and untenable.

Religion as a social force cannot be ignored. Religion has been aptly described by Hebert Spencer as "the weft which everywhere crosses the warp of history". This is true of every Society. But Religion has not only crossed everywhere the warp of Indian History it forms the warp and woof of the Hindu mind. The life of the Hindu is regulated by Religion at every moment of his life. It orders him how during life he should conduct himself and how on death his body shall be disposed of. It tells him how and when he shall indulge in his sexual impulses. It tells him what ceremonies are to be performed when a child is born-how he should name, how he should cut the hair on its head, how he should perform its first feeding. It tells him what occupation he can take to, what woman he should marry.

It tells him with whom he should dine and what food he should eat, what vegetables are lawful and what are forbidden. It tells how he should spend his day, how many times he should eat, how many times he should pray. There is no act of the Hindu which is not covered or ordained by Religion. It seems strange that the educated Hindus should come to look upon it as though it was a matter of indifference. Besides, Religion is a social force. As has been pointed out Religion stands for a scheme of divine governance. The scheme becomes an ideal for society to follow. The ideal may be nonexistent in the sense that it is something which is constructed. But although nonexistent, it is real. For an ideal it has full operative force which is inherent in every ideal. Those who deny the importance of religion not only forget this, they also fail to realize how great is the potency and sanction that lies behind a religious ideal as compound with that of a purely secular ideal. This is probably due to the lag which one sees between the real and the ideal which is always present whether the ideal is religious or secular.

But the relative potency of the two ideals is to be measured by another test-namely their power to override the practical instincts of man. The ideal is concerned with something that is remote. The practical instincts of man are concerned with the immediate present. Now placed as against the force of the practical instincts of man the two ideals show their difference in an unmistaken manner. The practical instincts of man do yield to the prescriptions of a religious ideal however much the two are opposed to each other. The practical instincts of man do not on the other hand yield to the secular ideal if the two are in conflict. This means that a religious ideal has a hold on mankind, irrespective of an earthly gain. This can never be said of a purely secular ideal. Its power depends upon its power to confer material benefit. This shows how great the difference in the potency and sanction of the two ideals is over the human mind. A religious ideal never fails to work so long as there is faith in that ideal. To ignore religion is to ignore a live wire.

Again to hold that all religions are true and good is to cherish a belief which is positively and demonstrably wrong. This belief, one is sorry to say, is the result of what is known as the study of comparative religion. Comparative religion has done one great service to humanity. It has broken down the claim and arrogance of revealed religions as being the only true and good religions of study. While it is true that comparative religion has abrogated the capricious distinction between true and false religions based on purely arbitrary and a priori considerations, it has brought in its wake some false notions about religion. The most harmful one is the one mentioned namely that all religions are equally good and that there is no necessity of discriminating between them. Nothing can be a greater error than this. Religion is an institution or an influence and like all social influences and institutions, it may help or it may harm a society which is in its grip.

As pointed out by Prof. Tiele religion is "one of the mightiest motors in the history of mankind, which formed as well as tore asunder nations, united as well as divided empires, which sanctioned the most atrocious and barbarous deeds, the most libinous customs, inspired the most admirable acts of heroism, self renunciation, and devotion, which occasioned the most sanguinary wars, rebellions and persecutions, as well as brought about the freedom, happiness and peace of nations-at one time a partisan of tyranny, at another breaking its chains, now calling into existence and fostering a new and brilliant civilization, then the deadly foe to progress, science and art." A force which shows such a strange contrast in its result can be accepted as good without examining the form it takes and the ideal it serves. Everything depends upon what social ideal a given religion as a divine scheme of governance hold out. This is a question which is not avowed by the science of comparative religion. Indeed it begins where comparative religion ends. The Hindu is merely trying to avoid it by saying that although religions are many they are equally good. For they are not.

However much the Hindu may seek to burke the inquiry into the philosophy of Hinduism there is no escape. He must face it. Now to begin with the subject let us to apply both the tests, the test of justice and the test of utility to judge the philosophy of Hinduism. First I will apply the test of justice. Before doing so principle of gustic needs to be explained. No one has expounded it better than Professor Bergbon As interpreted by him the principle of justice is a compendious one and includes most of the other principles which have become the foundation of a moral order. Justice has always evoked ideas of equality, of proportion of "compensation". Equity signifies equality. Rules and regulations, right and righteousness are concerned with equality in value. If all men are equal, all men are of the same essence and the common essence entitled them to the same fundamental rights and to equal liberty. In short justice is simply another name for liberty, equality and fraternity. Which of these tenets does Hinduism recognize? Let us take the question one by one.

Equality of Hinduism

In the scheme of Manu the Brahmin is placed at the first in rank. Below him is the Kshatriya. Below Kshatriya is the Vaishya. Below Vaishya is the Sudra and Below Sudra is the Ati-Sudra (the Untouchables). This system of rank and gradation is, simply another way of enunciating the principle of inequality so that it may be truly said that Hinduism does not recognize equality. This inequality in status is not merely the inequality that one sees in the warrant of precedence prescribed for a ceremonial gathering at a King's Court. It is a permanent social relationship among the classes to be observed-to be enforced-at all times in all places and for all purposes. It will take too long to show how in every phase of life Manu has introduced and made inequality the vital force of life. But it will illustrate it by taking a few examples such as slavery, marriage and Rule of Law. Manu recognizes Slavery. But he confined it to the Sudras.

Only Sudras could be made slaves of the three higher classes. But the higher classes could not be the slaves of the Sudra. But evidently practice differed from the law of Manu and not only Sudras happened to become slaves but members of the other three classes also become slaves. When this was discovered to be the case a new rule was enacted by a Successor of Manu namely Narada. This new rule of Narada runs as follows: "In the inverse order of the four castes slavery is not ordained except where a man violates the duties peculiar to his caste. Slavery (in that respect) is analogous to the condition of a wife." Recognition of slavery was bad enough. But if the rule of slavery had been left free to take its own course it would have had at least one beneficial effect. It would have been a levelling force. The foundation of caste would have been destroyed. For under it a Brahmin might have become the slave of the Untouchable and the Untouchable would have become the master of the Brahmin. But it was seen that unfettered slavery was an equalitarian principle and an attempt was made to nullify it. Manu and his successors therefore while recognising slavery ordains that it shall not be recognised in its inverse order to the Varna System. That means that a Brahmin may become the slave of another Brahmin. But he shall not be the slave of a person of another Varna i.e. of the Kshatriya, Vaishya, Sudra, or Ati-Sudra. On the other hand a Brahmin may hold as his slave any one belonging to the four Varnas. A Kshatriya can have a Kshatriya, Vaisha, Sudra and Ati-Sudra as his slaves but not one who is a Brahmin. A Vaishya can have a Vaishya, Sudra and Ati-Sudra as his slaves but not one who is a Brahmin or a Kshatriya.

A Sudra can hold a Sudra and Ati-sudra can hold an Ati-Sudra as his slave but not one who is a Brahmin, Kshatriya, Vaishya or Sudra. Challenge Conversion and Hindu Response: Again at a moment of history of our ancient nation when the Hindu foundation of the nation is being challenged and sought to be undermined. But never before in our history has the challenge been as dangerously deceptive, pernicious, and sophisticated as it is now. It is therefore difficult to respond to this challenge since it cannot be easily perceived.

Hence, the response to this challenge and the implicit threat has to be well thought out and profound, but as before in our history, the response to be fruitful has to be designed and structured by the confluence of spiritual guidance and political resolve. Such a confluence has been the fundamental basis of our past responses to such challenges in history, from the installation by rishis of Adi Raja Prithu as King of Bharatvarsh, Chanakya's founding of the Mauryan kingdom, the establishment of the Vijayanagaram empire at Hampi by Sringeri Shankaracharya, to inspiring the fighting armies of Shivaji by Swami Ramdass. Even Mahatma Gandhi and Jayaprakash Narayan in their respective struggles for independence of the nation from colonialism, and for the restoration of democracy in a nation that was drowned in the darkness of the Emergency, had followed this unique Hindu model of spiritually guiding a political movement without seeking the fruits of office for themselves. The Hindu foundation of modern India is why India has been and is even today referred to, in India and abroad, as Hindustan. Hindustan is defined as a nation of Hindus and those who accept that their ancestors are Hindus. The concept also includes refugee minorities who accept the core values of the

Hindu culture and therefore recognised as a part of the Hindustan nation. Thus, when the Dwarka Mutt Shankaracharya gave the arriving Parsi refugees in Sanjaan [Kutch coast] a five-point requirement for settling in the country, they readily accepted and have not deviated from it even today.

These five points were: Giving up Persian language and adopting Gujarati; wearing Indian clothes instead of Persian; treating the cow as sacred; reciting some select Sanskrit shlokas in their marriage ceremony; and laying down of weapons. Despite being the smallest minority, with disproportionate share in offices of power and national wealth, and perhaps also the wealthiest community, there is and has been no tension or conflict between Hindus and Parsis. Today Hindus despite de facto in power and in the organs of the state, are victims of that same targeting, but of course in a very subtle and sophisticated manner. In furthering the objective of this targeting, Islam and Christianity, more so the latter, have been able to leverage the influence of prominent Hindus themselves.

Parsis and Jews do not threaten the Hindu character of the nation. They do not seek to proselytise or convert Hindus by monetary inducements or by obscurantist preachings such as curing persons who convert, of incurable terminal diseases. But on the other hand, the preachings of the religious leaders of Islam and Christianity in India, altogether for a thousand years, had targeted Hindus and sought the religious conversions to their faiths by creating deprivation and loss of self-esteem, through the abuse of the power of the state against Hindus.

They were not subtle about it. For example, in 1545, King John III of Portugal gave a command to the then Governor of Goa that neither public nor private 'idols' of Hindu heathens be tolerated on the island of Goa and that severe punishment be meted out to those who persist in keeping them. Thereafter, a terrible inquisition followed during which Hindus were killed, brutalised and their temples razed to the ground. Still we must not forget only a minority of Hindus converted to Christianity. No other religious community other than Hindus suffered such prolonged and atrocious persecution and survived as a religion of a vast majority on their own soil. Let us not forget this defiance in our past. Today Hindus despite de facto in power and in the organs of the state, are victims of that same targeting, but of course in a very subtle and sophisticated manner. In furthering the objective of this targeting, Islam and Christianity, more so the latter, have been able to leverage the influence of prominent Hindus themselves, who wittingly for money or unwittingly because of a programmed mindset of being defensive about being a Hindu [thereby ready to ape the West] are tools of this targeting. What is the nature and scope of this targeting, and is there a way for us to end it by conciliation with Christians and Muslims? In other words, can we seek to end religious conversion in India today by the ancient Hindu way of shashtrarthas as Hindu saints did, as for example Adi Sankara did with Buddhism and Uttara Mimamsa theologies and Azhwars and Nayanars saints in the south did with Jainism? Will indeed Christians and Muslims recognise the sanctity of shashtrarthas?

There is a serious problem here because as an interesting study of Sarah Claerhout and Jakob De Roover titled: The Question of Conversion in India [Economic and Political Weekly, July 9, 2005] concludes, Hindus and Christians have fundamentally different and mutually exclusive concepts of religion and thus also in their approaches to the question of conversion. Hence, say the authors, for Hindus and Christians to dialogue on conversion would be fruitless because they will have "great difficulties making sense of each other's statements and arguments". This is because Hindus do not consider any religion as wholly false, and as Gandhiji put it, all religions have some errors in them. Since all religions lead to God, hence there is no need for forcing a conversion. Christians [and Muslims] think that their's is the only true religion, and it is God's work to convert heathens and kafirs to their only true religion. Therefore, either Hindus will have to capitulate on this question by permitting religious conversion in India, or in the alternative be united and assertive to ensure that laws are enacted and effectively enforced against religious conversion of Hindus. There is no third way.

It is urgent now that Hindus be mobilised to assertively oppose any further conversion from Hinduism to any other non-Indian religion. There is no room for indifference here. This is because that status quo is damaging to the Hindu faith, since the Christian missionaries and Muslim mullahs are already fully at work, funds being no constraint, to convert Hindus. If conversions are not explicitly opposed, then Hindus are implicitly acquiescing in the atrocity. There is a fundamental disconnect between the religious outlook of Hindus and the Christians and Muslims which makes it impossible for a fruitful debate and mutual understanding on the question of religious conversion.

Reflect on the past trends: In 1000 A.D., Muslims and Christians in undivided India were in negligible numbers. By 1400, they had become 3.5 per cent of the subcontinent. In 1700, they rose to 11 per cent, and by 1891 to 13 per cent. By the time of Partition, they were 23 per cent, and today in South Asia, the Christian and Muslim population is 36 per cent. What will it be in 2050 or 2150? This is an extraordinary rise, which has continued even after freedom from British colonial rule. De facto power in the hands of Hindu majority has not changed the attitude of the proselytisers, only their strategy has changed and become invisible for most Hindus. And those Hindus who have been in power in government have been soft on this issue entrapped by the lack of a Hindu mindset and bloc voting by the Muslims and Christians.

Even the most secular Hindus should however worry about this demographic trend, because secularism is itself under threat, if the Hindus lose their majority share in population. That is why even Gandhiji and Dr. Ambedkar [no Hindu fundamentalists but highly regarded secularists], during the freedom struggle had stoutly opposed religious conversions. In Mahatma's interview given to The Hindu in 1931.

4 Legal Definition of Hinduism

HINDU LAW

India's Constitution does not give a definition of the term Hindu, but it does define to whom the "Hindu Law" applies. It has to do this because in spite of its pretence to secularism, the Indian Constitution allows Muslims, Christians and Parsis a separate Personal Law. In a way, this separate treatment of different communities merely continues the communal autonomy of castes and sects accepted in pre-modern Hindu states, but it exposes the credibility deficit of Indian secularism. At any rate, the situation is that Personal Law is divided on the basis of religion, and that one of the legal subsystems is called Hindu Law. Article 25 (2)(b) of the Constitution stipulates that "the reference to Hindus shall be construed as including a reference to persons professing the Sikh, Jain or Buddhist religion". The Hindu Marriage Act of 1955 goes in greater detail to define this "legal Hindu", by stipulating in Section 2 that the Act applies:

(a) To any person who is a Hindu by religion in any of its forms and developments, including a Viashaiva, a Lingayat or a follower of the Brahmo, Prarthana or Arya Samaj.

(b) To any person who is a Buddhist, Jain or Sikh by religion.

(c) To any other person domiciled in the territories to which this Act extends who is not a Muslim, Christian, Parsi or Jew by religion.

This definition of the "legal Hindu", though explicitly not equating him with the "Hindu by religion", is exactly coterminous with the original Islamic use of the term Hindu: all Indian Pagans are legally Hindus. The Buddhists, Jains and Sikhs are explicitly included in the "Hindus by law" but separated from the "Hindus by religion": at this point, the law follows the usage established by Western scholars, contrary to the original usage. Note that the changes in Hindu Law imposed by an Act of Parliament (on top of the very existence of separate Hindu and Muslim Law regimes) constitute a further measure of communal inequality. The secular government would not dare to touch the other religion-based law systems, as has repeatedly been shown in the past decades regarding items of Christian and Muslim Personal Law. An interference in Hindu Law by a national legislative body only makes sense in an avowedly Hindu state; in a sense, therefore, the Hindu Marriage Act constitutes an admission by Jawaharlal Nehru that ultimately India is a Hindu state.

Semi-Hindus

Separatist Sikhs have at times criticized the inclusion of the Sikhs in the "legal Hindu" category. When Law Minister Dr. Bhimrao Ambedkar first introduced the Hindu Code Bill in 1951, Sikh spokesman Sardar Hukum Singh regarded the Bill as "a dubious attempt on the part of the Hindus to absorb the Sikhs". Dr. Ambedkar replied: "The application of the Hindu Code to Sikhs, Buddhists and Jains was a historical development and it would be too late, sociologically, to object to it. When the Buddha differed from the Vedic Brahmins, he did so only in matters of creed, but left the Hindu legal framework intact. He did not propound a separate law for his followers. The same was the case with Mahavir and the ten Sikh gurus. The Privy Council had as early as 1830 laid down that the Sikhs were governed by the Hindu law."

This at once explains why Ambedkar's neo-Buddhist followers have not objected to their inclusion in the "legal Hindu" category. On the contrary, this inclusion later served to justify their inclusion in reservation schemes and other benefits for Hindu ex-Untouchables: as Untouchability was a problem of Hindu society, it was reasonable that special benefits for this section of Hindu society only apply to ex-Untouchable members of the Hindu, or at least the "legal Hindu" category. When the Ramakrishna Mission went to court to have itself declared a non-Hindu minority (in order to escape the legal anti-Hindu discriminations esp. in education), it claimed that its members could legally still be treated as Hindus in matters of marriage and inheritance, even while being recognized as non-Hindus in the religious sense.

In effect, the Ramakrishnaites wanted to have the same status as Sikhs and Buddhists: legal recognition as "legal Hindus and religious non-Hindus". They rightly understood that the law has created a category of semi-Hindus who have no separate traditions of personal law but have nevertheless a separate religious identity entitling them to the privileges accorded to the minorities. The Indian laws make a distinction between what we may call the "Hindu in the broad sense", to whom Hindu Law applies, and who is coterminous with the Hindu of Persian-Islamic usage, viz. every Indian Pagan; and the "Hindu in the narrow sense", a category which may not include Buddhism and Sikhism. Though the law does not mention them, the tribal traditions are also taken to fall partly (except for a measure of accomplished sanskritization) outside this narrow category. Of course, the claims by different groups of belonging to this broad-Hindu but non-narrow-Hindu category should be considered separately and on their own merits, e.g. Buddhism's claim to a distinct identity does not imply an endorsement of Sikhism's claim to the same. The debate over whether certain communities come under the definition of Hinduism is largely a debate over whether it is the narrow or the broad definition that should be considered as the "true" definition.

The Scheduled Castes

A contentious point, esp. since the institution and expansion of caste-based reservation schemes, is the religious factor in defining the Scheduled Castes, the former Untouchables. The legal situation is as follows: "The Constitution (Scheduled Castes) Order 1950 said in so many words that a non-Hindu could never be a Scheduled Caste (even if belonging to a particular caste included in the official list of Scheduled Castes). By an amendment introduced in 1956, it was provided that only a Hindu or a Sikh could be a Scheduled Caste. The Scheduled Caste law is, thus, clearly religion-based and its religious basis has generated abundant case law. The Supreme Court has held that a Scheduled

Caste Hindu on ceasing to be a Hindu also ceases to be a Scheduled Caste and, should he ever reconvert to Hinduism, he will also regain forthwith the Scheduled Caste status." Meanwhile, Buddhists have also been explicitly included (and had already been implicitly treated) as belonging to the Hindu category in this regard, i.e. entitled to Scheduled Caste status if belonging to such a caste. Jains need no mention here, as they belong to the Vaishya upper castes; but the rare Scheduled Caste convert to Jainism would likewise remain entitled to benefits earmarked for the Scheduled Castes.

In contemporary anti-Hindu polemic, chiefly by Christian missionaries, and here by the Muslim chairman of the Minorities' Commission (an intrinsically anti-Hindu institution), it is frequently claimed that: "This law has been clearly designed with the object of preventing low caste Hindus, even if disgruntled with religion-based social inequalities, from converting to Christianity or Islam." If this seems plausible, and is hence repeated faithfully in most Western publications, it is nonetheless untrue. The Government of India Act (1935), enacted by the British who had other concerns, already excluded Christian converts from the Scheduled Castes category. This was done after consultation with the missionaries, who were honest enough to acknowledge this as the obvious implication of their own boast that conversion brought freedom from caste disabilities. As long as Christians and Muslims propagate the notion that their own religion is egalitarian and caste-free, it is only logical that converts have to give up their Scheduled Caste status. Today, all while propagating the necessary connection between Hinduism and caste disabilities, the Churches are clamouring for the recognition of their SC converts as "Dalit Christians". If they haven't had their way so far, it is mainly due to the opposition not from the Hindutva forces but from the neo-Buddhists and the legitimate Scheduled Castes themselves. At the time of writing, the legal position remains that only followers of Indic religions are classified by caste, with the concomitant legal benefits in case of low castes.

The Scheduled Tribes

The Scheduled Tribes as such are not mentioned in the context of defining the borders of the Hindu community, for "tribal" is only recognized in law as a sociological rather than a religious category. A Christian tribal is consequently still entitled to all the special privileges of Scheduled Tribe status. Or to put it in Tahir Mahmood's partisan language: "The law on Scheduled Tribes is, on the contrary, wholly free from religious shackles. The 'No non-Hindu please' clause of the Constitution (Scheduled Castes) Order 1950 has no parallel in the Constitution (Scheduled Tribe) Order 1950. Nor is there any judicial decision saying that all Scheduled Tribes are born Hindus. Any change of religion on the part of a member of a Scheduled Tribe does not legally alter his or her Scheduled Tribe status. The modem Hindu code of 1955-56 does not apply to Scheduled Tribes.

In respect of several tribal communities there have been judicial decisions specifically affirming that the four Hindu law enactments of 1955-56 do not extend to the Scheduled Tribes." This means, for example, that customary marriage systems including polygamy (abolished in the Hindu Marriage Act) are condoned in the case of tribals. There is undeniably a contradiction here, for the Hindu Marriage Act had defined the legal Hindu as including (apart from Hindus in the narrow sense, Buddhists, Jains and Sikhs) "any other person domiciled in the territories to which this Act extends who is not a Muslim, Christian, Parsi or Jew by religion". In spite of that definition, Indian law in general treats tribals as non-Hindus. The 1991 census also separated tribal religion from Hinduism. It divided the population into eight different categories: Hindus, Muslim, Christians, Sikhs, Buddhists, Jains, "Other Religions and Persuasions", and "Religion non stated".

In appendix, the "other religions and persuasions" are detailed, and about 60 tribal religions are specified. The prevalent academic and mediatic dicourse takes this line further, e.g. by redefining the sanskritization of the tribals (the gradual adoption of elements of Sanskritic civilization, which has been a natural and ongoing process since many centuries) as "conversion to Hinduism", on the same footing as "conversion to Christianity"; and by describing Hindu social activists working in tribal areas as a kind of missionaries, outsiders propagating a religion that is quite foreign to the tribals. So, against the historical definition of "Hindu" which includes all Indian Pagans, and against the specific definition in the Hindu Marriage Act, which is coterminous with the historical definition, official India treats tribal religions as separate from Hinduism.

DOES HINDUISM RECOGNISE FRATERNITY?

There are two forces prevalent in Society. Individualism and Fraternity. Individualism is ever present. Every individual is ever asking "I and my neighbours, are we all brothers, are we even fiftieth cousins, am I their keeper, why should I do right to them" and under the pressure of his own particular interests acting as though he was an end to himself, thereby developing a non-social and even an antisocial self. Fraternity is a force of opposite character. Fraternity is another name for fellow feeling. It consists in a sentiment which leads an individual to identify himself with the good of others whereby "the good of others becomes to him a thing naturally and necessarily to be attended to like any of the physical conditions of our existence". It is because of this sentiment of fraternity that the individual does not "bring himself to think of the rest of his fellow-creatures as struggling rivals with him for the means of happiness, whom he must desire to see defeated in their object in order that he may succeed in his own." Individualism would produce anarchy. It is only fraternity, which prevents it and helps to sustain the moral order among men. Of this there can be no doubt.

How does this sentiment of Fraternity of fellow feeling arise? J. S. Mill says that this sentiment is a natural sentiment. "The social state is at once so natural, so necessary, and so habitual to man, that, except in some unusual circumstances or by an effort of voluntary abstraction he never conceives himself otherwise than as a member of a body; and this association is riveted more and more, as mankind are further removed from the state of savage independence. Any condition, therefore, which is essential to a state of society, becomes more and more an inseparable part of every person's conception of the state of things which he is born into, and which is the destiny of a human being. Now, society between human beings, except in the relation of master and slave, is manifestly impossible on any other footing than that the interests of all are to be consulted. Society between equals can only exist on the understanding that the interests of all are to be regarded equally. And since in all states of civilisation, every person, except an absolute monarch, has equals, every one is obliged to live on these terms with some body; and in every age some advance is made towards a state in which it will be impossible to live permanently on other terms with any body. In this way people grow up unable to conceive as possible to them a state of total disregard of other people's interests."

Does this sentiment of fellow feeling find a place among the Hindus? The following facts throw a flood of light on this question. The first fact that strikes one is the number of castes. No body has made an exact computation of their number. But it is estimated that total is not less than 2000. It might be 3000. This is not the only distressing aspect of this fact. There are others. Castes are divided into sub-castes. Their number is legion. The total population of the Brahmin Caste is about core and a half. But there are 1886 sub-castes of the Brahmin Caste. In the Punjab alone the Saraswat Brahmins of the Province of Punjab are divided into 469 sub-castes. The Kayasthas of Punjab are divided into 590 sub-castes. One could go on giving figures to show this infinite process of splitting social life into small fragments.

The third aspect of this splitting process is the infinitely small fragments into which the Castes are split. Some of the Baniya sub-castes can count no more than 100 families. They are so inter related they find extremely difficult to marry within their castes without transgressing the rules of consanguinity. It is noteworthy what small excuses suffice to bring about this splitting. Equally noteworthy is the hierarchical character of the Caste System. Castes form an hierarchy in which one caste is at the top and is the highest, another at the bottom and it is the lowest and in between there are castes every one of which is at once above some castes and below some castes.

The caste system is a system of gradation in which every caste except the highest and the lowest has a priority and precedence over some other castes. How is this precedence or this superiority determined? This order of superiority and inferiority or this insubordination is determined by rules: (1) which are connected with religious rites and (2) which are connected with commensuality. Religion as a basis of Rules of precedence manifests itself in three ways. Firstly through religious ceremonies, secondly through incantations that accompany the religious ceremonies and thirdly through the position of the priest. Beginning with the ceremonies as a source of rules of precedence it should be noted that the Hindu Scriptures prescribe sixteen religious ceremonies.

Although those are Hindu ceremonies every Hindu Caste cannot by right claim to perform all the sixteen ceremonies. Few can claim the right to perform all. Some are allowed to perform certain ceremonies; some are not allowed to perform certain of the ceremonies. For instance take the ceremony of Upanayan, wearing of the sacred thread. Some castes can't. Precedence follows this distinction in the matter of right to perform the ceremonies. A caste which can claim to perform all the ceremonies is higher in status than the caste which has a right to perform a few. Turning to the Mantras, it is another source for rules of precedence.

According to the Hindu Religion the same ceremony can be performed in two different ways: (1) Vedokta and (2) Puranokta. In the Vedokta form the ceremonies are performed with Mantras (incantations) from the Vedas. In the Puranokta form the ceremony is performed with Mantras (incantations) from the Puranas. Hindu Religious Scriptures fall into two distinct categories: (1) The Vedas which are four, and (2) the Puranas which are eighteen. Although they are all respected as scriptures they do not all have the same sanctity. The Vedas have the highest sanctity and the Puranas have the lowest sanctity. The way the Mantras give rise to social precedence will be obvious if it is borne in mind that not every caste is entitled to have the ceremony performed in the Vedokta form. Three castes may well claim the right to the performance of one of the sixteen ceremonies. But it will be that one of it is entitled to perform it in the Vedokta form, another in the Puranokta form. Precedence goes with the kind of Mantra that a caste is entitled to use in the performance of a religious ceremony. A caste which is entitled to use Vedic Mantras is superior to a caste which is entitled to use only Puranokta Mantras.

Taking the priest as a second source of precedence connected with Religion, Hinduism requires the instrumentality of a priest for the derivation of the full benefit from the performance of a religious ceremony. The priest appointed by the scripture is the Brahmin. A Brahmin therefore is indispensable. But the scriptures do not require-that a Brahmin shall accept the invitation of any and every Hindu irrespective of his caste to officiate at a religious ceremony. The invitation of which caste he will accept and of which he will refuse is a matter left to the wishes of the Brahmin. By long and well-established custom it is now settled at which caste he will officiate and at which caste he will not. This fact has become the basis of precedence as between castes.

The caste at which a Brahmin will officiate is held as superior to a caste at whose religious functions a Brahmin will not officiate. There is no sharing among Hindus of joys and sorrows involved in the vital facts of life. Everything is separate and exclusive. The Hindu is separate and exclusive all through his life. A foreigner coming to India will not find men crying Hindu Pani (water for Hindus) and Musalman Pani (water for Musalmans). He will find Brahmin Coffee This view of the caste is due to taking the separate aspects of caste separately. One must take them in conjunction. The resultant social utility or distillate of caste can be ascertained only by putting together the separate aspects of caste and judge them in their combination. Following this line of attacking the problem, the following conclusions follow:

(1) Caste divides Labourers
(2) Caste disassociates work from interest
(3) Caste disconnects intelligence from manual labour
(4) Caste devitalises by denying to him the right to cultivate vital interest and
(5) Caste prevents mobilisation. Caste System is not merely division of labour.

DIVISION OF LABOUR

Civilised society undoubtedly needs division of labour. But in no civilised society is division of labour accompanied by this unnatural division of labourers into watertight compartments. Caste System is not merely a division of labourers, which is quite different from division of labour it is an hierarchy in which the divisions of labourers are graded one above the other. In no other country is the division of labour accompanied by this gradation of labourers. There is also a third point of criticism against this view of the Caste System. This division of labour is not spontaneous, it is not based on natural aptitudes. Social and individual efficiency requires us to develop the capacity of an individual to the point of competency to chose and to make his own career. This principle is violated in the Caste System in so far as it involves an attempt to appoint tasks to individuals in advance, selected not on the basis of trained original capacities, but on that of the social status of the parents.

Looked at from another point of view this stratification of occupations which is the result of the Caste System is positively pernicious. Industry is never static. It undergoes rapid and abrupt changes. With such changes an individual must be free to change his occupations. Without such freedom to adjust himself to changing circumstances it would be impossible for him to gain his livelihood. Now the Caste System will not allow Hindus to take occupations where they are wanted if they do not belong to them by heredity. If a Hindu is seen to starve rather than take to new occupations not assigned to his Caste, the reason is to be found in the Caste System. By not permitting readjustment of occupations, caste becomes a direct cause of much of the unemployment we see in the country. As a form of division of labour the Caste System suffers from another serious defect.

The division of labour brought about by the Caste System is not a division based on choice. Individual sentiment, individual preference has no place in it. It is based on the dogma of predestination. Considerations of social efficiency would compel us to recognise that the greatest evil in the industrial system is not so much poverty and the suffering that it involves, as the fact that so many persons have callings which make no appeal to those who are engaged in them. Such callings constantly provoke one to aversion, ill will and the desire to evade.

There are many occupations in India which on account of the fact that they are regarded as degraded by the Hindus provoke those who are engaged in it to aversion. There is a constant desire to evade and escape from such occupations which arises solely because of the blighting effect which they produce upon those who follow them owing to the slight and stigma cast upon them by the Hindu religion. The second mischief it dose is to dissociate intelligence from work and create contempt for labour. The theory of the Caste is that a Brahmin who is permitted to cultivate his intellect is not permitted to labour, indeed is taught to look down upon labour. While the Sudra who is required to labour is not permitted to cultivate his intelligence. The disastrous consequences of this have been well portrayed by Mr. R.C.Dutt. Wealth without education and wealth is brutal. Each is necessary to every one. They are necessary for the growth of a man. That the Brahmin should cultivate knowledge, Kshatriya should bear arms, the Vaishya should trade and that the Sudra should serve is presented as a theory of mutual interdependence found in the family.

It is asked why should the Sudra need trouble to acquire wealth when the three Varnas are there to support him; Why need the Sudra bother to take to education when the Brahmin to whom he can go when the occasion for reading or writing arises; Why need the Sudra worry to arm himself because there is the Kshatriya to protect him? The theory of Chaturvarnya understood in this sense may be said to look upon the Sudra as the ward and the three Varnas as his guardians. Thus interpreted it is a simple and alluring theory. Assuming this to be the correct view of the underlying conception of Chaturvarnya it seems to me that the system is neither foolproof nor knave-proof. What is to happen if the Brahmins, Vaishyas and Kshatriyas fail to pursue knowledge, to engage in economic enterprises and to be efficient soldiers which are their respective functions? Contrary-wise, suppose that they discharge their functions but flout their duty to the Sudra or to one another? What is to happen to the Sudra if the three classes refuse to support him on fair terms or combine to keep him down? Who is to safeguard the interests of the Sudra or for the matter of that of the Vaishya and Kshatriya when the person who is trying to take advantage of his ignorance is the Brahmin?

Who is to defend the liberty of the Sudra or that of the Brahmin and the Vaishya, when the person who is robbing him of is the Kshatriya? Interdependence of one class on another class is inevitable. Even dependence of one class upon another may sometimes become allowable. But why make one person depend upon another in the matter of his vital needs? Education every one must have. Means of defence every one must have. These are the paramount requirements of every man for his self-preservation. How can the fact that his neighbour is educated and armed, help a man who is uneducated and disarmed. The whole theory is absurd. These are the questions which the defenders of Chaturvarnya do not seem to be troubled about. But they are very pertinent questions. Assuming their conception of Chaturvarnya that the relationship between the different classes is that of ward and guardian is the real conception underlying Chaturvarnya, it must be admitted that it makes no provision to safeguard the interests of the ward from the misdeeds of the guardian. Whether the relationship of guardian and ward was the real underlying conception on which Chaturvarnya was based there is no doubt that in practice the relation was that of master and servant.

The three classes, Brahmins, Kshatriyas and Vaishyas although not very happy in their mutual relationship managed to work by compromise. The Brahmin flattered the Kshatriya and both let the Vaishya live in order to be able to live upon him. But the three agreed to beat down the Sudra. He was not allowed to acquire wealth lest he should be independent of the three Varnas. He was prohibited from acquiring knowledge lest he should keep a steady vigil regarding his interests. He was prohibited from bearing arms lest he should have the means to rebel against their authority. That this is how the Sudras were treated by the Trayavarnikas is evidenced by the Laws of Manu. There is no code of laws more infamous regarding social rights than the Laws of Manu.

Any instance from anywhere of social injustice must pale before it. Why have the mass of people tolerated the social evils to which they have been subjected? There have been social revolutions in other countries of the world. Why have there not been social revolutions in India is a question which has incessantly troubled many. There is only one answer, it is that the lower classes of Hindus have been completely disabled for direct action on account of this wretched system of Chaturvarnya. They could not bear arms and without arms they could not rebel. They were all ploughmen or rather condemned to be ploughmen and they were not allowed to convert their ploughshares into swords. They had no bayonets and therefore everyone who chose ploughs did sit upon them. On account of the Chaturvarnya they could receive no education. They could not think out or know the way to their salvation. They were condemned to be lowly and not knowing the way of escape and not having the means of escape, they became reconciled to eternal servitude which they accepted as their inescapable fate. It is true that even in Europe the strong has not shrunk from the exploitation, nay the spoliation of the weak but in Europe, the strong have never contrived to make the weak helpless against exploitation so shamelessly as was the case in India among the Hindus.

Social war has been raging between the strong and the weak far more violently in Europe than it has ever been in India. Yet the weak in Europe has had in him freedom of military service his physical weapon, in suffrage his political weapon and in education his moral weapon. Three weapons for emancipation were never withheld by the strong from the weak in Europe. All these weapons were however denied to the masses in India by Chaturvarnya. There cannot be a more degrading system of social organisation than Chaturvarnya. It is the system, which deadens, paralyses and cripples the people from helpful activity. This is no exaggeration. History bears ample evidence.

There is only one period in Indian history, which is a period of freedom, greatness and glory. That is the period of the Maurya Empire. At all other times the country suffered from defeat and darkness. But the Maurya period was a period when Chaturvarnya was completely annihilated, when the Sudras, who constituted the mass of the people came into their own and became the rulers of the country. The period of defeat and darkness is the period when Chaturvarnya flourished to the damnation of the greater part of the people of the country.

Caste prevents mobilisation. Occasions arise when society must mobilise all its resources to one end in order to save itself from a catastrophe. To take a catastrophe like war, Society must mobilise all its resources for militarization. Every one must do war. Every one must be a soldier. Is this possible under the theory of caste? Obviously not. Indeed the destiny of a defeat which has been the lot of India throughout history is due to caste. Caste prevented general mobilisation. Or the extent of mobilisation was of a very limited character. Only the Kshatriyas were expected to fight. The rest the Brahmins and the Vaishyas were not armed and the Sudras who formed the large majority of the country were disarmed.

The result was that once the small class of Kshatriyas were defeated by a foreign foe, the whole country fell at his feet. It could offer no resistance. It was not capable of resistance. Indian wars have been mostly wars of single battles or single campaigns. This was due to the fact that once the Kshatriyas fell everything fell. Why? Simply because there was no general mobilisation and the theory deeply imbedded in the psychology of the people.

If these conclusions are sound, how can a philosophy which dissects society in fragments, which dissociates work from interest, which disconnects intelligence from labour, which expropriates the rights of man to interests vital to life and which prevented society from mobilising resources for common action in the hour of danger, be said to satisfy the test of Social Utility. The Philosophy of Hinduism therefore neither satisfies the test of social utility nor does it satisfy the test of individual justice. The result of this analysis is so odd that it will surprise many. Astonished some may even say that if the conclusions are so odd then there must be something wrong in the analysis of the philosophy of Hinduism. To those who refuse to accept this analysis because they do not have a correct notion what is central in the philosophy of Hinduism. If they do they will feel no surprise at the conclusions.

HUMAN SOCIETY FALL INTO TWO CLASSES

This matter is so important that it needs to be explained. It may be recalled that the foregoing analysis of the religious revolution showed that religious ideals as forms of divine governance for human Society fall into two classes, one in which Society is the centre and the other in which the Individual is the centre. The same anaiysis showed that for the former the appropriate test of what is good and what is right i.e. the test of the moral order is utility while for the latter the test is justice. Now the reason why the philosophy of Hinduism does not answer the test either of utility or of justice is because the religious ideal of

Hinduism for divine governance of human society is an ideal, which falls into a separate class by itself. It is an ideal in which the individual is not the centre.

The centre of the ideal is neither individual nor society. It is a class-the class of Supermen called Brahmins. Those who will bear the dominant and devastating fact in mind will understand why the philosophy of Hinduism is not founded on individual justice or social utility. The philosophy of Hinduism is founded on a totally different principle. To the question what is right and what is good the answer, which the philosophy of Hinduism gives, is remarkable. It holds that to be right and good the act must serve the interest of this class of supermen, namely, the Brahmins. Oscar Wilde said that to be intelligible is to be found out. Manu is neither afraid nor ashamed of being found out. Indeed Manu does not leave it to be found out. He expresses his view in resonant and majestic notes as who are the Supermen and anything which serves the interest of the Supermen is alone entitled to be called right and good.

The Original Home of the Hindus (Interview of Dr. Ambedkar)

The Father of the Indian Constitution, Dr. B. R. Ambedkar, was the foremost nationalist leader of the oppressed classes and an erudite scholar. The following is an account of the enlightening dialogue with him. Though the one may not agree with all of Sri Ambedkar's conclusions, the dialogue is significant for the fact of Sri Ambedkar's total rejection of the theory of Aryan invasion as "a perversion of scientific investigation".

Question: Do you believe that the Sudras were a non-Aryan aboriginal race?

Dr. Ambedkar: No. After deep study of the subject I have come to conclude:

(i) That, the Sudras were Aryans;

(ii) That the Sudras belonged to the Kshatriya Class; and

(iii) That the Sudras were so important a class of Kshatriyas that some of the most eminent and powerful kings of the ancient Aryan Communities were Sudras.

Western Theories

Q: I know you are well acquainted with the various theories of Western writers about the origin of the non-Traivarnikas whom they describe as 'Non-Aryans'. Are there any points on which there seems to be a certain amount of unity among all of them?

A: Yes. Such points comprise the following:

1. The people who created the Vedic literature belonged to the Aryan race.
2. This Aryan race came from outside India and invaded India.
3. The natives of India were known as Dasas and Dasyus who were racially different from Aryans.
4. The Aryans were a white race. The Dasas and Dasyus were a dark race.
5. The Aryans conquered the Dasas and Dasyus.
6. The Dasas and Dasyus after they were conquered and enslaved were called Sudras.
7. The Aryans cherished colour prejudice and therefore formed the chaturvarnya whereby they separated the white race from the black race such as the Dasas and the Dasyus.

Q: What is the basis for these Western Theories?

A: The foundation on which the whole fabric of the theory rests is the proposition that there lived a people who were Aryan by race.

Q: Is this proposition correct?

A: The Vedas do not know any such race as the Aryan race. A race may be defined as a body of people possessing certain typical traits which are hereditary. An examination of the Vedic literature shows that there occur two words in the Rig Veda-one is Arya with a short A and the other is Arya with a long A. The word Arya with a short A is used in the Rig Veda in 88 places. The word is used in four different senses; as (1) enemy, (2) respectable person, (3) name for India and (4) owner, Vaishya or citizen. The word Arya with a long A is used in the Rig Veda in 31 places. But in none of these is the word used in the sense of race. The one indisputable conclusion which follows is that the terms Arya and Arya which occur in the Vedas have not been used in the racial sense at call. This is what Prof. Max Mueller says on the subject: "There is no Aryan race in blood', Aryan, in scientific language, is utterly inapplicable to race." The Aryan Race Theory is so absurd that it ought to have been dead long ago.

Q: From where did the so-called 'Aryan race' come into India? What was the original home of the 'Aryan race'? Is the theory of Aryan invasion of India a historical fact?

A: There is no evidence in the Vedas of any invasion of India by the Aryan race and its having conquered the Dasas and Dasyus supposed to be natives of India. There is no evidence to show that the distinction between Aryans, Dasas and Dasyus was a racial distinction. The Vedas do not support the contention that the Aryans were different in colour from the Dasas and Dasyus. The word 'Varna' originally meant a class holding to a particular faith, and it had nothing to do with colour or complexion. The Vedic Aryans had no colour prejudice. They were not of one colour. Rama, Krishna, Dirghatamas, Kanva etc. have been described as dark in complexion. The assertion that the Aryans came from outside and invaded India is not proved and the premise that the Dasas and Dasyus are aboriginal tribes of India is demonstrably false.

INVASION THEORY A CONCOCTION

The theory of invasion is an invention. This invention is necessary because of a gratuitous assumption that the Indo-Germanic people are the purest of the modern representatives of the original Aryan race. The theory is based upon nothing but pleasing assumptions and inferences based on such assumptions. The theory is a perversion of scientific investigation. It is not allowed to evolve out of facts. On the contrary, the theory is preconceived and facts are selected to prove it. It falls to the ground at every point. The Western theory is in conflict with the Rig Veda on a major issue. The Rig Veda being the best evidence on the subject, the theory which is in conflict with it must be rejected. There is no escape.

Q: Are there any Hindu scholars who supported this Western theory?

A: This theory has received support from some Brahmin scholars. This is a very strange phenomenon. As Hindus, they should ordinarily show a dislike for the Aryan theory with its express avowal of the superiority of the European races over the Asiatic races. But the Brahmin scholar has not only no such aversion but he most willingly hails it. He claims to be the representative of the Aryan race and he regards the rest of the Hindus as descendants of the non-Aryans.

Q: What is your opinion about the suggestion of Lokamanya Tilak that the original home of the Aryan race was in the Arctic region?

A: This is of course a very original theory. There is only one point which seems to have been overlooked. The horse is a favourite animal of the Vedic Aryans. It was most intimately connected with their life and their religion. The question is: Was the horse to be found in the Arctic region?

If the answer is in the negative, the Arctic Home theory becomes very precarious, So far as the testimony of the Vedic literature is concerned, it is against the theory that the original horde of the Aryans was outside India.

The language in which reference to the seven rivers is made in the Rig Veda (x. 75.5) is very significant. No foreigner would ever address a river in such familiar and endearing terms as 'My Ganga, my Yamuna, my Sarasvati', unless by long association he had developed an emotion about it. In the face of such statements from the Rig-Veda, there is obviously no room for a theory of a military conquest by the Aryan race of the non-Aryan races of Dasas and Dasyus.

As Mr. P.T. Srinivasa Iyengar Points Out: "A careful examination of the Mantras where the words Arya, Dasas and Dasyus occur, indicates that they refer not to race but to cult. These words occur mostly in Rig Veda Samhita where Arya occurs about 33 times in mantras which contain 153,972 words on the whole. This rare occurrence is itself a proof that the tribes that called themselves Aryas were not invaders that conquered the country and exterminated the people. For an invading tribe would naturally boast of its achievements constantly."

The Fourth Varna

Q: If the theories of European scholars are incorrect, how can one explain the emergence of the Fourth Varna suffering from a number of social disabilities and degradations?

A: The whole position can be stated briefly as follows:

1. The Sudras were one of the Aryan Communities of the Solar race.
2. The Sudras ranked as the Kshatriya Varna in the Indo-Aryan Society.
3. There was a time when the Aryan Society recognised only three Varnas, namely, Brahmins, Kshatriyas and Vaishyas. The Sudras were not a separate Varna but a part of the Kshatriya Varna.
4. There was a continuous feud between the Sudra Kings and the Brahmins, in which the Brahmins were subjected to many tyrannies and indignities.
5. As a result of the hatred towards the Sudras due to their tyrannies and oppressions, the Brahmins refused to invest the Sudras with the Sacred Thread.
6. Owing to the loss of the Sacred Thread the Sudras became socially degraded, fell below the rank of the Vaishyas and came to form the Fourth Varna.

Q: What about the origin of the Fifth Varna known as untouchables?

A: In Vedic times there was no untouchability. As to the period of the Dharmasutras, there was 'Impurity' but there was no untouchability. Manu's decision is that there is no Fifth Varna. There was no untouchability at the time of Manu. We can definitely say that Manusmriti did not enjoin untouchability. While untouchability did not exist in 200 A.D., it had emerged by 600 A.D. As has been shown by Dr. D.R. Bhandarkar, cow-killing was made a capital offence by the Gupta kings sometime in the 4th Century A.D. We can, therefore say with some confidence that untouchability was born sometimes about 400 A.D.

Q: Can the hatred between Buddhism and Brahminism be taken to be the sole cause why 'Broken Men' became untouchables?

A: Obviously, it cannot be' The propaganda of the Brahmins was directed against Buddhists in general and not against the 'Broken Men' in particular. Since untouchability struck to 'Broken Men' only, it is obvious that there was some additional circumstance which has played its part in fastening untouchability upon them.

Q: Can we say that the 'Broken Men' came to he treated as untouchables because they ate beef?

A: There need be no hesitation in returning an affirmative answer to this question. No other answer is consistent with facts as we know them.

Q: Do the untouchables, belong to a separate, non-Aryan race?

A: As I said earlier, historians have made a mistake in proceeding on assumption that the Aryans were a separate race. In this connection, reference may be made to verse 23 of Adhyaya 65 of the Shanti Parva of Mahabharata. The verse says: "In all the Varnas and in all the Ashramas one finds the existence of Dasyus." This indicates that the term 'Dasyus' is not used for a non-Aryan.

If anthropometry is a science which can be depended upon to determine the race of a people, then the results obtained by the application of anthropometry to the various strata of Hindu society disprove that the untouchables belong to a race different from the Aryans and the Dravidians. The measurements establish that the Brahmins and untouchables belong to the same race. If the Brahmins are Aryans, the untouchables are also Aryans. If the Brahmins are Dravidians, the untouchables are also Dravidians. The racial theory of untouchability finds very little support from such facts as we know about the ethnology of India. Racial theory of the origin of untouchability must therefore be abandoned. According to Nehru, Mahatma Gandhi was a Hindu and an Indian, the greatest in many generations, and he was proud of being a Hindu and an Indian. (He broadcast this on 14 February, 1948). What the Mahatma wrote, said and did is widely known. The track record of Dr. BR Ambedkar as a Hindu is not so well known. His popular image is that of a Dalit leader and a constitutional guru. How much he felt, thought and pleaded for the interests of the Hindus therefore deserves recounting. Baba Saheb was one of the few Hindus, if not the only one, who foresaw the consequences of not letting the Muslims have their Dar-ul Islam.

He therefore openly and in cold print favoured a partition and in almost exact details by 1940. He did this almost on the morrow of the resolution demanding Pakistan which was passed by the Muslim League at its Lahore session on 26 March, 1940. He was clear in his view that Partition without an exchange of population was worse than Partition. His reasoning was interesting. To him dividing the subcontinent was to solve its communal conflict. The Communal Award was given in 1930 when Ramsay McDonald was the prime minister of Great Britain. The award gave the Muslims what they had demanded at the Round Table Conference. Their weightage as well as their separate electorates were retained and in addition they were given the statutory majority of seats in the provinces.

In those provinces they were in majority in the population. The Hindus were also awarded similar privileges. At the time there were five Muslim majority provinces and nine Hindu majority provinces. Since the Hindus had nothing comparable to the Muslim League to lead them, the Congress represented every one including the Hindus. They did not believe in separate electorates. In fact, they had continually insisted on joint electorates for all communities and had strongly objected to any community being given the majority of seats guaranteed by the Constitution.

The privileges which the Muslims celebrated had no meaning for the Congress and its followers. In Dr. Ambedkar's perception, in the provinces of Punjab, NWF, Sindh, Bengal and Baluchistan, the Muslim governments could treat Hindu minorities as they wished knowing fully well that there was no fear of retaliation in the other provinces because they would have the secular governments as distinct from Hindu ministries, as quoted by Dr.

Ambedkar in his book, Thoughts on Pakistan. The Hindu minorities in the Muslim provinces also insisted on joint electorates although the Communal Award ignored their feelings. It is interesting to recall what Maulana Abul Kalam Azad had to say as president of the Muslim Session held in Calcutta during 1927. In that speech the Maulana declared:

"That by the Lucknow Pact they had sold away their interests. The Delhi proposals of March last opened the door for the first time to the recognition of the real rights of Mussalmans in India. The separate electorates granted by the Pact of 1916 only ensured Muslim representation, but what was vital for the existence of the community was the recognition of its numerical strength. Delhi opened the way to the creation of such a state of affairs as would guarantee to them in the future of India a proper share.

Their existing small majority in Bengal and the Punjab was only a census figure, but the Delhi proposals gave them for the first time five provinces of which no less than three (Sindh, the Frontier Province and Baluchistan) contained a real overwhelming Muslim majority. If the Muslims did not recognise this great step they were not fit to live. There would now be nine Hindu provinces against five Muslim provinces, and whatever treatment Hindus accorded in the nine provinces Muslims would accord the same treatment to Hindus in the five provinces. Was not this a great gain? Was not a new weapon gained for the assertion of Muslim rights?"

Baba Saheb felt that the Communal Award meant that the Hindu Minorities would be hostages at the mercy of the five Muslim majority provincial governments. This he felt was a strong enough argument in favour of Partition. Incidentally, the Muslim League at its Lahore Session on 16th March, 1940 passed a resolution which amounted to the demand of a separate state called Pakistan. The scheme had been conceived by one Mr. Rehmat Ali in 1933 having advocated a partition. Dr. Ambedkar immediately noted that merely the formation of Pakistan would not ensure safety for the Hindus in the Muslim majority areas. In fact their condition may worsen because at the time the hostages could at least appeal to the Central Government about their grievances whereas in Pakistan, there would be no impartial Central Government to turn to. He recalled that the Hindus in Pakistan could then be given into the position of the Armenians under the Turks or of the Jews in Nazi Germany.

Baba Saheb was perceptive enough to realise that the evil was not Partition but the boundaries of the current provinces which did not reflect or were not consistent with the profile of the

Hindu-Muslim population. The boundaries had to be altered; the Punjab and Bengal had to be bifurcated. Even then some Hindus would get left behind in Pakistan and many of the Muslims would be scattered across Hindustan. All these would then have to be moved in a planned manner so that the Hindus and Sikhs came away to Hindustan and the Muslims moved to Pakistan. This was the gist of Dr. Ambedkar's formula. Nevertheless it is useful to quote him "that the transfer of minorities is the only lasting remedy for communal peace is beyond doubt.

If that is so, there is no reason why Hindus and Muslims should keep on trading in safeguards which have proved so unsafe. That, if small countries with limited resources like Greece, Turkey and Bulgaria were capable of such an undertaking, there is no reason to suppose that what they did cannot be accomplished by Indians. After all, the population involved is inconsiderable and it would be a height of folly to give up a sure way to communal peace because some obstacles in it require to be removed." Baba Saheb was convinced that the secret of a happy and successful state lay in homogeneity. That was the lesson taught also by the histories of Turkey, Greece and Bulgaria. Many a constituent of postwar era have given safeguard for the welfare of the minorities. Their experience, however, showed that these did not save the minorities. Even after safeguards the same old policy exterminating the minorities continued. Hence an exchange of minorities was found to be about the only solution. There was another factor which caused Dr. Ambedkar a great deal of anxiety. Basing his conclusions on the facts provided in the Simon Commission Report, he found that more than half the soldiers of the then Indian Army were from the North-West Frontier and West Punjab, most of them being Muslim.

British Indian Government

Although the British Indian Government justified the profile of recruitment with their theory of marshal and non-marshal classes, the fact was that during the rebellion of 1857, the people of these areas remained loyal to the British whereas soldiers recruited by the East India Company from the Indo-Gangetic plane were the ones that actually revolted. This was the view of a Special Army Survey in 1879 which observed that the distinction between marshal and non-marshal classes were indistinct. The khilafat committee, in its anxiety to safeguard pan-Islamism, had enunciated the principle that the Indian Army should not be used against a Muslim power. The Muslim League had endorsed this principle.

In the words of Dr. Ambedkar: "Even Theodore Morrison, writing in 1899, was of the opinion that 'the views held by the Mahomedans (certainly the most aggressive and truculent of the peoples of India) are alone sufficient to prevent the establishment of an independent Indian Government. Were the Afghan to descend from the north upon an autonomous India, the Mahomedans, instead of uniting with the Sikhs and Hindus to repel him, would be drawn by all the ties of kinship and religion to join his flag'." The Hindus, he continued, could find themselves between the devil and the deep sea so far as the defence of India was concerned. If India remains as one whole, what would happen? The issue might sound remote today but remember in 1919 the protagonists of the Khilafat movement had actually gone to the extent of inviting the Amir of Afghanistan to invade India.

Even the cost benefit factor did not escape Baba Saheb although he was not a financial expert: "The Pakistan area, which is the main recruiting ground of the present Indian Army, contributes very little to the central exchequer. The main contribution comes from the provinces of Hindustan. In fact, it is the money contributed by the provinces of Hindustan which enables the Government of India to carry out its activities in the Pakistan provinces. The Pakistan provinces are a drain on the provinces of Hindustan. Not only do they contribute very little to the Central Government but they receive a great deal from the Central Government. The revenue of the Central Government amounts to Rs 121 crore. Of this about Rs 52 crore are yearly spent on the army. In what area is this amount spent? Who pays the bulk of this amount of Rs 52 crore? The bulk of this amount of Rs 52 crore which is spent on the army is spent over the Muslim army drawn from the Pakistan area. Now the bulk of this amount of Rs 52 crore is contributed by the Hindu provinces and is spent on an army from which the Hindus, who pay for it, are excluded!! How many Hindus are aware of this tragedy?"

Hindu Reaction to Ambedkar's Conversion: Dr. Ambedkar was an unforgiving critic of Hinduism and the most prominent among formal converts out of Hinduism in the modern age. One might, therefore, expect the Hindu movement to be equally critical of Dr. Ambedkar. However, this is not the case, quite the contrary. Except for the arch-traditionalist like Swami Karapatri, the predominant approach is to co-opt Ambedkar. At Sangh Parivar functions, a picture of Ambedkar is mostly displayed along with pictures of Maharana Pratap, Shivaji, Guru Govind Singh, Hedgewar, Golwalkar and other more obvious Hindutva heroes.

Before elaborating on this general policy, we will first consider the handful of exceptions to the rule. In reaction to the mass conversion, the traditionalist Swami Karapatri arranged a big meeting in Kanpur to oppose "Buddhism and materialism". In Maharashtra, the heartland of both Ambedkarism and Hindutva, violent altercations between the two movements have taken place, mostly in the agitation for the renaming of Marathwada University as Dr. Ambedkar University in the late 1980s and early 90s. This renaming was opposed not by the Sangh Parivar but by the Shiv Sena; as this is an action movement with no intellectual dimension at all, it did not bother to back up this agitation with any reasoned argumentation in writing against Ambedkar. Ambedkarites of the Dalit Panther movement have allegedly made two failed attempts on the life of the late Jeevan Kulkarni, an amateur-historian belonging to the Hindu Mahasabha.

His crime was that he had developed a critique of Dr. Ambedkar's understanding of Buddhism, along the same lines as that quoted above from Buddhist sources. The mainstream approach is to neutralize Ambedkar's attack on Hinduism by "putting it into context" and emphasizing the nationalist motive of his conversion to Buddhism rather than a foreign religion. The embarrassing fact of his formal break with Hinduism is rendered harmless by means of the typically Hindu method of incorporation: Buddhism is defined as simply one of the sects of Hinduism. Even Veer Savarkar, in spite of his earlier invective against Buddhism, called Ambedkar's conversion "a sure jump into the Hindu fold", and said that "Buddhist Ambedkar is Hindu Ambedkar". Fact is that Ambedkar's choice of Buddhism, after two decades of suspense starting with his announcement in 1935 that he would not die as a Hindu, came as a great relief to the Hindu movement.

One reason for his embracing Buddhism was that he wanted a rational and humanist religion, for which he thought Christianity and Islam did not qualify. This did not evoke much interest in Hindutva circles, but they showed all the more sympathy for the second reason: that Buddhism was an indigenous religion which would not bring with it extraterritorial loyalties. Ambedkar has explained: "I will choose only the least harmful way for the country. And that is the greatest benefit I am conferring on the country by embracing Buddhism; for Buddhism is a part and parcel of Bharatiya culture. I have taken care that my conversion will not harm the tradition of the culture and history of this land." Another fact which genuinely endears Dr. Ambedkar to Hindutva activists, is his sincere patriotism.

He had a lively concern for the well-being and safety of India, e.g., while Jawaharlal Nehru stopped the army from reconquering all of Kashmir from Pakistan and allowed the Chinese to overrun Tibet in his mindless Hindi-Chini-bhai-bhai euphoria, Dr. Ambedkar warned against the danger of Islamic and Communist aggression and even suggested that India join the pro-Western SEATO (South-East-Asian Treaty Organization): "The Prime Minister has practically helped the Chinese to bring their border down to the Indian border. Looking at all these things, it would be an act of levity not to believe that India, if it is not exposed to aggression right now, is exposed to aggression and that aggression might well be committed by people who are always in the habit of committing aggression." During the framing of Indian Constitution, he advocated and succeeded in providing for a strong centre as he said that a week centre had invited foreign invasions in the past. In 1954, when Jawaharlal Nehru was wilfully being fooled by the Chinese who were silently occupying Aksai Chin, Dr. Ambedkar said in an election speech in Nagpur that "Nehru's foreign policy had made India a friendless country, that Nehru had bungled the Kashmir issue and had sheltered men who were dishonest, and that India was encircled by a kind of United States of Islam on one side and on the other side Russia and China in a combination for the conquest of Asia."

He was proven right on this score in 1962 and 1965. Dr. Ambedkar's conversion provoked a few Hindu authors to publish reflections on Buddhism and its relation with Hinduism. Thus, Ram Swarup wrote his Buddhism vis-a-vis Hinduism (1958), which is on the same wavelength as Ananda Coomaraswamy's approach. His focus is on the spiritual common ground of the two traditions (or the Hindu tradition and its Buddhist offshoot), though he acknowledges a difference in style and atmosphere. "Buddhism is returning home to India after a long exile of a thousand years and, like the proverbial prodigal son, is being received with open arms. Religious tolerance of the average Hindu partly explains the warm reception. But a more important reason is the fact that Buddha and Buddhism form an intimate part of Hindu consciousness. Buddha was a Hindu. Buddhism is Hindu in its origin and development, in its art and architecture, iconography, language, beliefs, psychology, names, nomenclature, religious vows and spiritual discipline. Hinduism is not all Buddhism, but Buddhism forms part of the ethos which is essentially Hindu."

5 Morality of Hinduism

SOUL OF HINDUISM

Inequality is the soul of Hinduism. The morality of Hinduism is only social. It is unmoral and inhuman to say the least. What is unmoral and inhuman easily becomes immoral, inhuman and infamous. This is what Hinduism has become. Those who doubt this or deny this proposition should examine the social composition of the Hindu Society and ponder over the condition of some of the elements in it. Take the following cases.

First as to the Primitive Tribes. In what state of civilisation are they? The history of human civilisation includes the entire period of human progress from Savagery to Barbarism and from Barbarism to Civilisation. The transition from one to other has been marked by some discovery or intention in some department of knowledge of Art resulting in advancing the onward march of man. The development of articulate speech was the first thing which, from the point of view of human progress, divided man from the brute. It marks the first stage of savagery. The Middle period of the state of savagery began with the knowledge of the manufacture and use of fire. This wonderful discovery enabled man to extend his habit almost indefinitely. He could leave his forest home, go to different and colder climates, and increase his food supply by including flesh and fish. The next discovery was the Bow and Arrow. This was the greatest achievement of primitive man and marks the highest state of savage man. It was indeed a wonderful implement.

The possessor of this device could bring down the fleetest animal and could defend himself against the most predatory. The transition from Savagery to Barbarism was marked by the discovery of pottery. Hitherto man had no utensils that could withstand the action of fire. Without utensils man could not store nor could he cook. Undoubtedly pottery was a great civilising influence. The Middle State of Barbarism began when man learned to domesticate wild animals. Man learned that captive animals could be of service to him. Man now became a herdsman, no longer dependent for food upon the precarious chase of wild animals. Milk procurable at all seasons made a highly important addition to his dietary. With the aid of horse and camel he traversed wide areas hitherto impassable. The captive animals became aids to commerce, which resulted in the dissemination of commodities as well as of ideas. The next discovery was of the Art of smelting iron.

This marks the highest stage of advancement of barbaric man. With this discovery man became a "tool-making animal" who with his tool could fashion wood and stone and build houses and bridges. This marks the close of the advancement made by barbaric man. The dividing line which marks off Barbaric people from Civilised people, in the fullest sense of the word Civilisation, is the art of making ideas tangible by means of graphic signs—which is called the art of writing. With this man conquered time as he had with the earlier inventions conquered space. He could now record his deeds and his thoughts. Henceforth, his knowledge, his poetical dreams, his moral aspirations might be recorded in such form as to be read not merely by his contemporaries but by successive generations of remote posterity. For man his history became safe and secure. This was the steepest assent and the climbing of it marks the beginnings of civilisation. Stopping here for the moment let us ask in what state of civilisation are the Primitive Tribes. The name Primitive Tribes is expressive of the present state of people who are called by that name. They live in small-scattered huts in forests.

They live on wild fruits, nuts and roots. Fishing and hunting are also resorted to for the purpose of securing food. Agriculture plays a very small part in their social economy. Food supplies being extremely precarious, they lead a life of semi-starvation from which there is no escape. As to clothes they economise them to a vanishing point. They move almost in a state of complete nakedness. There is a tribe, which is known as "Bonda Porajas" which, means "Naked Porajas". Of these people it is said that the women wear a very narrow strip which serves as a petticoat almost identical with what is worn by the Momjak Nagas in Assam, the ends hardly meeting at the top on the left thigh. These petticoats are woven at home out of the fibre of a forest tree. Girls wear a fillet of beads and of palmyra leaf and an enormous quantity of beads and neck ornaments extremely like those worn by many Komjak women. Otherwise the women wear nothing.

The women shave their heads entirely..... Of these Chenchus, a tribe residing near Farhabad in the Nizam's Dominions it is said that "their houses are conical, rather slight in structure made of bamboo sloping to the central point and covered with a thin layer of thatch..... They have very little, indeed, in the way of material effects, the scanty clothes they wear, consisting of a *langoti* and a cloth in the case of men, and a short bodice and a petticoat in the case of women, being practically all, besides a few cooking pots and a basket or two which perhaps sometimes contains grain. They keep cattle and goats and in this particular village do a little cultivation, elsewhere subsisting on honey and forest produce which they sell". Regarding the Morias, another Primitive tribe, it is stated the men generally wear a single cloth round the waist with a slap coming down in the front. They also have a necklace of beads and when they dance put on cock's plumes and peacock's feathers in their turbans. Many girls are profusely tattooed, especially on their faces, and some of them on their legs as well. The type of tattooing is said to be according to the taste of the individual and it is done with thorns and needles. In their hair many of them stick the feathers of jungle cocks and their heads are also adorned with combs of wood and tin and brass. These Primitive Tribes have no hesitation about eating anything, even worms and insects, and, in fact, there is very little meat that they will not eat, whether the animal has died a natural death or has been killed four days or more before by a tiger.

The next groups of the people he will come across are the Criminal Tribes. The Criminal Tribes live not in Forests as the Primitive Tribes do but in the plains in close proximity to, and often in the midst of civilised life. Hollis in his "Criminal Tribes of the United Provinces" gives an account of their activities. They live entirely by crime. A few may be ostensibly engaged in agriculture, but this is only to cover up their real activities. Their nefarious practices find largest scope in dacoity or robbery by violence, but being a community organised for crime, nothing comes amiss to them. On deciding to commit a dacoity in any particular locality spies are sent out to select a suitable victim, study the general habits of the villagers, and the distance from any effective aid, and enumerate the number of men and firearms. The raid usually takes place at midnight. Acting on the information given by the spies, men are posted at various points in the village and by firing off their guns attract attention from the main gang which attacks the particular house or houses previously appointed. The gang usually consists of 30 to 40 men.

It is essential to emphasis the great part played by crime in the general life of these peoples. A boy is initiated into crime as soon as he is able to walk and talk. No doubt the motive is practical, to a great extent, in so far as it is always better to risk a child in petty theft, who, if he is caught, would probably be cuffed, while an adult would immediately be arrested. An important part is also played by women, who, although they do not participate in the actual raids, have many heavy responsibilities. Besides being clever in disposing off stolen property the women of the Criminal Tribes are experts in shop lifting. At one time the Criminal Tribes included such well-organised Confederacies of Professional Criminals as the Pindharies and the Thugs.

The Pindharies were a predatory body of armed gangsters. Their organisation was an open military organisation of freebooters who could muster 20000 fine horse and even more. They were under the command of brigand chiefs. Chitu one of the most powerful commanders had under his single command 10000 horse, including 5000 good cavalry, besides infantry and guns. The Pindharies had no military projects for employing their loose bands of irregular soldiery, which developed into bodies of professional plunderers. The Pindharies aimed at no conquests. Their object was to secure booty and cash for themselves. General loot and rapine was their occupation. They recognised no rulers. They were subjects of none. They rendered loyalty to none. They respected none, and plundered all, high and low, rich and poor, without fear or compunction. The Thugs were a well organised body of professional assassins, who, in gangs of from 10 to 100 wandered in various guises throughout India, worked themselves into the confidence of wayfarers of the wealthier class, and, when a favourable opportunity occurred, strangled them by throwing a handkerchief or noose round their necks, and then plundered and buried them.

All this was done according to certain ancient and rigidly prescribed forms and after the performance of special religious rites, in which was the consecration of the package, and the sacrifice of sugar. They were staunch worshippers of Kali, the Hindu Goddess of destruction. Assassination for gain was with them a religious duty, and was considered a holy and honourable profession. They had, in fact, no idea of doing wrong, and their moral feelings did not come into play. The will of the Goddess, by whose command and in whose honour they followed there calling, was revealed to them through a very complicated system of omens. In obedience to these they often travelled even the distance of hundred miles in company with, or in the wake of, their intended victims before a safe opportunity had presented itself for executing their design; and when the deed was done, rites were performed in honour of that tutelary deity, and a goodly portion of the spoil was set apart for her. The Thugs had also a jargon of their own, as well as certain signs by which its members recognised each other in the remotest part of India.

Even those who from age or infirmities could no longer take an active part in the operations used to aid the cause as watchmen, spies or dressers of food. It was owing to their thorough organisation, the secrecy and security with which they went to work, but chiefly to the religious garb in which they shrouded their murders, that they could continue for centuries to practise their craft.

The extraordinary fact was that Thugee was regarded as a regular profession by Indian Rulers of the day, both Hindu and Mahomedans. The Thugs paid taxes to the state and the state left them unmolested. It was not until the British became rulers of the country that an attempt was made to suppress the Thugs.

By 1835, 382 Thugs were hanged and 986 were transported or imprisoned for life. Even as late as 1879 the number of registered Thugs was 344 and the Thugee and the Dacoity department of the Government of India continued to exist until 1904 when its place was taken by the Central Criminal Intelligence Department. While it is not possible for the criminal tribes to live by organized bodies of criminals, crime continues to be their main occupation. Besides these two classes there is a third class which comprises a body of people who are known as Untouchables. Below the Untouchables there are others who are known as unapproachable.

Untouchables are those who cause pollution only if they touch. The Unapproachable are those who cause pollution if they come within a certain distance. It is said of the Nayadis—a people, who fall into the category of the Unapproachable, "that they are the lowest caste among the Hindus—the dog-eaters. They are the most persistent in their clamour for charity, and will follow at a respectful distance, for miles together any person walking, driving or boating. If any thing is given to them, it must be laid down, and after the person offering it has proceeded a sufficient distance, the recipient comes timidly forward, and removes it. "Of the same people Mr. Thurston says, "The subject (i.e. the Nayadis) whom I examined and measured at Shoranus, though living only about three miles off, had, by reason of the pollution which they traditionally carry with them to avoid walking over the long bridge which spans the river, and follow a circuitous route of many miles". Below the Unapproachable are the Unseeables. In the Tinnevelley District of the Madras Presidency there is a class of unseeables called Purada Vannans. Of them it is said, "that they are not allowed to come out during day time because their sight is enough to cause pollution. These unfortunate people are `compelled' to follow the nocturnal habits, leaving their dens after dark and scuttling home at the false dawn like the badger, the hyena, the avordvark." Consider the total population of these classes.

The Primitive Tribes form a total of 25 million souls. The Criminal Tribes number 41/2 millions and the Untouchables number 50 millions. This makes a grand total of 791/2 millions. Now ask how these people could have remained in the state of moral, material, social and spiritual degradation surrounded as they have been by Hinduism. Hindus say that their civilisation is older than any civilisation, that Hinduism as a religion is superior to any other religion. If this is so how is that Hinduism failed to elevate these people, bring them enlightenment and hope; how is it that it failed even to reclaim them; how is it that it stood with folded hands when millions and millions were taking to life to shame and crime? What is the answer to this? The only answer is that Hinduism is overwhelmed with the fear of pollution. It has not got the power to purify. It has not the impulse to serve and that is because by its very nature it is inhuman and unmoral. It is a misnomer to call it religion. Its philosophy is opposed to very thing for which religion stands.

JOINT V/S SEPARATE ELECTORATES

The Hindus have after a long struggle accepted the view that a purely territorial constituency will not do in a country like India. In the previous discussion regarding the controversy between territorial constituency and communal constituency as two rival methods of bringing about a truly representative legislature was unnecessary. But I stated the case for and against because I felt that the foreigners who are not aware of Indian Political conditions ought to know the basic conceptions underlying that controversy. Unfortunately, however, the fact is that although the Hindus have accepted the basic argument in favour of communal scheme of representation they have not accepted all what the Untouchables are demanding. The Untouchables demand that their representation shall be by separate electorates. A separate electorate means an electorate composed exclusively of Untouchable voters who are to elect an Untouchable as their representative to the legislature.

The Hindus agree that certain number of seats are to be reserved for Untouchables to be filled only by Untouchables. But they insist that the Untouchables who is to be the representative of the Untouchables in the Legislature should be elected by a mixed electorate consisting both of the Hindus as well as of the Untouchables and not by an electorate exclusively of the Untouchables. In other words there is still a controversy over the question of joint versus separate electorates. Here again I want to set out the pros and cons of this controversy. The objection to separate electorate raised by the Hindus is that separate electorate means the fragmentation of the nation. The reply is obvious. First of all, there is no nation of Indians in the real sense of the word. The nation does not exist, it is to be created, and I think it will be admitted that the suppression of a distinct and a separate community is not the method of creating a nation.

Secondly, it is conceded-as the Hindus have done-that Untouchables should be represented in that Legislature by Untouchable then it cannot be denied that the Untouchable must be a true representative of the Untouchable voters. If this is a correct position then separate electorate is the only mechanism by which real representation can be guaranteed to the Untouchables. The Hindu argument against separate electorate is insubstantial and unsupportable. The premises on which the political demands of the Untouchables are based are admitted by the Hindus. Separate electorate is only a consequence which logically follows from those premises. How can you admit the premise and deny the conclusion?

Special electorates are devised as a means of protecting the minorities. Why not permit a minority like the Untouchables to determine what kind of electorate is necessary for its protection? If the Untouchables decide to have separate electorates why should their choice not prevail? These are questions to which the Hindus can give no answer. The reason is that the real objection to separate electorates by the Hindus is different from this ostensible objection raised in the name of a nation. The real objection is that separate electorate does not permit the Hindus to capture the seats reserved for the Untouchables. On the Other hand the joint electorate does. Let me illustrate the point by a few examples of how joint and separate electorate would work in the constituency. Take the following constituencies from the Madras Presidency. The figures of the voting strength given in the above table for the seven constituencies taken at random in the Madras Presidency are illuminating.

A scrutiny of the above figures is sufficient to show any disinterested person that if there is a separate electorate for the

Untouchables in these seven constituencies they would be in a position to elect a man in whom they had complete confidence and who would be independent to fight the battle of the Untouchables on the floor of the Legislature against the representatives of the Hindus. If, on the other hand, there is a joint electorate in these constituencies the representative of the Untouchables would be only a nominal representative and not a real representative, for no Untouchable who did not AGree to be a nominee of the Hindus and a tool in their hands could be elected in a joint eiectorate in which the Untouchable voter was out numbered in ratio of 1 to 24 or in some cases 1 to 49. The joint electorate is from the point of the Hindus to use a familiar phrase a "rotten borough" in which the Hindus get the right to nominate an Untouchable to set nominally as a representative of the Untouchables but really as a tool of the Hindus.

6 Riddle in Hinduism

THE DIFFICULTY OF KNOWING WHY ONE IS A HINDU

India is a conjeries of communities. There are in it Parsis, Christians, Mohammedans and Hindus. The basis of these communities is not racial. It is of course religious. This is a superficial view. What is interesting to know is why is a Parsi a Parsi and why is a Christian a Christian, why is a Muslim a Muslim and why is a Hindu a Hindu? With regard to the Parsi, the Christian and the Muslim it is smooth sailing. Ask a Parsi why he calls himself a Parsi he will have no difficulty in answering the question. He will say he is a Parsi because he is a follower of Zoraster. Ask the same question to a Christian. He too will have no difficulty in answering the question. He is a Christian because he believes in Jesus Christ. Put the same question to a Muslim. He too will have no hesitation in answering it. He will say he is a believer in Islam and that is why he is a Muslim. Now ask the same question to a Hindu and there is no doubt that he will be completely bewildered and would not know what to say.

If he says that he is a Hindu because he worships the same God as the Hindu Community does his answer cannot be true. All Hindus do not worship one God. Some Hindus are monotheists, some are polytheists and some are pantheists. Even those Hindus who are monotheists are not worshippers of the same Gods. Some worship the God Vishnu, some Shiva, some Rama, some Krishna. Some do not worship the male Gods. They worship a goddess. Even then they do not worship the same Goddesses. They worship different Goddesses. Some worship Kali, some worship Parvati, some worship Laxmi. Coming to the Polytheists they worship all the Gods. They will worship Vishnu and Shiva, also Rama and Krishna. They will worship Kali, Parvati and Laxmi. A Hindu will fast on the Shivaratri day because it is sacred to Shiva. He will fast on Ekadashi day because it is sacred to Vishnu. He will plant a Bel tree because it is sacred to Shiva and he will plant a Tulsi because it is dear to Vishnu. Polytheists among the Hindus do not confine their homage to the Hindu Gods. No Hindu hesitates to worship a Muslim Pir or a Christian Goddess.

Thousands of Hindus go to a Muslim Pir and make offerings. Actually there are in some places Brahmins who own the office of a hereditary priesthood of a Muslim Pir and wear a Muslim Pir's dress. Thousands of Hindus go to make offerings to the Christian Goddess Mant Mauli near Bombay. The worship of the Christian or Muslim Gods is only on occasions. But there are more permanent transfer of religious allegiance. There are many so-called Hindus whose religion has a strong Muhammadan content. Notable amongst these are the followers of the strange Panchpiriya cult, who worship five Muhammadan saints, of uncertain name and identity, and sacrifice cocks to them, employing for the purpose as their priest a Muhammadan Dafali fakir. Throughout India many Hindus make pilgrimages to Muhammadan shrines, such as that of Sakhi Sarwar in the Punjab. Speaking of the Malkanas Mr. Blunt says that they are converted Hindus of various castes belonging to Agra and the adjoining districts, chiefly Muttra, Ettah and Mainpuri. They are of Rajput, Jat and Bania descent.

They are reluctant to describe themselves as Musalmans, and generally give their original caste name and scarcely recognize the name Malkana. Their names are Hindu; they mostly worship in Hindu temples: they use the salutation Ram-Ram: they intermarry amongst themselves only. On the other hand, they sometimes frequent a mosque, practise circumcision and bury their dead: they will eat with Muhammadans if they are particular friends. In Gujarat there are several similar communities such as the Matia Kunbis, who call in Brahmans for their chief ceremonies, but are followers of the Pirana saint Imam Shah and his successors, and bury their dead as do the Muhammadans: the Sheikhadas at their weddings employ both Hindu and a Muhammadan priest, and the Momans who practise circumcision, bury their dead and read the Gujarati Koran, but in other respects follow Hindu custom and ceremonial.

If he says that "I am a Hindu because I hold to the beliefs of the Hindus" his answer cannot be right for here one is confronted with the fact that Hinduism has no definite creed. The beliefs of persons who are by all admitted to be Hindus often differ more widely from each other than do those of Christians and Muhammadans. Limiting the issue to cardinal beliefs the Hindus differ among themselves as to the beliefs which arc of cardinal importance. Some say that all the Hindu scriptures must be accepted, but some would exclude the Tantras, while others would regard only the Vedas as of primary importance; some again think that the sole essential is belief in the doctrine of karma and metempsychosis. A complex congeries of creeds and doctrines is Hinduism. It shelters within its portals monotheists, polytheists and pantheists; worshippers of the great Gods Shiva and Vishnu or of their female counterparts,.as well as worshippers of the divine mothers or the spirits of trees, rocks and streams and the tutelary village deities; persons who propitiate their deity by all manner of bloody sacrifices, and persons who will not only kill no living creature but who must not even use the word 'cut'; those whose ritual consists mainly of prayers and hymns, and those who indulge in unspeakable orgies in the name of religion; and a host of more or less heterodox sectaries, many of whom deny the supremacy of the Brahmans, or at least have non-Brahmanical religious leaders.

If he says that he is a Hindu because he observes the same customs as other Hindus do his answer cannot be true. For all Hindus do not observe the same customs. In the north near relatives are forbidden to marry; but in the south cousin marriage is prescribed, and even closer alliances are sometimes permitted. As a rule female chastity is highly valued, but some communities set little store by it, at any rate prior to marriage, and others make it a rule to dedicate one daughter to a life of religious prostitution. In some parts the women move about freely; in others they are kept secluded. In some parts they wear skirts; in others trousers. Again if he said that he is a Hindu because he believes in the caste system his answer cannot be accepted as satisfactory.

It is quite true that no Hindu is interested in what his neighbour believes, but he is very much interested in knowing whether he can eat with him or take water from his hands. In other words it means that the caste system is an essential feature of Hinduism and a man who does not belong to a recognized Hindu Caste cannot be a Hindu. While all this is *true* it must not be forgotten that observance of caste is not enough. Many Musalmans and many Christians observe caste if not in the matter of inter-dining certainly in the matter of inter-marriage. But they cannot be called Hindus on that account. Both elements must be present. He must be a Hindu and he must also observe caste. This brings us back to the old question who is a Hindu? It leaves us where we are. Is it not a question for every Hindu to consider why in the matter of his own religion his position is so embarrassing and so puzzling? Why is he not able to answer so simple a question which every Parsi, every Christian, and every Muslim can answer? Is it not time that he should ask himself what are the causes that has brought about this Religious chaos?

THE ORIGIN OF THE VEDAS— THE BRAHMINIC EXPLANATION OR AN EXERCISE IN THE ART OF CIRCUMLOCUTION

There is hardly any Hindu who does not regard the Vedas as the most sacred Book of his religion. And yet ask any Hindu what is the origin of the Vedas and it would be difficult to find one who can give a clear and a definite answer to the simple question. Of course, if the question was addressed to a Vedic Brahmin he would say that the Vedas are Sanatan. But this is no answer to the question. For first of all what does the word *Sanatan* means? The best explanation of the word *Sanatan* is to be found in the Commentary by Kalluka Bhatt on Chapter I Shiokas 22-23 of the Manu Smriti.

This is what Kulluka Bhatt defines the word Sanatan. "The word Sanatana he says, means 'eternally pre-existing'. The doctrine of the superhuman origin of the Vedas is maintained by Manu. The same Vedas which (existed) in the previous mundane era (Kalpa) were preserved in the memory of the omniscient Brahma, who was one with the supreme spirit. It was those same Vedas that, in the beginning of the present Kalpa, he drew forth from

Agni, Vayu and Surya; and this dogma, which is founded upon the Veda, is not to be questioned, for the Veda says, 'the Rig-Veda comes from Agni, the Yajur-Veda from Vayu, and the *Sama-Veda* from Surya. " To understand the explanation by *Kulluka Bhatt* it is necessary to explain what Kalpa means. A Kalpa is a reckoning of time adopted by the Vedic Brahmins.

The Brahmanic reckoning of time divides time into (1) Varsha, (2) Yuga, (3) Mahayuga, (4) Manvantara and (5) Kalpa. Varsha is easy enough to understand. It corresponds to the term year. What exactly the period of time covered by the term Yuga covers there is no unanimity. A Mahayuga is a period covered by a group of four Yugas: (1) Krita Yuga, (2) Treta Yuga, (3) Dwapar Yuga and (4) Kali Yuga. The four Yugas follow one another in a cycle, when the period of the first Yuga is spent it is followed by the second and so on in the order given.

When the cycle is complete one Mahayuga is completed and a new Mahayuga opens. Every Mahayuga begins with the Krita Yuga and ends with Kali Yuga. There is no uncertainty as to the time relation of a Mahayuga and a Kalpa. 71 Mahayugas make one Kalpa. There is however some uncertainty as to the time relation between Mahayuga and Manvantara. A Manvantara is equal to 71 Mahayugas "and something more"'. What exact period of time that 'something more' means, the Brahmins have not been able to state categorically. Consequently the time relation between Manvantara and Kalpa is uncertain. But this does not matter very much for our present purposes. For the present it is enough to confine our attention to Kalpa. The idea underlying ' Kalpa ' is closely connected with the creation and dissolution of the Universe. The creation of the world is called *Srashti*. The dissolution of the universe is called *Pralaya*. Time between *Srashti and Pralaya* is called *Kalpa*. The idea of the origin of the Vedas is thus more intimately connected with the idea of Kalpa. According to this scheme of things, what is supposed to happen is that when a *Kalpa* begins creation begins.

With the beginning of the creation there comes into being a new series of Vedas. What Kulluka Bhatt wants to convey is that though in a sense every new Kalpa has a new series of Vedas the same old Vedas are reproduced by Brahma from his memory.

That is why he says the Vedas are Sanatan i.e., eternally pre-existing. What Kalluka Bhatt says is that the Vedas are reproduced from memory. The real question is who made them and not who reproduced them. Even if one accepts the theory of reproduction at the beginning of each Kalpa the question still remains who made the Vedas when the First Kalpa began. The Vedas could not have come into being *ex-nihilo*. They must have a beginning though they may have no end. Why don't the Brahmins say openly? Why this circumlocution?

RIDDLE NO. 3: THE TESTIMONY OF OTHER SHASTRAS ON THE ORIGIN OF THE VEDAS

The search for the origin of the Vedas may well begin with the Vedas themselves. The Rig-Veda propounds a theory of the origin of the Vedas. It is set out in the famous Purusha Sukta. According to it, there was a mystic sacrifice of the Purusha a mythical being and it is out of this sacrifice that the three Vedas namely. Rig, Sama, Yajus came into being. The Sama-Veda and Yajur-Veda have nothing to say about the origin of the Vedas. The only other Veda that refers to this question is the Atharva-Veda. It has many explanations regarding the origin of the Vedas. One explanation reads as follows: "From Time the Rig verses sprang; the Yajus sprang from Time. " There are also two other views propounded in the Atharva-Veda on this subject. The first of these is not very intelligent and may be given in its own language which runs as follows : "Declare who that Skamba (supporting principle) is in whom the primeval rishis, the rick, saman, and yajush, the earth and the one rishi, are sustained.... "Declare who is that Skamba from whom they cut off the rick verses, from whom they scrapped off the yajush, of whom the saman verses are the hairs and the verses of Atharvan and Angiras the mouth." Obviously this statement is a challenge to some one who had proclaimed that the Rig, Sama and Yajur Veda were born out of a Skamba. The second explanation given in the Atharva-Veda is that the Vedas sprang from Indra.

This is all that the Vedas have to say about their own origin. Next in order of the Vedas come the Brahmanas. We must therefore inquire into what they have to say on this subject. The only

Brahmanas which attempt to explain the origin of the Vedas are the Satapatha Brahmana, the Taitteriya Brahmana. Aitereya Brahmana and Kaushitaki Brahmana. The Satapatha Brahmana has a variety of explanations. One attributes the origin of the Vedas to Prajapati. According to it: "Prajapati, was formerly this universe (i.e., the sole existence) one only. He desired, 'may I become, may I be propagated'. He toiled in devotion, he performed austerity. "From him, when he had so toiled and performed austerity, three worlds were created—earth, air and sky.

He infused warmth into these three worlds. From them, thus heated, three lights were produced,— Agni (fire), this which purifies i.e., Pavana, or Vayu, (the Wind), and Surya (the Sun). He infused heat into these three lights. From them so heated the three Vedas were produced,— the Rig-Veda from Agni (fire), the Yajur-Veda from Vayu (Wind) and the Sama-Veda from Surya (the Sun). He infused warmth into these three Vedas. From them so heated three luminous essences were produced, *bhuh*, from the Rig-Veda, *bhuvah* from the Yajur-Veda, and *svar* from the Sama-Veda. Hence, with the Rig-Veda, the office of the *adhvaryu;* with the Sama-Veda, the duty of the *udgatri;* while the function of the brahman arose through the luminous essence of the triple science (i.e., the three Vedas combined).'" The Satapatha Brahmana gives another variant of this explanation of the origin of the Veda from Prajapati. The explanation is that Prajapati created the Vedas from waters. Says the Satapatha Brahmana:

"This male, Prajapati, desired, 'May I multiply, may I be propagated'. He toiled in devotion; he practised austere-fervour. Having done so he first of all created sacred knowledge, the triple Vedic science. This became a basis for him. Wherefore men say, 'sacred knowledge is the basis of this universe'. Hence after studying the Veda a man has a standing ground; for sacred knowledge is his foundation. Resting on this basis he (Prajapati) practised austere-fervour. He created the waters from Vach (speech) as their world. Vach was his; she was created. As she pervaded (apnot) waters were called 'apah'. As she covered (avrinot) all, water was called 'Var'. He desired, 'May I be propagated from these waters'. Along with this triple Vedic science he entered the waters. Thence sprang an egg. He gave it an impulse; and said 'let there be, let there be, let there be again '.Thence was first created sacred knowledge, the triple Vedic science. Wherefore men say, 'Sacred knowledge is the first-born thing' in this universe. Moreover, it was sacred knowledge which was created from that Male in front, wherefore it was created as his mouth. Hence they say of a man learned in the Veda, 'he is like Agni; for the sacred knowledge is Agni's mouth '. "

There is a third explanation given in the Satapatha Brahmana: " I settle thee in the ocean as they seat."

"Mind is the ocean. From the mind-ocean with speech for a shovel the Gods dug out the triple Vedic science. Hence this verse has been uttered; 'May the brilliant deity today know where they placed that offering which the Gods dug out with sharp shovels. Mind is the ocean; speech is the sharp shovel; the triple Vedic Science is the offering. In reference to this the verse has been uttered. He settles it in Mind." The Taitteriya-Brahmana has three explanations to offer. It speaks of the Vedas as being derived from Prajapati. It also says Prajapati created king Soma and after him the three. Vedas were created. This Brahmana has another explanation quite unconnected with Prajapati. According to it: "Vach (speech) is an imperishable thing, and the first-born of the ceremonial, the mother of the Vedas, and the centre-point of immortality. Delighting in us, she came to the sacrifice. May the protecting goddess be ready to listen to my invocation, she whom the wise rishis, the composers of hymns, the Gods sought by austere-fervour, and by laborious devotion. " To crown all this the Taitteriya Brahmana offers a third explanation. It says that the Vedas came from the beard of Prajapati.

The Upanishads have also attempted to explain the origin of the Vedas. The explanation offered by the Chhandogya Upanishad is the same as that given by the Satapatha Brahmana—namely that the Rig-Veda originated from Agni, Yajus from Vayu and Sam from the Sun. The Brahad Aranyaka Upanishad has two explanations to offer. In one place, it says: "As from a fire made of moist wood, various modifications of smoke proceed, so is the breathing of this great Being the Rig-Veda, the Yajur-Veda, the Sama-Veda, the Atharvangirases, the Itihasas, Puranas, science, the Upanishads, verses (slokas), aphorisms, comments of different kinds—all these are his breathings. " In another place, it says "Prajapati (identified with Death or the Devourer) is said to have produced Vach (speech), and through her, together with soul, to have created all things, including the Vedas."

"By that speech and that soul he created all things whatsoever, rick, yajush, and saman texts, metres, sacrifices, creatures and animals." "The three Vedas are (identifiable with) these three things (speech, mind and breath). Speech is the Rig-Veda, mind the Yajur-Veda and breath the Sama-Veda."

Coming to the Smritis, there are two theories as to the origin of the Vedas to be found in the Manu Smriti. In one place, it is said that the Vedas were created by Brahma. "He (Brahma) in the beginning fashioned from the words of the Veda the several names, functions, and separate conditions of all (creatures). That Lord also created the subtle host of active and living deities, and of Sadhyas, and eternal sacrifice. And in order to the performance of sacrifice, he drew forth from Agni, from Vayu and from Surya, the triple eternal Veda, distinguished as Rick, Yajush and Saman." In another place he seems to accept the story of Prajapati being the originator of the Vedas as would be evident from the following: "Prajapati also milked out of the three Vedas the letters, *'a '*, *' u '*, and *"m '* together with the words *'bhuh '*, *' bhuvah '*and *' svar '*. The same supreme Prajapati also milked from each of the three Vedas one of the three portions of the text called Savitri (or gayatri), beginning with the word *tat*.... The three great imperishable particles (bhuh,bhuvah, svar) preceded by om, and the gayatri of three lines, are to be regarded as he mouth of Brahma."

It is also interesting to note what the Puranas have to say about the origin of the Vedas. The Vishnu Purana says: "From his eastern mouth Brahma formed the gayatra, the rick verses, the trivrit, the soma-rathantara, and of sacrifices, the agnishtoma. From his southern mouth he created the yajush verses, the trishtubh metre, the panchadasa-stoma, the vrihat-saman and the ukthya. From his western mouth he formed the saman verses, the jagatimetre, the saptadasa-stoma, the vairupa, and the atiratra. From his northern mouth he framed the ekavinsa, the atharvan, the aptoryaman, with the anushtubh and biraj metres." The Bhagvat Purana says: "Once the Vedas sprang from the four-faced creator, as he was meditating ' how shall I create the aggregate worlds as before?... He formed from his eastern and other mouths the Vedas called rick, yajush, saman, and atharvan, together with praise, sacrifice, hymns and expiation."

"Entering between her eyes. From her there was then produced a quadruple being in the form of a Male, lustrous as Brahma, undefined, eternal, undecaying, devoid of bodily senses or qualities, distinguished by the attribute of brilliancy, pure as the rays of the moon, radiant, and embodied in letters. The God fashioned the Rig-Veda, with the Yajush from his eyes, the Sama-Veda from the tip of his tongue, and the Atharvan from his head. These Vedas, as soon as they are born, find a body, (kshetra). Hence they obtain their character of Vedas, because they find (vindanti) that abode. These Vedas then create the pre-existent eternal Brahma (sacred science), a Male of celestial form, with their own mind-born qualities. " It also accepts Prajapati as the origin.

It says that when the Supreme being was intent on creating the Universe, Hiranyagarbha, or Prajapati, issued from his mouth the sound ' Om ', and was desired to divide himself—a process which he was in great doubt how he should effect— the Harivamsa proceeds: "While he was thus reflecting, the sound ' om ' issued from him, and resounded through the earth, air and sky. While the God of Gods was again and again repeating this, the essence of mind, the vashatkara proceeded from his heart. Next, the sacred and transcendent vyahritis, (bhuh, bhuvah, svar), formed of the great smriti, in the form of sound, were produced from earth, air, and sky. Then appeared the goddess, the most excellent of meters, with twenty-four syllables (the gayatri). Reflecting on the divine text (beginning with) 'tat', the Lord formed the Savitri. He then produced all the Vedas, the Rick, Saman, Atharvan, and Yajush, with their prayers and rites."

Here we have eleven different explanations regarding the origin of the Vedas—(1) as originating from the mystical sacrifice of Purusha, (2) as resting on Skambha, (3) as cut or scraped off from him, as being his hair and his mouth, (4) as springing from Indra, (5) as produced from Time, (6) as produced from Agni, Vayu and Surya, (7) as springing from Prajapati, and the Waters, (8) as being the breath of Brahma, (9) as being dug by the Gods out of mind-ocean, (10) as being the hair of Prajapati's beard and (II) as being the offspring of Vach. This bewildering multiplicity of answers to a simple question is a riddle. The writers who have come forward to furnish these answers are all Brahmins. They belong to the same Vaidik school of thought. They alone were the guardians of the ancient religious lore. Why should they have given such incoherent and chaotic answers to a very simple question?

RIDDLE No. 4: WHY SUDDENLY THE BRAHMINS DECLARE THE VEDAS TO BE INFALLIBLE AND NOT TO BE QUESTIONED?

To say that the Vedas occupy a very high position in the Religious literature of the Hindus is to make an understatement. To say that the Vedas form the sacred literature of the Hindus will also be an inadequate statement. For the Vedas besides being a sacred literature of the Hindus is a book whose authority cannot be questioned. The Vedas are infallible. Any argument based on the Vedas is final and conclusive. There is no appeal against it. This is the theory of the Vedic Brahmins and is accepted by the generality of the Hindus.

On what does this theory rest? The theory rests on the view that the Vedas are *Apaurusheya.* When the Vedic Brahmins say that the Vedas are *Apaurusheya* what they mean is that they were not made by man. Not being made by man, they are free from the failings, faults and frailties to which every man is subject and are therefore infallible.

It is difficult to understand how such a theory came to be propounded by the Vedic Brahmins. For there was a time when the Vedic Brahmins themselves thought quite differently on the question of the authority of the Vedas as being final and conclusive. These *Vaidik* Brahmins are no other than the authors of the various Dharma Sutras. The following are the views expressed by the Dharma Ṣutras on question of the authority of the Vedas: To begin with the Gautama Dharma Sutra. It lays down the following rule on the question of the infallibility of the Vedas. "The Veda is the source of the sacred law" 1-1.

"And the tradition and practice of those who know the Veda" I-2. "

"If authorities of equal force are conflicting, (either may be followed at) pleasure" I-4.

The Vashishta Dharma Sutra propounds the following view: "The sacred law has been settled by the revealed texts i.e., Vedas and by the tradition of the sages" I-4.

"On the failure of (rules given in) these (two sources) the practice of Shishtas (has) authority" I-5.

The views of Baudhayana are given below:

Prasna I, Adhyaya I, Kandika I.

(1) The sacred law is taught in each Veda.

(2) We will explain (it) in accordance with that.

(3) (The sacred law), taught in the tradition (Smriti) stands second.

(4) The practice of the Sishtas (stands) third.

(5) On failure of them an Assembly consisting at least of ten members (shall decide disputed points of law).

The view taken by the Apastamba Dharma Sutra is clear from the following extract from that Sutra: "Now, therefore, we will declare the acts productive of merit which form part of the customs of daily life" 1-1.

"The authority (for these duties) is the agreement (samaya) of those who know the law". 1-2.

"And (the authorities for the latter are) the Vedas alone" 1-3. With regard to the *Shishtas* both the Vashishtha Dharma Sutra and also the Baudhayana Dharma Sutra have taken particular care to define who can be regarded as *Shishtas.*

The Vashishta Dharma Sutra says: "He whose heart is free from desire (is called) a Shishta". I-6. Baudhayana goes into much greater details about the qualification of the Shishtas. This is what he says: "5. Shishtas, forsooth, (are those) who are free from envy, free from pride, contented with a store of grain sufficient for ten days, free from covetousness, and free from hypocrisy, arrogance, greed, perplexity and anger."

"6. Those are called Shishtas who, in accordance with the sacred law, have studied the Veda together with its appendages, know how to draw inferences from that (and) are able to adduce proofs perceptible by the senses from the revealed texts. " Baudhayana has also something very interesting to say about the assembly whom he authorises to decide. The following are his views on the matter: "8. Now they quote also (the following verses): 'Four men, who each know one of the four Vedas, a Mimansaka, one who knows the Angas, one who recites (the works on) the sacred law, and three Brahmanas belonging to (three different) orders, constitute an assembly consisting at least of ten members." "9. There may be five, or there may be three, or there may be one blameless man, who decides (questions regarding) the sacred law. But a thousand fools (can) not do it)." "As an elephant made of wood, as an antelope made of leather, such an unlearned Brahmana; those three having nothing but the name (of their kind)".

This review of Dharma Sutras' shows that the (1) Veda, (2) Tradition (Smriti), (3) Practice of Shishta and (4) Agreement in an assembly were the four different authorities which were required to be referred to in the decision of an issue which was in controversy. It also shows that there was a time when the Vedas were not the sole infallible authorities. That was the time represented by the Dharma Sutras of Vashishta and Baudhayana. Apastambha does not invest the Vedas with any authority at all. Knowledge of Vedas is made by him as an electoral qualification for membership of the Assembly whose agreed decision is the law and the only law. The Veda was not at all regarded as a book of authority and when the only recognized source of authority was an agreement arrived at in an Assembly of the learned. It is only in the time of Gautama that the Vedas came to be regarded as the only authority. There was a time when an agreed decision of the Assembly was admitted as one source of authority. That is the period represented by Baudhayana. This conclusion is reinforced by the following quotation from the Satapatha Brahmana.

Riddle No. 5: WHY DID THE BRAHMINS GO FURTHER AND DECLARE THAT THE VEDAS ARE NEITHER MADE BY MAN NOR BY GOD?

The Vedic Brahmins were not content with investing the Vedas with Infallibility. They went further and asserted that the Vedas were Apaurusheya. By this they meant the Vedas were not made by man. This doctrine no doubt leads to the doctrine of Infallibility. For not being made by man they are free from the failings, faults and frailties of man and are therefore infallible. All the same it is necessary to examine the theory separately for it is an independent theory. Is there really no human author of the Vedas?

Are they really Apaurusheya? The best evidence on the subject is the evidence of the *Anukramanis*— a special class of literature which forms part of the ancient Sanskrit literature. What are called Anukramanis are nothing but systematic indices to various portions of the ancient Vedic literature. Every Veda has an Anukramani, sometimes have more than one Anukramani. Seven Anukramanis for the Rig-Veda are known to be in existence, five by Shaunaka, one by Katyayana and one by an unknown author. For the Yajur-Veda there exist three Anukramanis, one for each of the three Shakhas, Atreyi, Charayaniyas and Madhyandina. For the Sama-Veda there are two Anukramanis, one is called Arsheya-Brahmana and the other is known by the name Parishistas. As to the Atharva-Veda one Anukramani is known to exist. It is known as Brihat-Sarvanukramani.

The most perfect Anukramani according to Prof. Max Muller is Katyayana's Sarvanukramani to the Rig-Veda. Its importance lies in the tact that it gives (1) the first words of each hymn, (2) the number of verses. (3) the name and the family of the Rishi who composed it, (4) the names of the deities and (5) the metres of every verse. What emerges from a reference to the Sarvanukramani is that the Rishis are the authors of the hymns which make up the Rig-Veda. The Rig-Veda therefore on the evidence of the Anukramani cannot but be regarded as a man-made work. The same must be the conclusion regarding the other Vedas. That the Anukramanis are realistic is proved by many passages in the Rig-Veda in which the Rishis describe themselves as the composers of the hymns.

Below are given a few of such passages: "The Kanvas make a prayer to you, hear well their invocation'. Thus, O, Indra, yoker of steeds, have the Gotamas made hymns for these efficaciously" "This hymn has efficaciously been made to you, O opulent Asvins, by the Manas" "These magnifying prayers, (this) hymn, 0 Asvins, the Gritsamadas have made for you " "Aspiring to heaven, the sage Kusikas have made a hymn with praises to thee, O Indra. " "Nodhas, descendant of Gotama, fashioned this new hymn for (thee). Indra, who are of old, and who yokest thy steeds" "Thus O, hero, have the Gritsamadas, desiring succour, fashioned for thee a hymn as men make works. " "The sages generated an efficacious production and a prayer for Indra." "These hymns, Agni, generated for thee, celebrate thy bounty in cows and horses. " "Our father hath discovered (or invented) this great, sevenheaded hymn, born of sacred truth; Ayasya, friend of all men celebrating Indra, has generated the fourth song of praise." "We, the Raghuanas, have uttered to Agni honied speech; we incessantly laud him with eulogies. " "Thus, all ye Adityas, Aditi, and ye ruling powers, has the wise son of Plati magnified you. The celestial race has been lauded by the immortal Gaya."

"He it is whom they call a rishi, a priest, a pious sacrificer, a chanter of prayers, a reciter of hymns, he it is who knows the three bodies of the brilliant (Agni), the man who is most prominent in bestowing gifts. "

Apart from the evidence of the Anukramanis there is another sort of evidence which militates against the theory of the Vedas being Apaurusheya. The Rishis themselves have treated the Vedas as a human and as a historical product. The hymns *of* Rig-Veda distinguish between ancient and modern Rishis. Here are a few of them: "Agni, who is worthy to be celebrated by former as well as modern rishis, will bring the gods hither. " "The former rishis who invoked thee for succour." "Hear the hymn of me this modern sage, of this modern (sage). " " Indra, as thou hast been like a joy to former worshippers who praised thee, like waters to the thirsty, I invoke thee again and again with this hymn."

"The ancient rishis, resplendent and sage, have placed in front of them (Brihaspati) with gladdening tongue." "Neither the ancients nor later men, nor any modern man, has attained to (conceived) thy prowess, O, Madhavan." "As (Indra's) former worshippers were, (may we be) blameless, irreproachable, and unharmed." "For, now, O energetic god, men are thy worshippers as the ancients born of old and the men of the middle and later ages have been thy friends. And O, much-invoked think of the most recent of all. "To Him (Indra) our ancient fathers, the seven Navagava sages desiring food, (resorted) with their hymns. " "Glorified by our newest hymn, do thou bring to us wealth and food with progeny."

A closer study of the Rig-Veda will show that the Rig-Veda itself makes a distinction between old hymns and new hymns. Some of them are given below: "Glorified by our newest hymn, do thou bring to us wealth and food and progeny." "Agni thou hast announced (or do thou announcest) among the gods this our offering, our newest hymn." "Through our new hymns, do thou, vigorous in action, destroyer of cities, sustain us with invigorating blessings. " "I bring to Agni, the son of strength, a new and energetic hymn, a production of, thought uttered by the voice (vachah)." "I present to the mighty protector a mental production, a new utterance (now) springing up" "May the new prayer impel thee, the heroic well-accourted, the loud-thundering to succour us. " "I seek like the ancients, to stimulate thee, the ancient, with a new hymn. " "May the new hymns made to praise you, may these prayers gratify you."

"Sing O, Sobhari, with a new hymn to these youthful, vigorous, and brilliant (gods) "Indra, slayer of Vritra, thunderer, invoked of many, we (thy) numerous (worshippers) bring to thee, as thy hire, hymns which never before existed. " "I will address to this ancient (deity) my new praises which he desires: May he listen to us" "Desiring horses, cattle, and wealth we invoke thee to approach us. "

Given this abundance of evidence to prove the human origin of the Vedas it is a riddle to find that the Brahmins should so strenuously propagate this extravagant view that the Vedas are not man made. What made the Brahmins propagate such a view? Notwithstanding this there were eminent philosophers who were prepared to accept the authority of the Vedas although they were not prepared to admit that the Vedas were *Sanatan* or *Apaurush.*

The Gautama the founder of what is called the Nyaya system of Philosopy said: "The authority of the Veda, like that of the formulas, and the Ayur-Veda (treatise on medicine) follows from the authority of the competent persons from whom they proceeded. Since the competent maker of the Veda possesses authority, inculcates truth, it results from the force of the terms that the Veda was uttered by a person of this character; and by this reasoning the authority of the Veda is to be inferred. He illustrates this by the case of the formulas and the Ayur-Veda. By formulas *(mantra)* are meant the sentences which neutralize poison etc., and the section containing the Ayur-Veda forms part of the Veda. Now as the authority of these two classes of writings is admitted by general consent, the authority of everything which possess the characteristics of the Veda must be inferred from this example. Some, however, explain the aphorism thus; a Veda is that in which authority is found or recognized. From such Vedicity (or Possession of the character of a Veda) the authority of any work is to be inferred. "

The Vaishashika system admits that the Vedas are authoritative. But the grounds on which it rests its conclusion are:

(1) That the Vedas are the product of an intelligent mind and

(2) That they have been uttered by God. Therefore they are authoritative.

The Sankhya system founded by Kapila held the view that eternity cannot be predicated of the Vedas, since various texts in the Vedas themselves declare them to have been produced. It expressly denies that the Vedas originated from the conscious effort of any divine being. According to the Sankhya, the Vedas like the Sun shine by their own light, and evince an inherent power both of revealing their own perfection and of elucidating all other things, past and future, great and small, near and remote. The system of Philosophy known as the Vedanta seems to support two distant views. It ascribes the origin of the Vedas to Brahma as its source or cause of source using the term Brahma as neuter denoting the supreme spirit and not as masculine designating the personal creator. It also speaks of the eternity of the Vedas and makes mention of a self-dependent author.

The Brahmins did not remain content with the argument that the Vedas were not made by man. They went much further and contended that the Vedas were not made even by God. This theory is propounded by Jaimini the author of the Purva Mimansa. Jaimini's arguments in favour of the thesis are so strange that one has to know them in order to realize their strangeness. It is in the

Purva Mimansa— a book of Brahmanic philosophy— that this doctrine of the Vedas being Apaurusheya is propounded. The following extracts from the book will reveal the nature of the argument. Jaimini the author of the Purva Mimamsa first deals with the argument of the Naiyayikas who assert that the Vedas are made by Parameshwara and states the case made out by the Naiyayikas. The argument of the Mimansakas is: "The Veda could not have been uttered by the incorporeal Paramesvara (God), who has no palate or other organs of speech, and therefore cannot be conceived to have pronounced the letters (of which it is composed.).

This objection (answers the Naiyayika) is not happy, because, though Paramesvara is by nature incorporeal, he can yet, by way of sport assume a body, in order to show kindness to his devoted worshippers. Consequently, the arguments in favour of the doctrine that the Veda had no personal author are inconclusive." He then proceeds to state his arguments in favour of the Doctrine of the Mimansakas— "I shall now clear up all these difficulties. What is meant by this *paurusheyatva* ('derivation from a personal author') which it is sought to prove? Is it (1) mere procession *(utpannatva)* from a person (purusha) like the procession of the Veda from persons such as ourselves, when we daily utter it? or (2) is it the arrangement— with a view to its manifestation—of knowledge acquired by other modes of proof, in the sense in which persons like ourselves compose a treatise? If the first meaning be intended, there will be no dispute.

If the second sense be meant, I ask whether the Veda is proved (to be authoritative) in virtue (a) of its being founded on inference, or (b) of its being founded on supernatural information *(agama-halat)?..* The former alternative (a) i.e., that the Veda derives its authority from being founded on inference cannot be correct, since this theory breaks down, if it be applied to the sentence of the Malati Madhava or any other secular poem (which may contain inferences destitute of authority). If, on the other hand, you say (b) that the contents of the Veda are distinguished from those of other books of having authority, this explanation also will fail to satisfy a philosopher. For the word of the Veda is (defined to be) a word which proves things that are not provable by any other evidence. Now if it could be established that this Vedic word did nothing more than prove things that are provable by other evidence, we should be involved in the same sort of contradiction as if a man were to say that his mother was a barren woman. And even if we conceded that Parameswara might in sport assume a body, it would not be conceivable that in that case he should perceive things beyond the reach of the senses, from the want of any means of apprehending objects removed from him in place, in time, and in nature.

Nor is it to be thought that his eyes and other sense alone would have the power of producing such knowledge, since men can only attain to conceptions corresponding with what they have perceived. This is what has been said by the Guru (Prabhakara) when he refutes this supposition of an omniscient author; 'Wherever any object is perceived (by the organ of sight) in its most perfect exercise, such perception can only have reference to the vision of something very distant or very minute, since no organ can go beyond its own proper objects, as e.g., the ear can never become cognizant of form '. Hence the authority of the Veda does not arise in virtue of any supernatural information acquired by the Deity in a corporeal shape." These are arguments urged by Jaimini to destroy the case of the Naiyayikas. Jaimini then proceeds to give his positive arguments to show why the Vedas are not the word of God but something superior to that. This is what he says: "In the preceding aphorism it was declared that the connection of words and their meanings is eternal. Desiring now to prove that this (eternity of connection) is dependent on the eternity of words (or sound), he begins by setting forth the first side of the question, viz., the doctrine of those who maintain that sound is not eternal."

"Some, i.e., the followers of the Nyaya philosophy, say that sound is a product, because we see that it is the result of effort, which it would not be if it were eternal." "That it is not eternal, on account of its transitoriness, i.e., because after a moment it ceases to be perceived." "Because, we employ in reference to it the expression 'making' i.e., we speak of 'making' a sound." "Because it is perceived by different persons at once, and is consequently in immediate contact with the organs of sense of those, both far and near, which it could not be if it were one and eternal." "Because sounds have both an original and a modified form; as e.g., in the case of *dadhi atra,* which is changed into *dadhy atra,* the original letter 'i ' being altered into ' *y* ' by the rules of permutation. Now, no substance which undergoes a change is eternal."

" Because sound is augmented by the number of those who make it. Consequently the opinion of the Mimansaka, who say that sound is merely manifested, and not created, by human effort, is wrong; since even a thousand manifesters do not increase the object which they manifest, as a jar is not made larger by a thousand lamps." These objections against the Mimansaka theory that sound is manifested, and not created, by those who utter it, are now answered by Jaimini. Says Jaimini: "But, according to both schools, viz., that which holds sound to be created, and that which regards it as merely manifested, the perception of it is alike momentary. But of these two views, the theory of manifestation is shown in the next aphorism to be the correct one."

"The non-perception at any particular time, of sound, which, in reality, perpetually exists, arises from the fact that the utterer of sound has not come into contact with his object i.e., sound. Sound is eternal, because we recognize the letter ' *k* ', for instance, to be the same sound which we have always heard, and because it is the simplest method of accounting for the phenomenon to suppose that it is the same. The still atmosphere which interferes with the perception of sound is removed by the conjunctions and disjunctions of air issuing from a speaker's mouth, and thus sound (which always exists, though unperceived) becomes perceptible. This is the reply to the objection of its 'transitoriness'. "The word, 'making' sounds, merely means employing or uttering them." "One sound is simultaneously heard by different persons, just as one Sun is seen by them at one and the same time. Sound like the Sun, is a vast, and not a minute object, and thus may be perceptible by different persons, though remote from one another." "The letter 'y', which is substituted for 'i' in the instance referred to under Sutra 10, is not a modification of 'i', but a distinct letter. Consequently, sound is not modified."

"It is an increase of 'noise ', not of sound, that is occasioned by a multitude of speakers. The word ' noise ' refers to the 'conjunctions ' and 'disjunctions' of the air which enter simultaneously into the hearer's ear from different quarters; and it is o.; these that an increase takes place." "Sound must be eternal, because its utterance is fitted to convey a meaning to other persons. If it were not eternal (or abiding), it would not continue till the hearer had learned its sense, and thus he would not learn the sense, because the cause had ceased to exist." "Sound is eternal, because it is in every case correctly and uniformly recognised by many persons simultaneously; and it is inconceivable that they should all at once fall into a mistake." "When the word *'go '* (cow) has been repeated ten times, the hearers will say that the word *'go"* has been ten times pronounced, not that ten words having the sound of *'go'* have been uttered; and this fact also is adduced as a proof of the eternity of sound. "Sound is eternal, because we have no ground for anticipating its destruction.

"But it may be urged that sound is a modification of air, since it arises from its conjunctions, and because the Siksha (or Vedanga treating of pronunciation) says that 'air arrives at the condition of sound' and as it is thus produced from air, it cannot be eternal." A reply to this difficulty is given in Sutra 22. " Sound is not a modification of air, because if it were, the organ of hearing would have no appropriate object which it could perceive. No modification of air (help by the Naiyayikas to be tangible) could be perceived by the organ of hearing, which deals only with intangible sound." "And the eternity of sound is established by the argument discoverable in the Vedic text, ' with an eternal voice, O Virupa '. Now, though this sentence had another object in view, it, nevertheless, declares the eternity of language, and hence sound is eternal." Such is the argument by Jaimini in favour of his thesis that the Vedas are eternal and not made by man, not even by God. The bases on which his thesis rests are simple.

Firstly God has no body and no palate and therefore he could not utter the Vedas.

Secondly, Assuming God had a body, God could not perceive things which are beyond the reach of the senses while the Vedas contain things beyond the reach of human senses.

Thirdly, The connection between a word and its meaning is eternal.

Fourthly, Sound is eternal.

Fifthly, Because sound is eternal words which are made up of sounds are also eternal.

Sixthly Because words are eternal therefore the Vedas are eternal and because the Vedas are eternal they are not made by man nor by God.

What can one say of these premises? Can there be anything more absurd? Who can accept that the Vedas contain something not comprehensible by human senses? Who can accept that there is an eternal connection between a word and its meaning? Who can accept that sound is not created nor manifested but is eternal? Having regard to these absurd premises one is led to ask why did the Brahmins make such a desparate attempt for establishing a desparate conclusion? What did they want to gain thereby? Was it because the Vedas had been made the exponent of the Chaturvarna with the Brahmins as the Lord of all?

RIDDLE NO. 6: THE CONTENTS OF THE VEDAS: HAVE THEY ANY MORAL OR SPIRITUAL VALUE?

If the Vedas are to be accepted as binding and Infallible then what they teach must have ethical and spiritual value. Nobody can regard a rag to be binding and infallible because a Philosopher like Jaimini came forward to lend his authority to such a proposal. Have the Vedas any ethical or spiritual value? Every Hindu who regards the Vedas are infallible is bound to consider this question. Modern writers have expressed views which deny any spiritual value to the Vedas. As an illustration one may refer to the views of Prof. Muir. According to Prof. Muir: "The whole character of these compositions and the circumstances under which, from internal evidence, they appear to have arisen, are in harmony with the supposition that they were nothing more than the natural expression of the personal hopes and feelings of those ancient bards of whom they were first recited. In these songs the Aryan sages celebrated the praises of their ancestral gods (while at the same time they sought to conciliate their goodwill by a variety of oblations supposed to be acceptable to them), and besought of them all the blessings which men in general desired— health, wealth, long life, cattle, offspring, victory over their enemies, foregiveness of sin, and in some cases also celestial felicity." It would no doubt be objected that all foreign scholars are prejudiced and that their views cannot therefore be accepted. Fortunately we are not altogether dependent upon the views of foreigners. There are leaders of indegeneous schools of thought which have taken the same view. The most notorious example is that of the Charvakas. The opposition of Charvaka can be seen from the following quotation which reproduces his line of argument against the Vaidikas: "

If you object that, if there be no such thing as happiness in a future world, then how should men of experienced wisdom engage in the agnihotra and other sacrifices, which can only be performed with great expenditure of money and bodily fatigue. Your objection cannot be accepted as any proof to the contrary, since the agnihotra, etc., are only useful as means of livelihood: for the Veda is tainted by three faults of untruth, self-contradiction, and tautology; then again the impostors who call themselves Vaidic pundits are mutually destructive, as the authority of the Jnan-Kanda is overthrown by those who maintain the authority of the Karma-Kanda and those who maintain the authority of the Jnan-Kanda reject that of the Karma-Kanda; and lastly, the three Vedas themselves are only the incoherent rhapsodies of knaves and to this effect runs the popular saying: "The Agnihotra, the three Vedas, the ascetic, three staves, and smearing oneself with ashes," Brihaspati says, "these are but means of livelihood for those who have no manliness nor sense.'" Brahaspati is another example of the same school of thought. Brahaspati was far more bold and militant in his opposition to the Vedas than the Charvakas. As reported by Madhava Acharya, Brahaspati argued:— "There is no heaven, no final liberation, nor any soul in another world: Nor do the actions of the four castes, orders etc., produce any real effect. The Agnihotra, the three Vedas, the ascetic's three stages and smearing one's self with ashes,.... were made by Nature as the livelihood of those destitute of knowledge and manliness; If a beast slain in the Jyotishtoma rite will itself go to heaven; why then does not the sacrificer forthwith offer his own father?

If the Sraddha produces gratification to beings who are dead, then here, too, in the case of travellers when they start, it is needless to give provisions for the journey. If beings in heaven are gratified by our offering the Sraddha here, then why not give the food down below to those who are standing on the housetop? While life remains let a man live happily, let him feed on ghee even though he runs in debt; When once the body becomes ashes, how can it ever return again? If he who departs from the body goes to another world, how is that he comes not back again restless for love of his kindred? Hence it is only a means of livelihood that Brahmans have established here. All these ceremonies are for the dead, there is no other fruit anywhere. The three authors of the Vedas were buffoons, knaves and demons. All the well-known formulas of the pundits Jarphari, Turphari, and all the obscene rites for the queen commanded in the Aswamedha: These were invented by buffoons, and so all the various kinds of present? to the priests. While the eating of flesh was similarly commended by night prowling demons."

If the opinions of the Charvaka and Brahaspati are not accepted there is plenty of other evidence. That evidence is recorded in the books of the various schools of philosophy such as the Nyaya, Vaishashikha, Purva and Uttar Mimamsa. It must be said to the credit of the authors of the text-books of these philosophies that before proceeding to defend the authority of the Vedas they have been very careful to set out the case of their opponents who were opposed to the authority of the. Vedas. This fact enables us to prove two things: (1) That there was a school of thought which was opposed to recognize the Vedas as books of authority; (2) That they were a respectable group of people whose opinions the defenders of the authority of the Vedas were bound to consider. I reproduce below the case of the opponents as set out in the Nyaya and the Purva Mirnarnsa.

Gotama the author of the Nyaya system of Philosophy was an upholder of the doctrine of the authority of the Vedas. He has summarized the arguments of his opponents in Sutra 57 which reads as follows: "The Veda has no authority, since it has the defects of falsehood, self-contradiction, and tautology. That verbal evidence, which is distinct from such as relates to visible objects, i.e., the Veda, has no authority. Why? Because it has the defects of falsehood etc." "Of these defects, that of falsehood is established by the fact that we sometimes observe that no fruit results from performing the sacrifice for a son, or the like. ' Self-contradiction ' is a discrepancy between a former and a later declaration. Thus the Veda says 'he sacrifices when the Sun is risen; he sacrifices when the Sun is not yet risen.

He sacrifices, (I cannot explain the next words says Muir,) A tawny (dog?) carries away the oblation of him who sacrifices before the Sun has risen: and both of these two carry off the oblation of him who sacrifices. Now here there is a contradiction between the words which enjoin sacrifices and the words which intimate by censure that those sacrifices will occasion disastrous results.

Again, the Veda has no authority, owing to its 'tautology', as where it is said, he repeats the first thrice, he repeats the last thrice. For as the lastness ultimately coincides with the firstness and as there is a triple repetition of the words, this sentence is tautological. Now since these particular sentences have no authority, the entire Veda will be proved by these specimens to stand in the same predicament, since all its other parts have the same author, or are of the same character, as these portions."

Coming to Jaimini. He summarises the views of the opponents of the Vedas in the first part of Sutras 28 and 32 of his Purva Mimamsa. Sutra 28 says: "It is also objected that the Vedas cannot be eternal, because we observe that persons, who are not eternal, but subject to birth and death, are mentioned in them. Thus it is said in the Veda ' Babara Pravahani desired ', ' Kusurvinda Auddalaki desired '. Now, as the sentences of the Veda in which they are mentioned, could not have existed before these persons were born, it is clear that these sentences had a beginning, and being thus non-eternal, they are proved to be of human composition."

Sutra 32 says: "It is asked how the Veda can constitute proof of duty when it contains such incoherent nonsense as the following: 'An old ox, in blanket and slippers, is standing at the door and singing benedictions. A Brahman female, desirous of offspring, asks, ' Pray O King, what is the meaning of intercourse on the day of the new moon?' or the following: 'the cows celebrated this sacrifice'."

This is also the view of Yaska the author of Nirukta who says: (Of the four kinds of verses specified in the preceding section), (a) those which address a god as absent, (b) those which address him as present, and (c) those which address the worshippers as present and the god as absent, are the most numerous, while (d) those which refer to the speaker himself are rare. It happens also that a god is praised without any blessing being invoked, as in the hymn. " I declare the heroic deeds of Indra," etc. Again, blessings are invoked without any praise being offered, as in the words, 'May, I see well with my eyes, be resplendent in my face, and hear well with my ears'. This frequently occurs in the Adhvaryava (Yajur), and in the sacrificial formula. Then again we find oaths and curses as in the words, 'May I die today, if I am a Yatudhana,' etc. Further, we observe the desire to describe some particular state of things, as in the verse. ' Death was not then, nor immortality,' etc. Then there is lamentation, arising out of a certain state of thing, as in the verse, 'The beautiful god will disappear and never return,' etc. Again we have blame and praise, as in the words. 'The man who eats alone, sins alone, etc. So, too, in the hymn to dice there is a censure upon dice, and a commendation of agriculture. Thus the objects for which the hymns were seen by the rishis were very various."

To quote the words of Yaska again— " Each particular hymn has for its deity the God to whom the Rishi, seeking to obtain any object of desire which he longs for, addresses his prayer." If this is not enough to prove that there is no ethical or spiritual Value in the Vedas further evidence could be added. As to morality there is hardly any discussion about it in the Rig-Veda. Nor does the Rig-Veda contain elevating examples of moral life. Three illustrations of cases on the other side may well be given:

First is the conversation between *Yama* and *Yami* who were brother and sister. "(Yami speaks). I invite my friend to friendship, having come over the vast and desert ocean may Vedhas, after reflecting, place in the earth the offspring (of thee) the father, endowed with excellent qualities." "(Yama speaks). Thy friend desires not this friendship, for although of one origin, she is of a different form; the hero sons of the great Asura (are) the upholders of heaven, enjoying vast renown." "(Yami speaks). The immortals take pleasure in (a union) like this which is forbidden to every mortal; let thy mind then concur with mine, and as the progenitor (of all) was the husband (of his daughter), do thou enjoy my person"

"(Yama speaks). We have not done what was done formerly; for how can we who speak truth, utter now that which is untrue? Gandharva (the sun) was in the watery (firmament), and the water was his bride. She is our common parent, hence our near affinity." "(Yami speaks). The divine omniform generator Twashtri, the progenitor, made us two husband and wife, even in the womb; none frustrate his undertaking; earth and heaven are conscious of this our (union)." "(Yama speaks). Who knows anything of this (his) first day (of existence)? Who has beheld it? Who has here revealed it? The dwelling of Mitra and of Varuna is vast. What sayest thou, who punishest men with hell?"

"(Yami speaks). The desire of Yama hath approached me Yami, to lie with him in the same bed; I will abandon my person as a wife to her husband; let us exert ourselves in union like the two wheels of a wagon." "(Yama speaks). The spies of the Gods, which wander upon earth, never stop, never close their eyes. Associate quickly, destructress with some other than with me, and exert yourselves in union, like the two wheels of a wagon." "(Yami speaks). To him (Yama) let every whorshipper sacrifice both day and night, on him let the eye of the Sun repeatedly rise; (for him may) the kindred pair (day and night unite) with heaven and earth. Yami will adhere to the non-affinity of Yama."

"(Yama speaks). The subsequent ages will come, when sisters will choose one who is not a brother (as a husband); therefore, auspicious one, choose another husband than me, and make thine arm a pillow for thy mate." "(Yami speaks). Is he a brother whose sister has no lord? Is she a sister (whose brother) misfortune approaches? Overcome by desire, I strongly urge this one request; unite thy person with mine." "(Yama speaks). I will not unite my person with thine; they call him who approaches a sister, a sinner. Enjoy pleasure with some other than me; thy brother, auspicious one, has no such desire."

"(Yami speaks). Alas, Yama, thou art feeble; we understand not thy mind or thy heart. Some other female exbrances thee as a girth a horse, or as a creeper a tree." "(Yama speaks). Do thou, Yami, embrace another; and let another embrace thee as a creeper a tree; seek his affection, let him seek thine; and make a happy union."

"May Agni, the destroyer of the Rakshasas consenting to our prayer, drive hence (the evil spirit) who (in the form of) sickness assails thine embryo, who, as the disease durnaman, assails thy womb." "May Agni concurring in our prayer, destroy the cannibal who, as sickness, assails thine embryo, who, as the disease durnaman, assails thy womb." "May we exterminate from hence (the evil spirit) who destroys the impregnating energy, the germ as it settles, the moving embryo, who seeks to destroy (the babe) when born." "May we exterminate from hence (the evil spirit), who separates thy thighs, who lies between husband and wife, who entering thy womb, devours (the seeds). May we exterminate from hence (the evil spirit), who in the form of brother, husband, or paramour, approaches thee, and seeks to destroy thy offspring." "May we exterminate from hence (the evil spirit) who, having beguiled thee by sleep or darkness, approaches thee, and seeks to destroy thy offspring."

Take some of the Hymns or prayers that are to be found in the Rig-Veda. The following are a few of them—

1. Oh ! God Vayu, how very beautiful you are. We have prepared the Somarasa (an intoxicating drink) with spices. Pray come and drink it and grant us our prayers—Rig. Ved. I. 1.2.1.
2. Oh! God Indra. Bring ye wealth for our protection. Let the wealth that you bring make us happy be increasing and everlasting and help us to kill our enemies—1. 1.8.1.
3. Oh! ye people whenever you are performing your yajna, fail not to praise the Gods Indra and Agni. Advance their position and sing their praises in the Gayatri Meter—I. 21.2.
4. Oh ! ye Agni, please bring the wives of the Gods and Twashta who are eager to come and drink Soma—I. 22.9.
5. We pray that the Gods' wives come to us with all available wings and with all happiness—I. 22.11.

6. I am praying the wives of Indra, Varuna and Agni to come to my place to drink Soma.
7. Oh! Varuna, we are supplicating before you to remove your anger. Oh! ye Asura, you are all wise, relieve us from our sins—I. 24.14.
8. Our Somarasa has been prepared by women who have churned it backward and forward. Oh! ye Indra we pray you to come and drink this Soma—1. 28.3.
9. Your enemies who do not make any offering to you may disappear and let your followers who do prosper. Oh ! Indra give us best cows and best horses and make us famous in the world.—1. 29.4.
10. Oh! Agni save us from Rakshasas, from cunning enemies, from those who hate us and want to kill us.—1. 36.15.
11. Oh! Indra, you are a hero. Come and drink the Soma we have prepared and be ready to give us wealth. Loot the wealth of those who do not make you any offering and give the same to us—1. 81-8-9.
12. Oh! Indra, drink this Soma which is the best, giving immortality and most intoxicating.—I. 84-4.
13. Oh ! Adityas, you come to give us your blessings. You give us victory in war. You are wealthy. You are charitable. Just as a chariot is pulled through a difficult path in the same way you pull us through our dangers.—1. 106-22.
14. Oh ! ye Marutas.....your followers are singing your praises. Be pleased to come and sit on the grass-cushion prepared for you for the purpose of drinking Soma.—VII. 57-1-2.
15. Oh! ye Mitra-Varuna we have offered you worship in the yajna. Be pleased to accept it and save us from all dangers—VII. 60-12.

These are only a few verses out of a large bundle which form the Rig-Veda. But there can be no doubt that this sample small as it is is true to bulk. I may state that I have deliberately omitted a good many obscene passages to be found in the Rig-Veda and Yajur-Veda.

Those who have any curiosity in the matter might look up the conversation between Surya and Pushan in Rig-Veda Mandal X.

85.37 and between Indra and Indrani in Rig-Veda. Mandal X. 86.6. A further obscenity will also be found in the Ashvamedha Section of the Yajur-Veda. Leaving these obscenities aside and confining oneself to the prayer portion of the Rig-Veda can any one say that these are morally or spiritually elevating prayers?

As to philosophy there is nothing of it in the Rig-Veda. As Prof. Wilson observes there is in the Rig-Veda, which is the stock Veda, scarcely any indication or doctrinal or philosophical speculation, no allusion to the later notions of the several schools, nor is there any hint of metempsychosis, or of the doctrine intimately allied to it, of the repeated renovation of the world.

The Vedas may be useful as a source of information regarding the social life of the Aryans. As a picture of primitive life it is full of curiosity but there is nothing elevating.

There are more vices and a few virtues. Atharva-Veda which contains black-magic and sorcery. The Rig-Veda is not altogether free from it. There are in it Mantras relating to black magic and sorcery. I give below three Suktas which deal with this matter:

SUKTA XVII (CXLV)

The deity or rather the aim of the hymn is the getting rid of a rival wife; the Rishi is Indrani, the metre of the last verse is Pankati, of the rest Anushtubh.

1. I dig up this most potent medicinal creeper, by which (a wife) destroys a rival wife, by which she secures to herself her husband.
2. O (plant) with up-turned leaves, auspicious, sent by the Gods, powerful, remove my rival and make my husband mine alone.
3. Excellent (plant) may I too be excellent amongst the excellent, and may she who is my rival be vile amongst the vile.
4. I will not even utter her name, no (woman) takes pleasure in that person: may we remove the other rival wife to a distance.
5. I am triumphing, thou art triumphant: we two being powerful will triumph over my rival.

6. I make thee the triumphant (herb) my pillow, I support thee with that more triumphant (pillow): let thy mind hasten to me as a cow to her calf, let it speed on its way like water.

SUKTA IV (CLV)

The deity of verses I and 4 is the averting of misfortune (Alakshmighna), of verses 2 and 3 Brahmanaspati, and of verse 5 the Viswadevas; the Rishi is Sirimbitha, the son of Bharadwaja, the metre is Anushtubh.

1. Miserable, ill-favoured, deformed ever-railing (goddess), go to thy mountain; with these exploits of Sirimbitha we scare thee away.
2. May she be scared away from this (world), scared away from the next (world), the destructress of all embryos; sharp-horned Brihaspati approach, driving away Distress.
3. The wood which floats by the seashore far off, remote from man, seize that, (O, goddess) hard to destroy, and therewith go to a distant shore.
4. Utterers of discordant sounds, when swiftly moving you departed, all the enemies of Indra were slain, disappearing like bubbles.
5. These (Viswadevas) have brought back the (stolen) cattle, they have built up the fire: they have provided food for the Gods. Who will overcome them?

SUKTA XII (CLXIII)

The deity is the cure of phthisis: the Rishi is Vivrihan, the son of Kasyapa, the metre is Anushtubh.

1. I banish disease from thine eyes, from thy head, from thy nose, from thy ears, from thy chin, from thy brain, from thy tongue.
2. I banish disease from thy neck, from thy sinews, from thy bones, from thy joints, from thy upper arms, from thy shoulders, and from thy fore-arms.
3. I banish disease from thine entrails, from thy anus, from thine abdomen, and from thy heart, from thy kidneys, from thy liver, from thy (other) viscera.

4. I banish disease from thy thighs, from thy knees, from thy heels, from thy toes, from thy loins, from thy buttocks, from thy private parts.
5. I banish disease from thy urethra, from thy bladder, from thy hair, from thy nails, from thy whole person.
6. I banish disease from each limb, from each hair, from each joint where it is generated, from thy whole person.

Enough has been extracted from the Vedas to show that they contain nothing that can be said to be spiritually or morally elevating. Neither the subject matter nor contents of the Vedas justify the infallibility with which they have been invested. Why then did the Brahmins struggle so hard to clothe them with sanctity and infallibility?

RIDDLE NO. 7: THE TURN OF THE TIDE OR HOW DID THE BRAHMINS DECEARE THE VEDAS TO BE LOWER THAN THE LOWEST OF THEIR SHASTRAS?

The religious literature *of* the Hindus includes (1) The Vedas, (2) The Brahmanas, (3) The Aranyakas, (4) Upanishads, (5) Sutras, (6) Itihas, (7) Smritis and (8) Puranas. As has been pointed out there was a time when they occupied the same status. There was no distinction of superior or inferior, sacred or profane, fallible or infallible. Eater on as we have shown the Vedic Brahmins felt that they must make a distinction between the Vedas and other classes of their religious literature. They made the Vedas not only superior to other classes of literature but they made them sacred and infallible. In evolving their dogma of the infallibility of the Vedas they made a distinction and divided their sacred writings in two classes (1) Shruti and (2) Non-Shruti. In the first division they placed only two of the eight classes of literature spoken of above namely-(1) Samhitas and (2) the Brahmanas. The rest they declared as Non-Shruti.

When this distinction was first made it is not possible to say. The more important question, however, is on what basis was this division made? Why were Itihas and Puranas excluded? Why were Aranyakas and Upanishads excluded? Why were the Sutras excluded? One can well understand why Itihas and Puranas were excluded from Shruti. At the time when the division took place they were too elementary and too undeveloped and in all probability included in the Brahmanas. Similarly one can well understand why the Aranyakas are not

This is a 21-page typed MS originally entitled ' The Supersession of the Vedas ', with several corrections and modifications by the author himself. This chapter seems complete as the last para of this chapter is concluded in the handwriting of the author.—Ed.

specifically mentioned as a part of the Shruti. They are a part of the Brahmanas and for that reason it was probably unnecessary to say expressly that they are part of the Shruti. The question of the Upanishads and the Sutras remains a puzzle. Why were they excluded from the Shruti? The question regarding the Upanishads is the subject matter of another chapter. Here it is proposed to deal with the question of the Sutras. Because the reasons for the exclusion of the Sutras it is not possible to comprehend. If there were good reasons for including the Brahmanas in the category of Shruti the same reasons could not fail to justify the inclusion of the Sutras. As Prof. Max Muller observes:

"We can understand how a nation might be led to ascribe a superhuman origin to their ancient national poetry, particularly if that poetry consisted chiefly of prayers and hymns addressed to their gods. But it is different with the prose compositions of the Brahmans. The reasons why the Brahmanas which are evidently so much more modern than the Mantras, were allowed to participate in the name of Sruti, could only have been because it was from these theological compositions, and not from the simple old poetry of the hymns, that a supposed divine authority could be derived for the greater number of the ambitious claims of the Brahmanas. But, although we need not ascribe any weight to the arguments by which the Brahmanas endeavoured to establish the contemporaneous origin of the Mantras and Brahmanas there seems to be no reason why we should reject as equally worthless the general opinion with regard to the more ancient date of both the Brahmanas and Mantras, if contrasted with the Sutras and the profane literature of India. It may easily happen, where there is a canon of sacred books, that later compositions become incorporated together with more ancient works, as was the case with the Brahmanas. But we can hardly imagine that old and genuine parts should ever have been excluded from a body of sacred writings, and a more modern date ascribed to them, unless it be in the interest of a party to deny the authority of certain doctrines contained in these rejected documents. There is nothing in the later literature of the Sutras to warrant a supposition of this kind. We can find no reason why the Sutras should not have been ranked as Sruti, except the lateness of their date, if compared with the Brahmanas, and still more with the Mantras. Whether the Brahmanas themselves were aware that ages must have elapsed between the period during which most of the poems of their Rishis were composed, and the times which gave rise to the Brahamanas, is a question which we need hardly hesitate to answer in the affirmative. But the recklessness with which Indian theologians claim for these Brahmanas the same title and the same age as for the Mantras, shows that the reason must have been peculiarly strong which deterred them from claiming the same divine authority for the Sutras."

The exclusion of the Sutras from the category of Shruti is a riddle that calls for explanation. There are other riddles which strike the student who cares to investigate into the subject. They relate to the changes in the content of the literature comprised in the term Shruti and their relative authority. One such riddle relates to the class of literature called the Brahmanas. At one time the Brahmanas were included in the term Shruti. But later on they seem to have lost this position. For Manu* seems to exclude the " Brahamanas " from the category of Shruti as may be seen from the following extract from his Smriti: "By Shruti is meant the Veda, and by Smriti the institutes of law; the contents of these are not to be questioned by reason, since from them (a knowledge of) duty has shown forth. The Brahman who, relying on rationalistic treatises, shall condemn these two primary sources of knowledge must be excommunicated by the virtuous as a sceptic and reviler of the Vedas.... To those who are seeking a knowledge of duty, the Sruti is the supreme authority." Why were the Brahmanas excluded from Shruti?

We may now turn to the class of literature called the Smritis, the most important of which are the Manu Smriti and the Yajnavalkya Smriti. The number of Smritis was ever on the increase and the composing of Smritis went on up to the advent of the British. Mitramistra refers to 57 Smritis, Nilakanta to 97 and Kamalakar to 131. The Smriti literature is bigger than any other class of religious literature regarded as sacred by the Hindus. There are several points regarding the relation of the Smritis to the Vedas. The first is that the Smriti was not recognized as part of the Dharma Shastra literature represented by the Dharma Sutras such as that of Baudhayana, Gautama or Apastambha. A Smruti originally dealt with social customs and conventions that were approved of and recommended by the learned leaders of society. As Prof. Altekar observes:

"In the beginning, Smritis were identical in nature and contents with *Sadacara* and were based upon it. When Smritis came into existence the scope of Sadacara became naturally reduced, as much of it was codified by Smritis. It began to denote those old practices which happened not to be codified in Smritis, or those new ones, which had acquired social approval at a period subsequent to the codification of the early Dharmasastras or Smritis." The second point to note is that the Smritis were treated as quite different from the Vedas or the Srutis. So far as their sanction and their authority were concerned they stood on absolutely different footing. The sanction behind the Sruti was divine. The sanction behind the Smriti was social. In the matter of their authority the Purva Mimarnsa lays down two rules. The first rule is that if there is a conflict between two texts of Sruti then both are authoritative and the presumption will be that the Vedas have given an option to follow one or the other. The second rule is that the text of a Smriti should be summarily rejected if it was opposed to the text of the Sruti. These rules were rigorously applied with the result that the Smritis could not acquire either the status or the authority of the Vedas.

Surprising as it may appear a time came when Brahmins took a summersault and gave the Smritis a status superior to that of the Vedas. As Prof. Altekar points out: "The Smritis have actually overruled some of the specific dicta of Srutis that were not in consonance with the spirit of the age, or were coming into direct conflict with it. The Vedic practice was to perform daiva *karma* in the morning and the *pitr karma* in the afternoon. In later times the modern *pitr tarpana* came into vogue and it began lo be offered in the morning, as the morning bath became the order of the day. Now this procedure is in direct conflict with the Vedic practice prescribed in the above-mentioned rule. Devamabhatta. the author ol the *Smrticandrika,* however says that there is nothing wrong in this: the Sruti rule must be presumed to be referring to pitr *karman* other than *tarpana.*

The Sruti literature shows that Visvamitra adopted Sunassepa, though he had a hundred sons living: this would thus permit a person to adopt a son even when he had a number ol his own sons living. But Mitramisra says that such a deduction would he wrong: we shall have to assume that the Smriti practice is also based upon a Sruti text, which is not now available but the existence of which will have to be assumed." "The Vedic passage, *na seso 'gne' nyajatamasti* certainly disapproves of the practice of the adoption of a son, which is clearly recommended in later times by the Smriti literature. This is a clear example of a Sruti being thrown overboard by a Srnriti. But Mitramisra says that there is nothing wrong about the procedure. The Sruti passage is a mere *arthavada;* it does not lay down any injunction. The Smritis on the other hand prescribe adoption so that *homas* etc. should be properly performed. *Arthavada Sruti* is thus being fittingly overruled by a Srnriti text, which has a *vidhi* for its purport."

"The custom of the Sati of the later age is in direct conflict with the vedic injunction prohibiting suicide. Apararka, however, argues that the conflict with Sruti should not invalidate the custom. For the Sruti passage lays down a general principle disapproving suicide, while the Smritis lay down a special exception in the case of a widow." Whether the customs of a Sati and adoption are good or not is a different question. Somehow or other society had come to approve of them. Smritis gave canonical, sanction to them and sought to defend them even against the authority of the Vedas. The question is why did the Brahmins after having struggled so hard for establishing the supremacy of the Vedas degrade the Vedas and invest the Smritis with authority superior to that of the Vedas? They did so much to raise the authority of the Vedas above the divine. Why did they drag them below the Smritis which had nothing but social sanction?

The steps they adopted were so ingenious and artificial that one cannot help feeling that there must have been some definite motive which led the Brahmins to give the Smritis a status superior to that of the Vedas. To give some idea as to how artificial, ingenious and desparate these arguments were it might be useful to give just a brief outline of them. As an illustration of an artificial argument, one may refer to the view propounded by Brahaspati. According to him, Sruti and Smriti are the two eyes of the Brahmana, if he is void of one of them he becomes a one-eyed person. As an illustration of an ingenious argument one may refer to the argument of Kumarila Bhatt. His argument is founded on the theory of lost Sruti. It was argued on behalf of the Smritis that their views cannot be set aside even when they are in direct conflict with the Srutis for they may quite possibly have been based upon a lost text of Sruti, and so the conflict is not a conflict between a text of Sruti and that of a Smriti. It is really a conflict between an existing and lost text of Sruti.

Smriti therefore came to be represented as lost Sruti. There is a third means adopted by the Brahmins to make the Smritis equal if not superior to the Vedas. It is to be found in the Atri Smriti. Atri says that those who do not respect the Smritis will be subject to curse. Atri's argument is that *Brahmanyam* arises only as a result of a joint study of the Sruti and Smriti and if a person studies the Vedas only but holds the Smriti in contempt he would be immediately condemned to be born as a beast for 21 generations. Why did the Brahmins adopt such desparate means to place the Smritis on the same footing as the Sruti? What was their purpose? What was their motive? Prof. Altekar's argument that the Smritis were given supremacy over the Vedas because they gave legal justification to customary law which was of later growth, cannot be accepted as adequate.

If the case was that, there was law in the Vedic period and custom had grown later on; and if there was a conflict between the two, one could have understood the argument that the Smritis were given predominance because they set right the conflict by recognizing the progressive doctrines of the custom. This is not the case. There was no such thing as law in the Vedas. As Professor Kane points out: "All law was customary and there was no necessity to give recognition to the customs because they were recognized by the people. Secondly the Smritis cannot be said to be more progressive than the Vedas. Barring the Chaturvarna doctrine which everybody knows the Vedas except in the matter of forms of worship left Society quite free to develop. What the Smritis have done is, take out the unprogressive element in the Vedas namely the Chaturvarna theory and to propagandize it and hammer it into the heads of the people." Therefore there must be some other reason why the Brahmins gave supremacy to the Smritis over the Vedas.

The Brahmins were not content with their first acrobatics. They performed another. The Smritis were followed in point of time by the Puranas. There are 18 Puranas and 18 Up-Puranas altogether 36. In one sense the subject matter of the Puranas is the same. They deal with the creation, preservation and destruction of the world. But in the rest of their contents they differ altogether. Some propagate the cult of Brahma, some the cult of Shiva, some the cult of Vishnu, some the cult of Vayu, some the cult of Agni, some the cult of Surya and some the cult of Goddesses and other deities. As has been noted there was a time when the Puranas were not included in the Shruti. In later times however a striking change seems to have taken place. The Puranas which were considered as too profane to be included in the Shruti were given a superiority over the Vedas. The Vayu Purana says: "First, of all the Shastras, the Purana was uttered by Brahma. Subsequently the Vedas issued from his mouth." The Matsya Purana not only claims priority of creation for the Puranas as against the Vedas, but also the qualities of eternity and identity with sound, which was once predicated of the Vedas alone. It says: "Pitamaha (Brahma), first of all the immortals, took shape; then the Vedas with their Angas and Upangas (appendages and minor appendages), and the various modes of their textual arrangements, were manifested. The Purana, eternal, formed of sound, pure, extending to the length of a hundred crores of verses, was the first of the Sastras which Brahma uttered; and afterwards the Vedas, issued from his mouth; and also the Mimansa and the Nyaya with its eightfold system of proofs.

The Bhagawat Purana claims equality of authority with the Vedas. It says: "(Bramharatra) declared the Purana called the

Bhagavata, which stands on an equality with the Veda." The Brahma-Vaivartta Purana has the audacity to claim superiority over the Vedas. It says: "That about which venerable sage, you have inquired, and which you desire, is all known to me, the essence of the Puranas, the preeminent Brahma-Vaivartta, which refutes the errors of the Puranas and Upa-puranas, and the Vedas." This is the second acrobatic performed by the Brahmins in assigning priority, precedence, and authority to their sacred books.

This does not complete the story of the suppression of the Vedas. The worse is yet to come. The Puranas were followed by another class of literature called the *Tantras*. Their number is also quite formidable. Shankaracharya refers to 64 Tantras. There might be many more. Traditionally the authorship of these works is attributed to Dattatreya, who was an incarnation of the Hindu trinity, Brahma, Vishnu and Shiva. They are therefore to be regarded as equally the revelation of the three supreme divinities. In form, however, they are dependent on Shiva alone, who in dialogue with his wife Durga, or Kali, reveals the mystical doctrines and observances which are *to* be received and practised by his worshippers. This authoritative or 'higher tradition' is further said to have been delivered from his central or fifth mouth. As such it is pre-eminently sacred and secret and may not be revealed to the uninitiated. They are also called by the name Agamas, and as such are sometimes distinguished from Nigama, the text of the Vedas, Dharmashastras, and other sacred books. The Tantras are regarded specially as the religious text-books of the Saktas and of their various sects. There are different Tantrik schools, with variant traditions, the distinctions between which are little understood outside of their immediate circle of adherents. The ritual of the Tantras of the Daksinacharins, however, is said to be pure and in harmony with the Vedas, while that of the Vamacharins is intended only for Shudras.

The teaching of the Tantras, as of the Puranas is essentially based on the Bhakti-Marga which is regarded by them as superior to the Karma-Marga and Jnana-Marga of the Brahmanas and Upanishads. Adoration of a personal deity is inculcated, especially of the wife of Shiva, who is worshipped as the source of all regenerative power. In all these writings the female principle is personified and made prominent, to the almost total exclusion of the male. What is the relation of the Tantras to the Vedas? Kalluka Bhatta the well known commentator of Manu Smriti has no hesitation in asserting that Shruti is two-fold-*Vaidik* and *Tantrik*— which means that the Vedas and the Tantras stand on equal footing. While the Vaidik Brahmins like Kalluka Bhatta admitted the equality of the Tantras to the Vedas, the authors of the Tantras went much beyond. They claimed that the Vedas, the Shastras, and the Puranas are alike a common woman, but the Tantras are like a highborn woman conveying thereby that the Tantras are superior to the Vedas.

From this survey one thing is clear. The Brahmins have not been very steadfast in their belief regarding the sacred character of what they called their books of religion. They fought to maintain the thesis that the Vedas were not only sacred but that they were infallible. Not only they maintained that the Vedas were infallible but they spent their ingenuity to invent strange arguments to support the doctrine of infallibility. Yet they had not the slightest compunction to overthrow the position of the Vedas and to subordinate them first to the Smritis, then to the Puranas and lastly to the Tantras. The question of all questions is what made the Brahmins degrade the Vedas and supersede them by Smritis, Puranas and the Tantras if they regarded their Vedas as the most sacred?

RIDDLE NO. 8: HOW THE UPANISHADS DECLARED WAR ON THE VEDAS?

What is the position of the Upanishads in relation to the Vedas? Are the two complimentary to each other or are they antagonistic? Of course, no Hindu would admit that the Vedas and Upanishads are repugnant to each other. On the contrary, it is the common belief of all Hindus that there is no antagonism between them and that both form part and parcel of the same single system of thought. Is this belief well-founded? The principal reason for the rise of such a belief is to be found in the fact that the Upanishads are also known by another name which is called Vedanta. The word Vedanta has got two meanings. In one sense, it means the last parts of the Vedas. In the second sense, it means the essence of the Vedas. The word Vedanta being another name for the Upanishads, the Upanishads themselves have come to acquire these meanings. It is these meanings which are responsible for the common belief that there is no antagonism between the Vedas and the Upanishads.

The subject matter of the LJpanishads is not the same as that of the Vedas. This is also another reason why the Upanishads are not a part of the Vedas. What is the origin of the word Upanishad? The point is somewhat obscure. Most European scholars are agreed in deriving Upanishad from the root *sad,* to sit down, preceded by the two prepositions *ni* down and *upa* near, so that it would express the idea of session or assembly of public sitting down near their teacher to listen to his instructions. This is because in the Trikandasesha, the word Upanishad is explained by *Samipasadana* as sitting down near a person. But as Prof. Max Muller points out there are two objections to the acceptance of this derivation. Firstly such a word, it would seem, would have been applicable to any other portion of the Veda as well as to the chapters called Upanishad, and it has never been explained how its meaning came thus to be restricted. Secondly, the word Upanishad, in the sense of session or assembly has never been met with.

Whenever the word occurs, it has the meaning of doctrine, secret doctrine, or is simply used as the title of the philosophic treatises which contain the secret doctrine. There is another explanation proposed by Sankara in his commentary on the Taittiriya-Upanishad II, 9, noted by Prof. Max Muller. According to it the highest bliss is contained in the Upanishad *(param sreyo 'syam nishannam).* That is why it is called Upanishad. Regarding this, Prof. Max Muller says: "The Aranyakas abound in such etymologies which probably were never intended as real as plays on words, helping, to account somehow for their meaning." Prof. Max Muller however favours a derivation of the word ' Upanishad ' from the root *sad* to destroy, and meant knowledge which destroys ignorance, the cause of Samsara, by revealing the knowledge of Brahmana as a means of salvation.

Prof. Max Muller points out that this is the meaning which the native scholars have unanimously given to the word Upanishad. If it be granted that the true derivation of the word

' Upanishad ' is what is suggested by Prof. Max Muller, then it would be one piece of evidence to show that the common belief of the Hindus is wrong and that the subject matter of the Vedas and the Upanishads are not complimentary but antagonistic. That the system of thought embodied in the Upanishads is repugnant to that of the Vedas is beyond doubt. A few citations from some of the Upanishads will suffice to show their opposition to the Vedas.

The Mundaka Upanishad says: " Bramha was produced the first among the gods, maker of the universe, the preserver of the world. He revealed to his eldest son Atharva, the science of Brahma the basis of all knowledge. (2) Atharvan of old declared to Angis this science, which Brahma had unfolded to him; and Angis, in turn, explained it to Satyavaha, descendant of Bharadvaja, who delivered this traditional lore, in succession, to Angiras. (3) Mahasala Saunaka, approaching Angiras with the proper formalities, inquired, 'What is that, O venerable sage, through the knowledge of which all this (universe) becomes known? (4) (Angiras) answered, 'Two sciences are to be known— this is what the sages versed in sacred knowledge declare—the superior and the inferior. (5) The inferior (consists of) the Rig Veda, the Yajur-Veda, the Sama-Veda, the Atharva-Veda, accentuation, ritual grammar, commentary, prosody and astronomy. The superior science is that by which the imperishable is apprehended." by which of course he means the Upanishads. The Chhandogya Upanishad says: "(1) Narada approached Sanatkumara, saying, "Instruct me, venerable sage.

He received for answer ' Approach me with (tell me) that which thou knowest; and I will declare to thee whatever more is to be learnt.' (2) Narada replied, 'I am instructed, venerable sage, in the Rig-veda, the Sama-veda, the Yajur-veda, the Atharvana (which is) the fourth, the Itihasas and Purana (which are) the fifth Veda of the Vedas, the rites of the pitris, arithmetic,, the knowledge of portents and of great periods, the art of reasoning, ethics, the science of the gods, the knowledge of Scripture, demonology, the science of war, the knowledge of the stars, the sciences of serpents and deities: this is what I have studied. (3) I, venerable man, know only the hymns (mantras); while I am ignorant of soul. But I have heard from reverend sages like thyself that 'the man who is acquainted with soul overpasses grief '. Now I, venerable man, am afflicted; but do thou transport me over my grief. Sanatkumara answered, ' That which thou hast studied is nothing but name. (4) The Rig-veda is name: and so are the Yajur-veda, the Sama-veda, the Atharvana, which is the fourth, and the Itihasas and Puranas, the fifth Veda of the Vedas, etc., (all the other branches of knowledge are here enumerated just as above),—all these are but names: worship name. (5) He who worships name (with the persuasion that it is) Brahma, ranges as it were at will over all which that name comprehends: such is the prerogative of him who worships name (with the persuasion that it is) Brahma, ' Is there anything, venerable man' asked Narada, 'which is more than name?' 'There is,' replied, 'something which is more than name'. 'Tell it to me', rejoined Narada."

The Brahadaranyaka Upanishad says: "In that (condition of profound slumber) a father is no father, a mother is no mother, the worlds are no worlds, the gods are no gods, and the Vedas are no Vedas, sacrifices are no sacrifices. In that condition a thief is no thief, a murderer of embryos is no murderer of embryos, a Pulkasa no Paulakasa, a Chandala no Chandala, a Sramana no Sramana, a devotee no devotee; the saint has then no relation, either of advantage or disadvantage, to merit or to sin; for he then crosses over all griefs of the heart."

This is what the Katha Upanishad has to say: "This soul is not to be attained by instruction, nor by understanding, nor by much scripture. He is attainable by him whom he chooses. The soul chooses that man's body as his own abode ". "Although this soul is difficult to know, still it may easily be known by the use of proper means. This is what (the author) proceeds to say. This soul is not to be attained, known, by instruction, by the acknowledgement of many Vedas; nor by. understanding, by the power of recollecting the contents of books; nor by much scripture alone. By what, then, is it to be attained? This he declares ".

How great was the repugnance to the Vpanishads and the philosophy contained in them will be realized if one takes note of the origin of the words Anuloma and Pratiloma which are usually applied to the marriage tie among the Hindus. Speaking of their origin Mr. Kane, points out that: "These two words Anuloma and Pratiloma (as applied to marriage or progeny) hardly ever occur in the Vedic literature. In the Br. Up. (II. 1.5) and Kausitaki Br. Up. IV. 8. the word ' Pratiloma ' is applied to the procedure adopted by a Brahmana of going to a Kshatriya for knowledge about ' *Brahman* '. Anuloma means according to the heir that is in the natural order of things, Pratiloma means against the heir that is contrary to the natural order. Reading the observations of Mr. Kane in the light of the definition of the word Pratiloma it is obvious that the Upanishads far from being acknowledged as part of the Vedic literature were if not despised, held in low esteem by the Vedic Brahmins. This is anadditional piece of evidence which shows that there was a time when the relation between the Vedas and the Upanishads was of antagonism.

Another illustration of the attitude of the Vaidik Brahmins towards Brahmins who had studied the Upanishads may be given. It is to be found in the texts of the Dharma Sutras of Baudhayana. Baudhayana in his Dharma Sutras says that at a Shradha ceremony a Rahasyavid is to be invited only if other Brahmins are not available. A Rahasyavid of course means a Brahmin versed in the Upanishads. The belief that the Vedas and the Upanishads are complimentary came into being is really a riddle.

RIDDLE NO. 9: HOW THE UPANISHADS CAME TO BE MADE SUBORDINATE TO THE VEDAS?

In the preceding chapter it was shown that originally the Upanishads were not a part of the Vedas and that the two in the matter of doctrine were opposed to each other. It is instructive to compare the later relations between the Vedas and the Upanishads. The later relations between them are best illustrated by the controversy between two philosophers, Jaimini and Badarayana. Jaimini is the author of a work called the Mimamsa Sutras while Badarayana is the author of Brahma Sutras. Jaimini is an upholder of the Vedas and Badarayana is an upholder of the Upanishads. The point of dispute was—Is it necessary to perform sacrifices? The Vedas say ' yes ' and the Upanishads say ' no '.

The position of Jaimini is stated by Badarayana in his Sutras 2-7, and explained by Shankaracharya in his commentary. Jaimini contends that*: " No one undertakes a sacrificial act unless he is conscious of the fact that he is different from the body and that after death he will go to heaven, where he will enjoy the result of his sacrifices. The Texts dealing with self-knowledge serve merely to enlighten the agent and so are subordinate to sacrificial acts." In short Jaimini says that all that Vedanta teaches is that self is different from the body and outlive the body. Such a knowledge is not enough. The self must have the aspiration to go to heaven. But it can't go to heaven unless it performs Vedic sacrifices which is what his Karmakand teaches. Therefore his Karmakand is the only Salvation and that the Jnankand from that point of view is quite useless. For this Jaimini relies on the conduct of men who have believed in Vedanta: "Janaka, emperor of Videha performed a sacrifice in which gifts were freely distributed. I am going to perform a sacrifice sirs. Now both Janaka and Asvapati were knowers of the Self. If by this knowledge of the Self they had attained Liberation, there was no need for them to perform sacrifices. But the two texts quoted show that they did perform sacrifices. This proves that it is through sacrificial acts alone that one attains Liberation and not through the knowledge of the Self as the Vedantins hold."

Jaimini makes a positive assertion that the scriptures unmistakably declare "that knowledge of the Self stands in a subordinate relation to sacrificial acts ". Jaimini justifies it because he says " the two (knowledge and work) go together (with the departing soul to produce the results)." Jaimini refuses to give an independent position to Badarayana's *Jnanakanda*. He takes his stand on two grounds.

First: " Knowledge of the Self does not independently produce any result."

Second: According to the authority of the Vedas "Knowledge (of Self) stands in a subordinate relation to work." This is the position of Jaimini towards Badarayana's *Jnanakanda*. What is the position of Badarayana towards Jaimini and his *Karma Kanda*^ This is explained by Badarayana in Sutras 8 to 17.

The first position taken up by Badarayana is that the Self spoken of by Jaimini is the limited self i.e., the soul is to be distinguished from the Supreme soul and that the Supreme soul is recognized by the Scriptures. The second position taken up by Badarayana is that the Vedas support both knowledge of Self as well as sacrifices.

The third position taken up by Badarayana is that only those who believe in the Vedas are required to perform sacrifices. But those who follow the Upanishads are not bound by that injunction. As Shankaracharya explains: "Those who have read the Vedas and known about the sacrifices are entitled to perform work (sacrifices).' No work (sacrifice) is prescribed for those who have knowledge of the Self from the Upanishads. Such a knowledge is incompatible with work."

The fourth position taken up by Badarayana is that *Karmakanda* is optional to those who have attained Bramhanand. As Shankaracharya explains: "That some have of their own accord given up all work. The point is that after knowledge some may choose to work to set an example to others, while others may give up all work. There is no binding on the knowers of the Self as regards work." His last and final position is that: "Knowledge of the Self is antagonistic to all work and so cannot possibly be subsidiary to work"

And as evidence in support of it he relies on the scriptures which recognizes Sannyas as the fourth Ashram and relieves the Sannyasi from performing sacrifices prescribed by the *Karmakanda*.

Many such Sutras can be found in Badarayana indicating the attitude of the two scholars of thought towards each other. But the one given above is enough as it is so very typical. If one stops to consider the matter the position wears a strange appearance. Jaimini denounces Vedanta as a false Shastra, a snare and a delusion, something superficial, unnecessary and unsubstantial. What does Badarayana do in the face of this attack? Does he denounce the *Karmakanda* of Jaimini as a false Shastra, a snare and a delusion, something superficial, unnecessary and unsubstantial as the Upanishads themselves did? No. He only defends his own Vedanta Shastra. But one would expect him to do more. One would expect from Badarayana a denunciation of the *Karmakanda* of Jaimini as a false religion. Badarayana shows no courage. On the contrary he is very apologetic. He concedes that Jaimini's *Karmakanda* is based on the scriptures and the scriptures have authority and sanctity which cannot be repudiated. All that he insists on is that his Vedanta doctrine is also true because it has also the support of the scriptures.

This is not all. What Badarayana does is to use the term Vedanta to cover two senses. He uses it so as to emphasize that the Upanishads do form a part *of* the Vedic literature. He uses it also to emphasize that Vedanta or the *Jnyanakanda* of the Upanishads is not opposed to the *Karmakanda* of the Vedas that the two are complimentary. Indeed this is the foundation on which Badarayana has raised the whole structure of his Vedanta Sutras.

This thesis of Badarayana—which underlies his Vedanta Sutras and according to which the Upanishads are a part of the Veda and there is no antagonism between the Vedas and Upanishads—is quite contrary to the tenor of the Upanishads and their relation to the Vedas. Badarayana's attitude is not easy to understand. But it is quite obvious that Badarayana's is a queer and a pathetic case of an opponent who begins his battle by admitting the validity of the premises of his adversary. Why did Badarayana concede to Jaimini on the question of infallibility of the Vedas which were opposed to the Upanishads? Why did he not stand for truth, the whole truth and nothing but the truth as expounded by the Upanishads? The Badarayana has in his Vedanta Sutras betrayed the Upanishads. Why did he do so?

RIDDLE NO. 10: WHY DID THE BRAHMINS MAKE THE HINDU GODS FIGHT AGAINST ONE ANOTHER?

The Hindu theology regarding the world is based upon the doctrine of Trimurti. According to this doctrine the world undergoes three stages. It is created, preserved and destroyed. It is endless series of cycles which goes on without stoppage. The three functions which comprise the cycle are discharged by three Gods, Brahma, Vishnu and Mahesh. Brahma creates the world, Vishnu-preserves and Mahesh destroys it for the purpose of creation. These gods are spoken of as forming what is called Trimurti. The doctrine of Trimurti postulates that three gods are co-equal in status and are engaged in functions which are contemporary and not competitive. They are friends and not rivals.

They are allies of one another and not enemies. When, however, one studies the literature which depicts the deeds of these three gods one finds a complete difference between the theory and the practice. The Gods far from being friends appear to be worse enemies of one another, competing for supremacy and sovereignty among themselves. A few illustrations from the Puranas will make the matter clear.

At one time Brahma appears to be the most supreme god as compared to Shiva and Vishnu. Brahma is said to be the creator of the universe—the first Prajapati. He is the progenitor of Shiva,* and the master of Vishnu because if Vishnu became the preserver of the universe it was because Brahma commanded him to do it. So supreme was Brahma that he was the arbitrator in the conflicts that took place between Rudra and Narayan and between Krishna and Shiva. Equally certain is the fact that at a subsequent stage Brahma came into conflict with Shiva and Vishnu and strangely enough lost his position and supremacy to his rivals. Two illustrations of his conflict with Vishnu may be given

The first may well be the story of the Avatars. On the issue of the Avatars there is a rivalry between Brahma and Vishnu. The theory of Avatars or incarnation assumed by God to save humanity from a calamity began with Brahma. He was said to have assumed two Avatars (1) Boar and (2) Fish. But the followers of Vishnu refused to allow this. They asserted that these Avatars were not the Avatars of Brahma but that they were the Avatars of Vishnu. Not only did they appropriate these Avatars of Vishnu they gave to Vishnu many more Avatars.

The second story may well be the issue of the first born. It is related in the Skanda Purana. The story says that at one time Vishnu lay asleep on the bosom of Devi, a lotus arose from his navel, and its ascending flower soon reached the surface of the flood. Brahma sprang from flower, and looking round without any creature on the boundless expanse, imagined himself to be first born, and entitled to rank above all future beings; yet resolved to investigate deep and to ascertain whether any being existed in its universe who could controvert his preeminence, he glided down the stock of the lotus and finding Vishnu asleep, asked loudly who he was 'I am the first born' answered Vishnu; and when Brahma denied his preprogeniture, they engaged in battle, till Mahadeo pressed between them in great wrath, saying ' It is I who am truly the first born '. But I will resign my place to either of you, who shall be able to reach and behind the summit of my head, or the soles of my foot.

Brahma instantly ascended but having fatigued himself to no purpose in the regions of immensity yet loath to abandon his claim, returned to Mahadeo declaring that he had attained and seen the crown of his head, and called as his witness the first born cow. For this union of pride and falsehood, the angry God Shiva ordained that no sacred rites should be performed to Brahma and that the mouth of cow should be defiled. When Vishnu returned, he acknowledged that he had not been able to see the feet of Mahadeo who then told him that he was the first born among the Gods, and should be raised above all. It was after this Mahadeo cut off the fifth head of Brahma who thus suffered the loss of his pride, his power and his influence. According to this story Brahma's claim to be the first born was false. He was punished by Shiva for making it. Vishnu gets the right to call himself the first born. But that is allowed to him by the grace of Shiva. The followers of Brahma had their revenge on Vishnu for stealing.what rightfully belonged to him with the help of Shiva. So they manufactured another legend according to which Vishnu emanated from Brahma's nostrils in the shape of a pig and grew naturally into a boar—a very mean explanation of Vishnu's Avatar as a boar.

After this Brahma tried to create enmity between Shiva and Vishnu evidently to better his own position. This story is told in the Ramayana. It says: "When King Dasaratha was returning to his capital, after taking leave of Janaka, the king of Mithila, whose daughter Sita had just been married to Rama, he was alarmed by the ill-omened sounds uttered by certain birds, which however were counteracted, as the sage Vasishtha assured the king, by the auspicious sign of his being perambulated by the wild animals of the forest. The alarming event indicated was the arrival of Parasurama, preceded by a hurricane which shook the earth and prostrated the trees, and by thick darkness which veiled the sun. He was fearful to behold, brilliant as fire, and bore the axe and a bow on his shoulder. Being received with honour, which he accepted, he proceeded to say to Rama, the son of Dasaratha that he had heard of his prowess in breaking the bow produced by Janaka and had brought another which he asked Rama to bend, and to fit an arrow on the string; and if he succeeded in doing so, he (Parasurama) would offer to engage with him in single combat. Dasaratha is rendered anxious by this speech, and adopts a suppliant tone towards Parasurama, but the latter again addresses Rama, and says that the bow he had broken was Siva's, but the one he himself had now brought was Vishnu's. Two celestial bows, he proceeds, were made by Visvakarma of which one was given by. the gods to Mahadeva, the other to Vishnu". The narrative then proceeds:

"The gods then all made a request to Brahma desiring to find out the strength and weakness of Sitikantha (Mahadeva) and Vishnu. Brahma, most excellent of the three learning the purpose of the gods, created enmity between the two. In this state of enmity a great and terrible fight ensued between Sitikantha and Vishnu each of whom was eager to conquer the other. Siva's bow of dreadful power was then relaxed and the three-eyed Mahadeva was arrested by a muttering. These two eminent deities being entreated by the assembled gods, rishis, and Charanas then became pacified. Seeing that the bow of Shiva had been relaxed by the prowess of Vishnu, the gods and rishis esteemed Vishnu to be superior." Thus Brahma managed to avenge the wrong done to him by Mahadeo. Even this stratagem did not avail Brahma to maintain his position against Vishnu. Brahma lost his position so completely to Vishnu that Vishnu who at one time was at the command of Brahma became the creator Of Brahma.

In his contest with Shiva for supremacy Brahma suffered equal defeat. Here again, the position became completely inverted. Instead of being created by Brahma, Shiva became the creator of Bramha. Brahma lost the power of giving salvation. The god who could give salvation was Shiva and Brahma became no more than a common devotee worshipping Shiva and his Linga in the hope of getting salvation. He was reduced to the position of a servant of Shiva doing the work of charioteer of Shiva. Ultimately Brahma was knocked out of the field of worship on a charge of having committed adultery with his own daughter. The charge is set out in the Bhagwat Purana in the following terms: "We have heard, O Kshatriya, that Swayambhu (Brahma) had a passion for Vach, his slender and enchanting daughter, who had no passion for him. The Munis, his sons, headed by Marichi, seeing their father bent upon wickedness, admonished him with affection; 'This is such a thing as has not been done by those before you, nor will those after you do it,— that you, being the lord, should sexually approach your daughter, not restraining your passion. This, O preceptor of the world, is not a laudable deed even in glorious personages, through limitation of whose actions men attain felicity. Glory to that divine being (Vishnu) who by his own lustre revealed this (universe) which abides in himself, he must maintain ' righteousness '. Seeing his sons, the Prajapatis, thus speaking before him the lord of the Prajapatis (Bramha) was ashamed, and abandoned his body. This dreadful body the regions received and it is known as foggy darkness."

The result of this degrading and defamatory attacks on Brahma was to damn him completely. No wonder that his cult disappeared from the face of India leaving him a nominal and theoretical member of the Trimurti. After Brahma was driven out of the field there remained in the field Shiva and Vishnu. The two however were never at peace. The rivalry and antagonism between the two is continuous. The Puranas are full of propaganda and counter-propaganda carried on by the Brahmins, protagonists of Shiva and Vishnu. How well matched the propaganda and counter-propaganda was, can be seen from the following few illustrations: Vishnu is connected with the Vedic God Sun. The worshippers of Shiva connect him with Agni. The motive was that if Vishnu has a Vedic origin Shiva must also have Vedic origin as well. One cannot be inferior to the other in the matter of nobility of origin. Shiva must be greater than Vishnu and Vishnu must not be less than Shiva. Vishnu has thousand names. So Shiva must have thousand names and he has them.

Vishnu has his emblems. They are four. So Shiva must have them and he has them. They are (1) flowing gauges, (2) Chandra (moon), (3) Shesh (snake) and (4) *Jata* (walled hair). The only point on which Shiva did not compete with Vishnu was the matter of *Avatars*. The reason is not that there was no desire to compete but that philosophically there was an impediment in the way of Shiva taking Avatars. The Saivas and Vaisnavas differed fundamentally in their conceptions of immortal bliss. As has been pointed out by Mr. Ayyer: "To the Shaiva the goal to be reached was final liberation from all fetters, bodily and mental, by their total annihilation.

Hence he conceived of Rudra as the inextinguishable, one who could never be destroyed, but who extinguished or destroyed everything else. That was why Rudra came to be called the Destroyer. In the final stage of the spiritual development of an individual, there ought to be no separateness at all from the supreme Shiva. He ought to transcend his body and mind, pleasure and pain, and all opposites or dualities. He should attain union or Sayujya with Shiva in which condition he would not be able to regard himself as separate from Shiva. Till he reached that stage, he was imperfect, however pure he might be, however eligible he might be, for the highest state of Sayujya: for, those who were eligible had attained only the subordinate stages of Salokya, Samipya and Sarupya. That was also the reason why the doctrine of Avatars did not appeal to the Shaiva. God as an Avatar was only a limited being, one who had the capacity perhaps, of releasing himself from his fetters but not one without letters. The Vaisnava believed differently. He had also an equally clear conception of the highest state that could be reached, and that ought to he reached. But there was, according to him, nothing appealing in the idea of losing one's own individuality totally.

One should be united with the supreme, and yet be conscious of the union. He should be united with the universe which again should be regarded as the other aspect of the supreme imperishable being. He was not, in other words, for the extinction of the universe as if it were something separate and distinct from the Supreme Purusha. He was rather in favour of the preservation of the universe which was neither more nor less than the manifestation of the Purusha so manifested. That was the reason why Vishnu was given the name of the Preserver. After all, it is but a difference in the way in which the truth is perceived or viewed. The Shaiva viewed the universe as an object of pain and misery—as *Pasha* or fetters (and one bound by it to be *Pasu)* which had to be broken and destroyed. The Vaisnava regarded it as evidencing the greatness of the Purusa and so to be preserved. The Shaiva, with his superior pessimism (if it could be so called) was not likely to respect the. Dharma Shastras, the Artha Shastras and other scriptures all of which were framed with the purpose of establishing orderliness in the world, inevitable for its welfare. He was bound to be a non-conformist, disdaining rules and conventions. Ideas of caste rigidity would be repugnant to the highly-evolved Shaiva who would at best tolerate such notions in others who had not reached his own stage of development.

He would pay respect to and cultivate the society of only such people, to whatever caste they might belong, as were eligible for Samipya, Salokya, Sarupya and Sayujya, with Shiva. The Vaisnava, on the other hand, was more concerned with the preservation of all rules and regulations which would have the effect of promoting peace and happiness in the world. If '*Dharma*' perished, the world would perish too, and since the world ought not to perish, for it was a manifestation of the glory of the cosmic Purusa, his duty consisted in doing everything he could for preserving the Dharma. If things went beyond his control he was sure Vishnu would take the matter up himself; for he would come into the world as an Avatar. But when Vishnu did come upon the earth, it would be to destroy the wicked, that is, all those who were instrumental in upsetting the Dharma, and so it was necessary that one should be careful not to deserve that terrible punishment from Vishnu. Hence, the Agamas or rules laid down for the guidance of Shiva bhaktas did not emphasise caste, and were concerned only with the duties of *bhaktas* in general, the proper fulfilment of which would render them fit to gain God vision, and ultimately union with Shiva. These were regarded as impure by the others because they were subversive of caste ideas, and as stated before, they were not alluded to in the orthodox scriptures." In the performance of deeds of glory the propaganda in favour of Shiva is fully, matched by counter-propaganda in favour of Vishnu.

One illustration of this is the story regarding the origin of the holy river Ganges. The devotees of Shiva attribute its origin to Shiva. They take its origin from Shiva's hair. But the Vaishnavas will not allow it. They have manufactured another legend.

According to the Vaishnavite legend the blessed and the blessing river flowed originally out of Vaikunth (the abode of Vishnu) from the foot of Vishnu, and descending upon Kailasa fell on the head of Shiva. There is a two-fold suggestion in the legend. In the first place Shiva is not the source of the Ganges. In the second place Shiva is lower than Vishnu and receives on his head water which flows from the foot of Vishnu. Another illustration is furnished by the story which relates to the churning of the oceans by the Devas and the Asuras. They used the Mandara mountain as the churning rod and mighty serpant Shesha as a rope to whirl the mountain. The earth began to shake and people became afraid that the world was coming to an end. Vishnu took the Avatar of Kurma (Tortoise) and held the earth on his back and prevented the earth from shaking while the churning was going on.

This story is told in glorification of Vishnu. To this the Shaivites add a supplement. According to this supplement the churning brought out fourteen articles from the depth of the ocean which are called fourteen jewels. Among these fourteen a deadly poison was one. This deadly poison would have destroyed the earth unless somebody was prepared to drink it. Shiva was the only person who came forward to drink it. The suggestion is that Vishnu's act was foolish in allowing the rivals— the Gods and Demons—to bring out this deadly poison. Glory to Shiva for he drank it and saved the world from the evil consequences of the folly of Vishnu. Third illustration is an attempt to show that Vishnu is a fool and that it is Shiva who with his greater wisdom and greater power saves Vishnu from his folly. It is the story of Akrurasura. Akrur was a demon with the face of a bear, who, nevertheless, was continuously reading the Vedas and performing acts of devotion. Vishnu was greatly pleased and promised him any boon that he would care to ask. Akrurasura requested that no creature, then existing in three worlds, might have power to deprive him of life, and Vishnu complied with his request; but the demon became so insolent that the Devatas, whom he oppressed, were obliged to conceal themselves, and he assumed the dominion of the world; Vishnu was then sitting on a bank of the Kali, greatly disquieted by the malignant ingratitude of the demon; and his wrath being kindled, a shape, which never before had existed, sprang from his eyes. It was Mahadeva, in his destructive character, who dispelled in a moment the anxiety of the Vishnu.

This is countered by the story of Bhasmasura intended to show that Shiva was a fool and Vishnu saved him from his folly. Bhasmasura having propitiated Shiva asked for a boon. The boon was to be the power to burn any one on whose head Bhasmasura laid his hands. Shiva granted the boon. Bhasmasura tried to use his boon power against Shiva himself. Shiva became terrified and ran to Vishnu for help. Vishnu promised to help him. Vishnu took the form of a beautiful woman and went to Bhasmasura who became completely enamoured of her. Vishnu asked Bhasmasura to agree to obey him in everything as a condition of surrender. Bhasmasura agreed. Vishnu then asked him to place his hands on his own head which Bhasmasura did with the result that Bhasmasura died and Vishnu got the credit of saving Shiva from the consequences of his folly.

"Is Isa (Mahadeva) the Cause of causes for any other reasons? We have not heard that the linga (male organ) of any other person is worshipped by the gods. Declare, if thou hast heard, what other being's linga except that of Mahesvara is now worshipped, or has formerly been worshipped, by the gods? He whose linga Brahma and Vishnu, and thou (Indra), with the deities, continually worship, is therefore then most eminent. Since children bear neither the mark of the lotus (Brahma's), nor of the discus (Vishnu's), nor of the thunderbolt (Indra's), but are marked with the male and the female organs,—therefore offspring is derived from Mahesvara. All women produced from the nature of Devi as their cause, are marked with the female organ, and all males are manifestly marked with the linga of Hara. He who asserts any other cause than Isvara (Mahadeva) or (affirms) that there is any (female) not marked by Devi in the three worlds, including all things movable or immovable, let that fool be thrust out. Know everything which is male to be Isara and all that is female *to* be Uma: for this whole world, movable and immovable, is pervaded by (these) two bodies."

The Greek Philosopher Zenophanes insists that polytheism or plurality of Gods is inconceivable and contradictory. That the only true doctrine was monotheism. Considered from a philosophical point of view, Zenophanes might be right. But from the historical point of view both are natural. Monotheism is natural where society is a single community. Where society is a federation of many communities polytheism is both natural and inevitable. Because every ancient community consisted not merely of men but of men and its Gods it was impossible for the various communities to merge and coalesce except on one condition that its God is also accepted by the rest. This is how polytheism has grown.

Consequently the existence of many Gods among the Hindus is quite understandable because the Hindu Society has been formed by the conglomeration of many tribes and many communities each of whom had their own separate Gods. What strikes one as a strange phenomenon is the sight of the Hindu Gods struggling one against the other, their combats and feuds and the ascriptions by one God *to* the other, all things that arc a shame and disgrace to common mortals. This is what requires explanation.

RIDDLE NO. 11: WHY DID THE BRAHMINS MAKE THE HINDU GODS SUFFER TO RISE AND FALL?

The Hindus are accused of idolatry. But there is nothing wrong in idolatry. Making an idol is nothing more than having a photograph of the deity and if there can be no objection to keeping a photograph what objection can there be to having an image. Real objection to Hindu idolatry is that it is not mere photography, not mere production of an image. It is more than that. The Hindu idol is a living being and is endowed with all the functions of a human being. A Hindu idol is given life by means of a ceremony called Pranapratishtha. The Buddhists also are idolatrous in as much as they too worship Buddha's idol. But the idol they worship is only a photograph, a mere image. There is no soul in it. Why the Brahmins endowed the Hindu Gods with souls and made them living beings opens out an inquiry which is bound to be revealing.

The second charge generally levelled against the Hindus is that they are polytheists i.e., they worship many Gods. Here again the Hindus are not the only people who are guilty of the practice of Polytheism. Other communities have also been known to have practised polytheism. To mention only two. The Romans and the Greeks were essentially polytheists. They too worshipped many Gods. There is therefore no force in this charge.

The real charge which can be levelled against the Hindus most people seem to have missed. That charge is that the Hindus are never steadfast in their devotion to their Gods. There is no such thing as loyalty or attachment or faith in one God. In the history of Hindu Gods one finds it a very common experience that some Gods have been worshipped for a time and subsequently their worship has been abandoned and the Gods themselves have been thrown on the scrap-heap. Quite new Gods are adopted and their worship goes with an intensity of devotion which is full and overflowing. Again the new Gods are abandoned and are replaced by a fresh crop of new Gods. So the cycle goes on. In this way the Hindu Gods are always undergoing rise and fall—a phenomenon which is unknown in the history of any other community in the world. The statement that the Hindus treat their Gods with such levity may not be accepted without demur.

Some evidence on this point is therefore necessary. Fortunately there is abundance of it. At present the Hindus worship four Gods (1) Shiva, (2) Vishnu, (3) Rama and (4) Krishna. The question that one has to consider is: are these the only Gods the Hindus have worshipped from the beginning? The Hindu Pantheon has the largest number of inmates. The Pantheon of no religion can rival it in point of population. At the time of the Rig-Veda the number of its inmates was colossal. At two places the Rig-Veda speaks of three thousand three hundred and nine Gods. For some reasons, which it is not possible for us now to know, this number came to be reduced to thirty-three. This is a considerable reduction. Nevertheless with thirty three, the Hindu Pantheon remains the largest.

The composition of this group of thirty-three Gods is explained by the Satapatha Brahmana as made up of 8 Vasus, 11 Rudras and 12 Adityas, together with Dyasus and Prithvi (heaven and earth). Of greater importance than the question of numbers is the question of their relative rank. Was their any distinction between the 33 Gods in point of their rank? There is a verse in the Rig-Veda which seems to suggest that these thirty-three Gods were divided for purposes of honours and precedence into two classes, one being great and small and the other being young and old. This view seems to be against an earlier view also contained in the Rig-Veda. The old rule says: " None of you O! Gods! is small or young: You are all great ". This is also the conclusion of Prof. Max Muller: "When these individual gods are invoked, they are not conceived as limited by the power of others, as superior or inferior in rank. Each god is to the mind of the supplicants as good as all the gods. He is felt, at the time, as a real divinity, as supreme and absolute, in spite of the necessary limitations which, to our mind, a plurality of gods must entail on every single god. All the rest disappear for a moment from the vision of the poet, and he only, who is to fulfil their desires stands in full light before the eyes of the worshippers" "Nowhere is any of the Gods represented as the slave of others". This is of course true only for a time.

A change seems to have come in the old angle of vision towards the Gods. For one finds numerous hymns of the Veda in which some gods are represented as supreme and absolute. In the first hymn of the second Mandala, Agni is called the ruler of the Universe, the Lord of men, the wise king, the father, the brother, the son, the friend of men; nay, all the powers and names of the others are distinctly ascribed to Agni. Then a second god came to be elevated above Agni.

He is Indra. Indra is spoken of as the strongest god in the hymns as well as in the Brahmanas, and the burden of one of the songs of the Tenth Book is: *Visvasmad Indra Uttarah* 'Indra is greater than all'. Then a third god is raised to the highest level. He is Soma. Of Soma, it is said that he was born great and that he conquers every one. He is called the king of the world, he has the power to prolong the life of men, and in one verse he is called the maker of heaven, and earth, of Agni, of Surya, of Indra and of Vishnu. Then Soma was forgotten and a fourth God was elevated. He is Varuna. Varuna was made the highest of all Gods. For what more could human language do than to express the idea of a divine and supreme power, than what the Vedic poet says of Varuna; ' Thou art Lord of all, of heaven, and earth ' or, as is said in another hymn, 'Thou art the king of all; of those who are gods, and of those who are men."

What is the present position as compared with that found in the Chula-Niddessa? Here again, three propositions are well-established. *First*: the cults of Agni, Indra, Brahma and Surya have disappeared. *Second:* Krishna has retained his position. *Three:* The cults of Vishnu, Shiva and Rama are new cults which have come into existence since the time of the Chula-Niddessa. Given this situation it raises three questions for considerations: *One* is why have the old cults of Agni, Indra, Brahma and Surya disappeared? Why was the worship of these Gods abandoned? *Second* is what are the circumstances that gave rise to the new cults of Krishna, Rama, Shiva and Vishnu. Third what is the relative position of these new Gods, Krishna, Rama, Shiva and Vishnu? For the first question we can find no answer.

The Brahmanic literature gives us no clue whatsoever as to why the Brahmins abandoned the worship of Agni, Indra, Surya and Brahma. There is some explanation as to why the cult of Brahma disappeared. It rests in a charge which is found to be levelled in the Brahmanic literature against Brahma. The charge is that he committed rape on his own daughter and hereby made himself unworthy of worship and devotion. Whatever be the truth in the charge it could not be regarded as sufficient to account for the abandonment of Brahma and for two reasons. In the first place, in that age such conduct was not unusual. In the second place, Krishna was guilty of greater immoralities than were charged to Brahma and yet they continued to worship him. While there is something to speculate about the abandonment of Brahma there is nothing to account for the abandonment of the others.

The disappearance of Agni, Indra, Surya and Brahma is thus a mystery. This is no place to solve this mystery. It is enough to say that the *Gods* of the Hindus had ceased to be Gods—a terrible thing. The second question is also enveloped in mystery. Brahmanic literature, to account for the importance of the cults of these new Gods, Krishna, Vishnu, Shiva and Rama, is full and overflowing. But there is nothing in the Brahmanic literature to account for the rise of these new Gods. Why these new Gods were brought into action is thus a mystery. The mystery however deepens when one finds that some of the new Gods were definitely anti-Vedic. Let us take the case of Shiva. That Shiva was originally an Anti-Vedic

God is abundently clear. The following two incidents recorded in the Bhagvata Purana (and also in the Mahabharata) throw a flood of light on the subject. The first incident shows how enmity arose between Shiva and his father-in-law Daksha. It appears that the Gods and Rishis were assembled at a sacrifice celebrated by the Prajapatis. On the entrance of Daksha, all the personages who were present, rose to salute him, except Brahma and Shiva. Daksha, after making his obeisance to Brahma, sat down by his command; but was offended at the treatment he received from Shiva.

This is how he addressed Shiva : " Beholding Mrida (Shiva) previously seated, Daksha did not brook his want of respect; and looking at him obliquely with his eyes, as if consuming him, thus spake: ' Hear me, ye Brahman rishis, with the Gods and the Agnis, While I, neither from ignorane nor from passion, describe what is the practice of virtuous persons. But this shameless being (Shiva) detracts from the reputation of the guardians of the world, he by whom, stubborn as he is, the course pursued by the good is transgressed. He assumed the position of my disciple, inasmuchas, like a virtuous person, in the face of Brahmans and of fire, he took the hand of my daughter, who resembled Savitri. This monkey-eyed (god), after having taken of (my) fawn-eyed (daughter), has not even by word shown suitable respect to me whom he ought to have risen and saluted. Though unwilling, I yet gave my daughter to this impure and proud abolisher of rites and demolisher of barriers, like the word of the Veda to a Sudra. He roams about in dreadful cemeteries, attended by hosts of ghosts and spirits, like a madman, naked, with dishevelled hair, laughing, weeping, bathed in the ashes of funeral piles, wearing a garland of dead men's (skulls), and ornaments of human bones, pretending to be Shiva (auspicious) but in reality Asiva (in-auspicious), insane, beloved by the insane the lord of Pramathas and Bhutas (spirits), beings whose nature is essentially darkness.

To this wicked-hearted lord of the infuriate, whose purity has perished. I have, alas ! given my virtuous daughter, at the instigation of Brahma'. Having thus reviled Girisa (Shiva), who did not oppose him, Daksha having then touched water, incensed, began to curse him (thus): 'Let this Bhava (Shiva), lowest of the gods, never, at the worship of the gods, receive any portion along with the gods Indra, Upendra (Vishnu), and others.' Having delivered his malediction, Daksha departed." The enmity between the father-in-law and son-in-law continues. Daksha being elevated by Brahma to the rank of the Chief of the Prajapatis decided to perform a great Sacrifice called Vrihaspatisava. Seeing the other Gods with their wives going to this Sacrifice, Parvati pressed her husband, Shiva, to accompany her thither. He refers to the insults which he had received from her father, and advises her not to go. She, however, being anxious to see her relatives, disregards his warning and goes: but being sighted by her father, Daksha, she reproaches him for his hostility to her husband, and threatens to abandon the corporeal frame by which she was connected with her pare .. She then voluntarily gives up the ghost. Seeing this, Shiva's attendants, who had followed her, rush on Daksha to kill him. Bhrigu, however, throws an oblation into the southern fire, pronouncing a Yajus text suited to destroy the destroyers of sacrifice *(yajna-ghnena yajusha dakshinagnau juhavaha)*. A troop of Ribhus in consequence spring up, who put Shiva's followers to flight. Shiva is filled with wrath when he hears of the death of Sati. From a lock of his hair, which he tore out, a gigantic demon arose, whom he commended to destroy Daksha and his sacrifice. This demon proceeds with a troop of Shiva's followers, and they all execute the mandate.

How they executed the mandate is described in the Bhagvat Purana in the following terms: "' Some broke the sacrificial vessels, others destroyed the fires, others made water in the ponds, others cut the boundary-cords of the sacrificial ground: others assaulted the Munis, others reviled their wives: others seized the gods who were near, and those who had fled.... 19. The divine Bhava (Shiva) plucked out the beard of Bhrigu, who was offering oblations with a ladle in his hand. and who had laughed in the assembly, showing his beard. He also tore out the eyes of Bhaga, whom in his wrath he had felled to the ground, and who, when in the assembly, had made a sign to (Daksha when) cursing (Shiva) He moreover knocked out the teeth of Pushan (as Bala did the king of Kalinga's). who (Pushan) had laughed, showing his teeth, when the great god was being cursed. Tryambaka (Shiva, or Virabhadra, according to the commentator) then cuts off the head of Daksha, but not without some difficulty. The gods report all that had passed to Svayambhu

(Brahma), who, with Vishnu, had not been present. Brahma advises the gods to propitiate Shiva, whom they had wrongfully excluded from a share in the sacrifice. The deities, headed by Aja (Brahma), accordingly proceed to Kailasa when they see Shiva " bearing the linga desired by devotees, ashes a staff, a tuft of hair an antelope's skin and a digit of the moon, his body shining like an evening cloud ". Brahma addresses Mahadeva "as the eternal Brahma, the lord of Shakti and Shiva, who are respectively the womb and the seed of the universe, who in sport, like a spider, forms all things from Shakti and Shiva, who are consubstantial with himself, and preserves and reabsorbs them". Brahma adds that it was this great being who had instituted sacrifice, and all the regulations which Brahmans devoutly observe and entreat him. Who is beyond all illusion, to have mercy on those who, overcome by its influence, had wrongly attached importance to ceremonial works, and to restore the sacrifice of Daksha, at which a share had been refused to him by evil priests. Mahadeva partly relents "

There can be no better evidence to prove that Shiva was an anti-vedic God than his destruction of Daksha's Yajna. Now let us take Krishna. There are four persons who go by the name *Krishna.* One Krishna is the son of Satyavati and father of Dhratarashtra, Pandu and Vidur. Second Krishna is the brother of Subhadra and friend of Arjuna. Third Krishna is the son of Vasudeva and Devaki and was resident of Mathura. Fourth Krishna is the one brought up by Nanda and Yeshoda at Gokul and it was he who killed Shishupal. If the Krishna of the Krishna cult is the same as the Krishna son of Devaki there can be no doubt that Krishna originally also was anti-Vedic. From the Chhandogya Upanishad it appears that he was a pupil of Ghora Angiras. What did Ghora Angiras teach him? This is what the Chhandogya Upanishad says on the subject: "Ghora, the descendant of Angiras, having declared this (the preceding mystical lore) to Krishna the son of Devaki, said to him that (which, when he heard) he became free from thirst (i.e. desire), viz., ' let a man at the time of his death have recourse to these three texts, ' Thou art the undecaying, thou art the imperishable, thou art the subtle principle of breath '.

The commentator on this text of the Upanishad explains: "A person, Ghora by name, and an Angirasa by family, having declared this doctrine of sacrifice to Krishna the son of Devaki, his pupil, then said etc. The connexion of the last word 'said', is with the words which occur some way below, 'these three etc.. And having heard this doctrine he became free from desire for any "kinds of knowledge. In this manner he praises this knowledge of the Purusha-sacrifice by saying that it was so distinguished that it destroyed all thirst in Krishna, the son of Devaki, for any other knowledge. He now tells us that Ghora Angirasa said after declaring this knowledge to Krishna. It was this: 'Let him who knows the aforesaid sacrifice, at the time of his death have recourse to, mutter, these three texts, *pranasamsitam* means, 'thou art the very minute, and subtle principle of breath." Obviously the doctrine taught by Ghora Angiras to Krishna was opposed to the Vedas and the Vedic sacrifices as a means of spiritual salvation. On the contrary Vishnu is a Vedic God. Yet his cult is established much later than that of Shiva. Why there has been so much neglect of Vishnu it is difficult to understand. Similarly Rama though not anti-vedic is unknown to the Vedas. What was the necessity of starting his cult and that too at so late a stage in the history of the country? We may now take up the third question—namely what is the relative position of these new Gods to the old Pauranic Gods. The rise and fall of Bramha, Vishnu and Shiva has already been told in a previous chapter called *Gods at War.*

Whatever happened, the struggle for place and power was confined to these three Gods. They were not dragged below any other. But a time came when they were placed below the Devi by name Shri. How this happened is told in the Devi Bhagwat. The Devi Bhagwat says that a Devi by name *Shri* created the whole world and that it is this Goddess who created Bramha, Vishnu and Shiva! The Devi Bhagwat goes on to state that the Devi desired to rub her palms. The rubbing of palms produced a blister. Out of this blister was born Bramha. When Bramha was born the Devi asked him to marry her. Bramha refused saying she was his mother. The Devi got angry and burned Bramha alive by her wrath and Bramha was reduced to ashes then and there. Devi rubbed her palms a second time and had a second blister. Out of this second blister a second son was born. This was Vishnu. The Devi asked Vishnu to marry her. Vishnu declined saying that she was his mother. Devi got angry and burned down Vishnu to ashes. Devi rubbed her palms a third time and had a third blister. Out of this third blister was born a third son. He was Shiva. The Devi asked Shiva to marry her. Shiva replied: ' I will, provided you assume another body '. Devi agreed. Just then Shiva's eyes fell on the two piles of ashes. Devi replied ' they are the ashes of his two brothers and that she burnt them because they refused to marry her. ' On this Shiva said, ' How can I alone marry? You create two other women so that we all three can marry '. The Devi did as she was told and the three Gods were married to the Devi and her female creations. There are two points in the story. One is that even in doing evil Shiva did not wish to appear more sinning than Bramha and Vishnu for fear that he may appear more degraded than his other two competitors. The more important point however is that Bramha, Vishnu and Shiva had fallen in rank and had become the creatures of the Devi. Having dealt with the rise and fall of Bramha, Vishnu and Shiva, there remains the vicissitudes in the cults of the two new Gods, Krishna and Rama. Obviously there is a certain amount of artificiality in the cult of Krishna as compared with the cult of Brahma, Vishnu and Shiva.

Bramha, Vishnu and Mahesh were born gods. Krishna was a man who was raised to godhood. It is probably to confer godhood on him that the theory was invented that he was the incarnation of Vishnu. But even then his godhood remained imperfect because he was regarded to be only a partial avatar of Vishnu largely because of his debaucheries with the *gopis* which would have been inexcusable if he had been a full and perfect *avatar* of Vishnu. Notwithstanding this humble beginning Krishna became elevated to the position of a supreme God above all others. How great a God he became can be seen by a reference to Chapter X and XIV of the Bhagvat Geeta. In these Chapters Krishna says: "Well then, O best of the Kauravas I will state to you my own divine emanations; but (only) the chief (ones) for there is no end to the extent of my (emanations). I am the self. O Gudakesa seated in the hearts of all beings; I am the beginning and the middle and the end also of all beings. I am Vishnu among the Adityas, the beaming Sun among the shining (bodies); I am Marichi among the Maruts, and the Moon among the lunar mansions. Among the

Vedas, I am the Sama-veda. I am Indra among the Gods. And I am mind among the senses. I am consciousness in (living) beings. And I am Shankara among the Rudras, the Lord of Wealth among Yakshas and Rakshasas. And I am *fire* among the Vasus, and Meru among the high-topped (mountains). And know me, O Arjuna to be Brihaspati, the chief among domestic priests. I am Skanda among generals. I am the ocean among reservoirs of water. I am Bhrigu among the great sages. I am the Single syllable (Om) among words. Among sacrifices I am the *Gapa* sacrifice; the Himalaya among the firmly fixed (mountains); the Asvattha among all trees, and Narada among divine sages; Chitraratha among the heavenly *choristers*, the sage Kapila among the Siddhas.

Among horses know me to be Uchhaissravas, brought forth by (the labour for) the nectar; and Airavata among the great elephants, and the ruler of men among men. I am the thunderbolt among weapons, the wish-giving (cow) among cows. And I am love which generates. Among serpents I am Vasuki. Among Naga snakes I am Ananta; I am Varuna among aquatic beings. And I am Aryaman among the manes, and Yama among rulers. Among demons, too, I am Pralhada. I am the king of death (kala, time) among those that count. "Among beasts I am the lord of beasts, and the son of Vinata among birds. I am the wind among those that blow. I am Rama among those that wield weapons. Among fishes I am Makara, and among streams the Janhavi. Of created things I am the beginning and the end and the middle also. O Arjuna, among sciences, I am the science of the Adhyatma, and I am the argument of controversialists. Among letters I am the letter A, and among the group of compounds the copulative compound. I myself am time inexhaustible and I the creator whose faces are in all directions. I am death who seizes all, and the source of what is to be. And among females, fame, fortune, speech, memory, intellect, courage, forgiveness. Likewise among Saman hymns, I am the Brihat-saman, and I the Gayatri among metres. I am Margasirsha among the months, the spring among the seasons, of cheats, I am the game of dice; I am the glory of the glorious; I am victory. I am industry, I am the goodness of the good. I am Vasudeva among the descendants of Vrishni and Arjuna among the Pandvas. Among sages also, I am Vyasa; and among the discerning ones, I am the discerning Usanas. I am the rod of those that restrain, and the policy of those that desire victory. I am silence respecting secrets. I am the knowledge of those that have knowledge. And O Arjuna! I am also that which is the seed of all things. There is nothing movable or immovable which can exist without me." "Know that glory (to be) mine which, dwelling in the Sun, lights up the whole world, or in the moon or fire. Entering the earth, I by my power support all things; and becoming the juicy moon, I nourish all herbs. I becoming the fire, and dwelling in the bodies of (all) creatures, and united with the upward and downward life-breaths cause digestion of the four-fold food. And I am placed in the heart of all."

" From me (come) memory, knowledge, and their removal; I alone am to be learnt from all the Vedas; I am the author of the Vedantas; and I alone know the Vedas. There are these two beings in the world, the destructible and the indestructible. The destructible (includes) all things. The unconcerned one is (what is) called the indestructible. But the being supreme is yet another, called the highest self, who as the inexhaustible lord, pervading the three worlds, supports (them). And since I transcend the destructible, and since I am higher also than the indestructible therefore am I celebrated in the world and in the Vedas as the best of things." It is therefore clear that so far as the Gita is concerned there is no God greater than Krishna. He is, Alla ho Akbar. He is greater than all other Gods. Let us now turn to the Mahabharata. What do we find? We find a change in the position of Krishna. There is a rise and fall in his position. In the first place we find Krishna elevated above Shiva. Not only that, Shiva is made to admit and acknowledge the greatness of Krishna. Along with this we also find Krishna degraded to a rank below that of Shiva and is made to acknowledge the greatness of Shiva.

As a piece of evidence in support of the elevation of Krishna above Shiva the following passage from the *Anusasana-Parvan* is very illuminating: "Superior even to Pitamaha (Bramha) is Hari, the eternal Purusha, Krishna, brilliant as gold, like the sun risen in a cloudless sky, ten-armed, of mighty force, slayer of the foes of the gods, marked with the *srivatsa*, Hrishikesa, adored by all the gods. Bramha is sprung from his belly and I (Mahadeva) from his head, the luminaries from the hair of his head, the gods, and

Asuras from the hairs of his body, and the rishis as well as everlasting worlds, have been produced from his body. He is the manifest abode of Pitamaha, and of all the deities. He is the creator of this entire earth, the lord of the three worlds, and the destroyer of creatures, of the stationary and the moveable. He is manifestly the most eminent of the gods, the lord of the deities, the vexer of his foes. He is omniscient, intimately united (with all things), omnipresent facing in every direction, the supreme spirit, Hrishikesa all-pervading, the mighty Lord. There is none superior to him in the three worlds. The slayer of Madhu is eternal, renowned as Govinda. He, the conferer of honour, born to fulfil the purposes of the gods, and assuming a human body, will slay all the kings in battle. For all the hosts of the gods, destitute of Trivikrama (the god who strode thrice), are unable to effect the purposes of the gods, devoid of a leader. He is the leader of all creatures, and worshipped by all creatures.

"Of this lord of the gods, devoted to the purposes of the gods, who is Brahma, and is the constant refuge of gods and rishis, Brahma dwells within the body, abiding in his face, and all the gods are easily sheltered in his body. This god is lotus-eyed, the producer of Sri, dwelling together with Sri... For the welfare of the gods, Govinda shall arise in the family of the great Manu, possessed of eminent intelligence and (walking) in the excellent path of the Prajapati Manu, charactcrized by righteousness (Govinda's ancestors are then detailed). In this family, esteemed by Brahmans, of men renowned for valour, distinguished by good conduct and excellent qualities, priests, most pure, this sura, the most eminent of Kshatriya heroic, renewed, conferring honour, shall beget a son Anakadundubhi, the prolonger of his race, known as Vasudev to him shall be born a four-armed son, Vasudeva, liberal, a benefactor of Brahmans, one with' 'Brahma, a lover of Brahmans." "You the gods, should, as is fit, worship this deity, like the eternal Brahma, approaching him with reverential and excellent garlands of praise. For the divine and glorious Vasudev should be beheld by him who desires to see me and Brahma and Parent. In regard to this, I have no hesitation, that when he is seen I am seen, or the Parent (Brahma), the lord of the gods: know this ye whose wealth is austerity."

We shall now see how Krishna after having been elevated to the position being highest among the Gods is being degraded. The Mahabharata is so full of incidents and occasions which demonstrate Krishna's inferiority to Shiva that it is difficult to recite the whole of them. One must be content with a few. The first incident relates to the view taken by Arjuna to slay Jayadratha on the following day. After the vow, Arjuna became very dejected thinking that Jayadratha's friends would do their utmost to save him and that unless he had sure weapons he would not be able to fulfil his vow. Arjuna goes to Krishna for advice. Krishna suggests to Arjuna that he should supplicate to Mahadeva for the Pasupata weapon with which Mahadev himself had formerly destroyed all the Daityas and which, if he obtained it, he would be sure to kill Jayadrath. The Drone-Parvan which relates the story proceeds to say: "The righteous Vasudeva (Krishna) then, together with the son of Pritha (Arjuna), reciting the eternal Veda, bowed his head to the ground, beholding him the source of the worlds, the maker of the universe, the unborn, the imperishable lord, the supreme source of mind, the sky, the wind, the abode of the luminaries, the creator of the oceans, the supreme substance of the earth, the framer of gods, Danavas, Yakshas and men, the supreme Brahma of meditative systems, the satisfied, the treasure of those who know Brahma, the creator of the world and also its destroyer, the great impersonated destructive Wrath, the original of the attributes of Indra and Surya. Krishna then reverenced him with voice, mind, understanding and act.

Those two (heroes) had recourse to Bhava (Mahadeva) as their refuge,—to him whom the wise, desiring the subtle spiritual abode, attain,—to him the unborn cause. Arjuna, too, again and again reverenced that deity, knowing him to be the beginning of all beings, the source of the past, the future, and the present. Beholding those two, Nara and Narayana, arrived Sarva (Mahadeva), then greatly gratified, said, as if smiling: 'Welcome, most eminent of men, rise up freed from fatigue, and tell me quickly, heroes, what your mind desires. Shall I accomplish for you the object for which you have come? Choose what is most for your welfare. I will give you all." Krishna and Arjuna then recite a hymn in honour of Mahadeva, in the course of which he is designated as the soul of all things, the creator of all things, and the pervader of all things. Arjuna now, after reverencing both Krishna and Mahadeva, asks the latter for the celestial weapon. They are thereupon sent by Mahadeva to a lake where he says he had formerly deposited his bow and arrows. They there saw two serpents, one of which was vomiting flames, and approached them, bowing to Mahadeva and uttering Satarudriya. Through the power of Mahadeva, the serpents change their shape and become a bow and arrow, which Krishna and Arjuna bring to Mahadeva. Eventually Arjuna receives as a boon from Mahadeva the Pasupata weapon, with the power of fulfilling his engagement to slay Jayadratha after which they both return to their camp." The Anusasana-Parvan of the Mahabharata contains a dialogue between Yudhishthira and Bhishma. Yudhishthira asks Bhishma to tell him the attributes of Mahadeva. This is what Bhishma says in reply:

"I am unable to declare the attributes of the wise Mahadeva, who is an all-pervading god, yet is nowhere seen, who is the creator and the lord of Brahma, Vishnu and Indra, whom the gods, from Brahma to the Pisachas, worship, who transcends material natures as well as spirit (Purusha), who is meditated upon by rishis versed in contemplation (yoga), and possesing an insight into truth, who is the supreme, imperishable Brahma, that which is both non-existent, and at once existent and non-existent. Having agitated matter and spirit by his power, this god of gods and lord of creatures (Prajapati) thence created Bramha. What human being like me, who has been subject to gestation in the womb, and to birth, and is liable to decay and death, can declare the attributes of Bhava, the supreme lord— (who can do this) except Narayana, the bearer of the shell, the discus, and the cub? This Vishnu, wise, eminent, in qualities, very hard to overcome, with divine insight, of mighty power, beholds (him) with the eye of contemplation. Through his devotion to Rudra, the world is pervaded by the mighty Krishna. Having then propitiated that deity (Mahadeva) at Badari, he (Krishna) obtained from the golden-eyed Mahesvara the quality of being in all worlds more dear than wealth. This Madhava (Krishna) performed austerity for a full thousand years, propitiating Shiva, the god who bestows boons, and the preceptor of the world. But in every mundane period (yuga) Mahesvara has been propitiated by Krishna and has been gratified by the eminent devotion Of that great personage. This unshaken Hari (Krishna) when seeking, for offspring, has beheld distinctly of what character is the glory of that great parent of the world. Than him I behold none higher. This large-armed (Krishna) is able to recount fully the names of the god of gods, to describe the qualities of the divine (being) and the real might of Mahesvara in all its extent".

This dialogue between Yudhishthira and Bhishma took place in the presence of Krishna. For immediately after his reply Bhishma calls upon Krishna to celebrate the greatness of Mahadeva. And this supreme Clod Krishna proceeds to do so without feeling any offence and says: "The course of the deeds of. Isa (Mahadeva) cannot he really known. He whose essence neither the gods headed by Hiranyagarhha nor the great rishis with Indra, nor the Adityas. The perceivers ol the minutest objects, understand,—how can he the refuge of saints he known by any mere man? I shall declare to you exactly some of the attributes of that divine slayer of the Asuras of the lord ol religious ceremonies."

Here not only do we find that Krishna acknowledges his inferiority to Shiva but we also find Shiva conscious of the fact that Krishna has been beaten down and is no longer his superior, indeed is not even his equal. This is evident from Sauptika-parvan where Mahadeva says to Asvathaman: " I have been duly worshipped by Krishna, the energetic in action with truth, purity, honesty, liberality, austerity, ceremonies patience, wisdom, self-control, understanding and words: Wherefore no one is dearer to me than Krishna ". Krisnna from being above Shiva, above every God indeed a Parmeshwar is reduced to the position of being a mere follower of Shiva begging for petty boons.

This does not complete the story of the degradation of Krishna. He is made to undergo further humiliation. Krishna not only accepted a position of infeiiority vis-a-vis Shiva hut he is sunk so low that he became a disciple of Upamanyu who was a great devotee of Shiva and took Diksha from him in Shaivism. Krishna himself says: "On the 8th day I was Initiated by that Brahamana (lJpamanyu) according to the Shastras. Having shaved my entire head.anointing myself with ghee, and taking the staff and kusa grass in my arms I dressed myself in bark fastened with the mekhala (the waist string)." Krishna then performs penance and has a sight, of Mahadeo. Can there be a more glaring instance of so great a rise and so much of a fall in the status of a God? Krishna who was a Parmeshwar as compared to Shiva who was only an Ishwar does not even remain an Ishwar. He actually becomes a devotee of Shiva and seeks initiation in the Shaiva Shastras from a common Brahmin like Upamanyu.

The case of Rama as a God is much more artificial than that of Krishna. Rama himself was unware of the fact that he was a God. After recovering Sita on the defeat and death of Ravana, Sita was suspected of unchastity, Rama felt very dejected on hearing the words of those who thus spoke about Sita. The Ramayana says: "Then King Kuvera, and Yama with the Pitris and Indra. Lord of the gods, and Varuna, lord of the waters, and the glorious three-eyed Mahadeva, whose ensign is a bull, and Bramha, the creator of the whole world, the most eminent of the knowers of the Veda: (and that King Dasaratha, moving in the air on a celestial car, arrived in that region, equal in lustre to the king of the gods); these all having come on cars brilliant as the Sun, and arrived in the city of Lanka, came near to Raghava (Rama). Then these most eminent gods, holding the large arms of Rama, adorned with armlets, addressed him as he stood with joined hands: How dost thou, the maker of the whole Universe, the most eminent of the wise, the pervading, disregard Sita's throwing herself into the fire?

How dost thou not perceive thyself to be the chief of the host of the gods? (Thou wast) formerly the Vasu Ritadhaman, and the Prajapati of the Vasus. Thou art the primal maker of the three worlds, the self dependent lord, the eighth Rudra of the Rudras, and the fifth of the Sadhyas. The Asvins are thine ears, the Moon and Sun thine eyes." "Thou, vexer of thy foes, art seen in the end and at the beginning of created beings. And yet thou disregardest Sita like a common man ". On being thus addressed by these Gods, Rama became surprized and replied: "I regard myself as a man, Rama, son of Dasharath; do you, divine being tell me who and whence I am ". On this, Brahma replying to Rama said:

"Hear my true word, O being of genuine power. Thou art the god, the glorious lord, Narayana, armed with the discus. Thou art the one-horned boar, the conqueror of thy foes, past and future, the true, imperishable Brahma, both in the middle and end. Thou art the supreme righteousness of the worlds, Vishvaksena, the four-armed; the bearer of the bow, Saranga, Hrishikesa (lord of the senses). Purusha (the male), the highest of Purushas, the unconquered, sword-wielding, Vishnu, and Krishna of mighty force, the general, the leader the true. Thou art intelligence, thou art patience, and self-restraint. Thou art the source of being and cause of destruction, Upendra (the younger Indra), the Madhusudana. Thou art Mahendra (the elder Indra) fulfilling the function of Indra, he from whose navel springs a lotus, the ender of battles. The great divine rishis call thee the refuge, the resort of suppliants. Thou art the hundred-horned, composed of the Veda, the thousand-headed the mighty.

Thou art the primal maker of the three worlds, the self-dependent lord, and the refuge of the Siddhas and Sahyas, O thou primevally born. Thou art sacrifice, thou art the vashatkara, and the omkara, higher than the highest. Men know not who thou art, the source of being, or the destroyer. Thou art seen in all creatures, in Brahmans and in cows, in all the regions, in the mountains and rivers, thousand-footed, glorious, hundred-headed, thousand-eyed. Thou sustainest creatures, and the earth with its mountains; thou art seen Rama at the extremity of the earth, in the waters, a mighty serpent supporting the three worlds, gods, Gandharvas, and Danavas. I am thy heart, Rama, the goddess Sarasvati is thy tongue. The gods have been made by Brahma the hairs on thy limbs. The night is called the closing, and the day the opening, of thine eyes. The Vedas are thy thoughts. This (universe) exists not without thee. The whole world is thy body; the earth is thy stability. Agni is thine anger, Soma is thy pleasure, O thou whose mark is the Srivatsa. By thee the three worlds were traversed of yore with thy three paces. and Mahendra was made king after thou hadst bound the terrible Bali. That which is known as the chiefest light, that which is known as the chiefest darkness, that which is the higher than the highest-thou art called the highest Soul. It is thou who art hymned as that which is called the highest, and is the highest. Men call thee the highest source of continuance, production and destruction." Obviously, there is the same degree of artificiality in the cult of Rama. Like Krishna he was a man who was made God. Unlike Brahma, Vishnu and Mahesh, he was not one who was born God. It is probably to make his Godhood perfect that the theory was invented that he was the incarnation of Vishnu and that Sita his wife was the incarnation of Lakshmi the wife of Vishnu.

In another respect, Rama was fortunate. He did not have to suffer degradation to other Gods as did Brahma, Vishnu and Krishna. There was however an attempt to degrade him below Parasurama the hero of the Brahmins. The story is told in the Ramayana which says: "When King Dasaratha was returning to his capital, after taking leave of Janaka the King of Mithila, whose daughter Sita had just been married to Rama he was alarmed by the ill-omened sounds by certain birds, which however were counteracted, as the sage Vasishta assured the king by the auspicious sign of his being perambulated by the wild animals of the forest. The alarming event indicated was the arrival of Parasurama, preceded by hurricane which shook the earth and prostrated the trees, and bythick darkness which veiled the Sun. He was fearful to behold, "brilliant as fire, and bore his axe and a bow on his shoulder. Being received with honour, which he accepted, he proceeded to say to Rama, the son of Dasaratha that he has heard of his prowess in breaking the bow produced by Janak and had brought another which he asked Rama to bend, and to fit an arrow on the string; and if he succeeded in doing so, he (Parasurama) would offer to engage with him in single combat." " Rama replied that though his warlike qualities are condemned by his rival, he will give him a proof of his powers. He then snatches, in anger, the bow from the hand of Parasurama, bends it, fits an arrow on the string; and tells his challenger that he will not shoot at him because he is a Brahman, and for the sake of his kinsman Visvamitra; but will either destory his superhuman capacity of movement, or deprive him of the blessed abodes he has acquired by austerity. The gods now arrive to be witnesses of the scene. Parasurama becomes disheartened and powerless and humbly entreats that he may not be deprived of his faculty of movement lest he should be incapacitated from fulfilling his promise to Kasyappa ' to leave the earth every night but consents that his blissful abodes may be destroyed."

With this exception Rama had no rivalry with any of the other Gods. He managed to be where he was. With regards to other Gods there is a different story to tell. Poor creatures they became nothing more than mere toys in the hands of the Brahmins. Why did the Brahmins treat the Gods with so scant a respect?

RIDDLE NO. 12: WHY DID THE BRAHMINS DETHRONE THE GODS AND ENTHRONE THE GODDESSES?

The worship of Gods is a thing common to all. But the worship of Goddesses is quite uncommon. The reason is that Gods are generally unmarried and have no wives who can be elevated to the position of Goddesses. How repugnant is the idea of a God being married is well illustrated by the difficulties which early Christians had in persuading the Jews to accept Jesus as the son of God. The Jews retorted saying God is not married and how can Jesus be the son of God. With the Hindus the position is quite otherwise.

They not only worship Gods they also worship Goddesses. This is so from the very beginning. In the Rig-Veda several Goddesses are mentioned such as *Prithvi, Adili, Diti, Nishtigri, Indrani, Prisni, Usha, Surya, Agnayi, Varunani, Rodasi, Raka, Sinivali, Sradha, Aramati, Apsaras and Sarasvati.* Prithvi is a very ancient Aryan Goddess. She is represented either as wife of *Dyaus* heaven or of *Parjanya.* Prithvi is an important Goddess because she is said to be the mother of many Gods. Aditi is chronologically one of the older Vedic Goddesses. She is described as the mighty mother of the Gods. The Gods, *Mitra, Aryaman* and *Varuna* are her sons. To whom Aditi was married does not appear from the Rig-Veda. We do not know much about *Diti* except that she is mentioned as a goddess along with and in contrast to *Aditi* and that the *Daityas* who were regarded in later Indian mythology as the enemies of the Devas were her sons. The goddess *Nishtigri* is the mother of Indra and the goddess *Indrani* is the wife of Indra.

Prisni is the mother of Maruts. *Usha* is described as the daughter of the sky, the sister of *Bhaga* and the kinswoman of *Varuna* and the wife of Surya. The goddess *Surya* is the daughter of *Surya* and the wife of the Gods *Asvins* or *Soma.* The goddesses *Agnayi, Varunani* and *Rodasi* are the wives of *Agni, Varuna* and *Rudra* respectively. Of the rest of the goddesses are mere personifications of rivers or are mentioned without any details. From this survey two things are clear. One is that a Hindu God can enter a married state and neither the God nor his worshipper need feel any embarrassment on account of the God acting as though he was no better than a common man. The second is that the God's wife automatically becomes a goddess worthy of worship by the followers of the God. Leaving the Vedic times and coming to the Pauranic times we come across the names of various Goddesses such as *Devi, Uma, Sati, Ambika, Parvati, Haimavati, Gauri, Kali, Nirriti, Chandi* and *Katyayini, Durga, Dassbhuja. Singhavahini, Mahishasuramardini, Jagaddhatri, Muktakesi, Tara, Chinnamustaka, Jagadgauri, Pratyangira, Annapurna, Ganeshjanani, Krishnakrora* and *Lakshmi.* It is very difficult to construct a who is who of these Goddesses.

In the first place it is difficult to say whether each name stands for a distinct and separate Goddess or they are the names of one Goddess. It is equally difficult to be sure of their parentage. Nor can any one say with certainty as to who their husbands are. According to one account *Vma, Devi, Sati, Parvati, Gauri* and *Ambika* are different names of the same Goddess. On the other hand *Devi* is said by some to be the daughter of Daksha, *Ambika* to be the sister of Rudra. Regarding *Parvati* the Varaha Purana in describing her origin says: "Brahma when on a visit to Shiva on Mount Kailasa is thus addressed by him: " Say, quickly, O, Brahma, what has induced you to come to me?' Brahma replies, 'There is a mighty Asura named Andhaka (Darkness), by whom all the gods, having been distressed, came for protection, and I have hastened to inform you of their complaints'.

Brahma then looked intently at Shiva, who bythought summoned Vishnu into their presence. As the three deities looked at each other, 'from their three refulgent glances sprang into being a virgin of celestial loveliness, of hue cerulean, like the petals of a blue lotus, and adorned with gems, who hashfully bowed before Brahma, Vishnu and Shiva. On their asking her who she was, and why she was distinguished by the three colours black, white and red, she said, ' From your glances was I produced: do you not know your own omnipotent energies?' Brahma then praising her said, 'Thou shalt be named the goddess of three times (past, present and future), the preserver of the universe, and under various appellations shalt thou be worshipped, as thou shalt be the cause of accomplishing the desires of thy votaries. But, O goddess, divide thyself into three forms, according to the colours by which thou art distinguished. She then, as Brahma had requested, divided herself into three parts: one white, one red, and one black. The white was ' Saraswati of a lovely, felicitious form, and the co-operator with Brahma increation: the red was Lakshmi, the beloved of Vishnu, who with him preserves the universe; the black was Parvati endowed with many qualities and energy of Shiva. "

Here is an attempt to suggest that *Saraswati, Lakshmi* and *Parvati* are different forms of one and the same divinity. When one remembers that *Sarasvati* is the wife of Brahma, Lakshmi is the wife of Vishnu and Parvati is the wife of Shiva, and also that Brahma. Vishnu and Shiva were at war, this explanation given by the Varah Puran seems very odd. Who is Gauri? The Purana says that Gauri is another name for Parvati. The reason how Parvati was called Gauri is that when Shiva and Parvati lived on mount Kailasa, occasionally there were quarrels between them, and on one occasion Shiva reproached her for the blackness of her skin. This taunt so grieved her that she left him for a time and, repairing to a deep forest, performed a most severe course of austerities, until Brahma granted her as a boon that her complexion should be golden and for this circumstance she is known as Gauri. Taking the other Goddesses it is not quite certain whether they are different names for one and the same Goddess or whether they are different Goddesses.

In the Mahabharata there is a hymn sung by Arjuna to Durga in which he says: "Reverence be to thee, Siddha-Senani (generalaless of the Siddhas), the noble, the dweller on Mandara, Kumari (Princess), Kali, Kapali, Kapila, Krishna-pingala. Reverence to thee, Bhadrakali; reverence to thee, Maha Kali, Chandi, Chanda, Tarini (deliveress), Varavarini (beautiful-coloured). O fortunate Kalyani, O Karali, O Vijaya, O Jaya (victory) younger sister of the chief of cowherds (Krishna), delighting always in Mahisha's blood'. O Uma, Sakambhari, thou white one, thou black one, O destroyer of Kaithabha! Of science, thou art the science of Brahma (or of the Vedas), the great sleep of embodied beings. O mother of Skanda (Kartikeya), divine Durga, dweller in wildernesses'. Thou, great goddess, art praised with a pure heart. By thy favour let me ever be victorious in battle." From this hymn it does appear that some of the Goddesses listed above are simply different names of Durga. Similarly, Dasabhuja, Singhavahini, Mahishamardini, Jagaddhatri, Chinnamustaka, Jagadgauri, Pratyangiri, Annapurna are the same as Durga or different forms of *Durga*.

There are thus two principal Goddesses. One is *Parvati* and the other is *Durga*. The rest are mere names. Parvati is the daughter of Daksha Prajapati and the wife of Shiva and Durga is the sister of Krishna and the wife of Shiva. The relationship of *Durga* and *Kali* is not quite clear. According to the hymn sung by Arjuna, Durga and Kali would appear to be one and the same. But the Linga Purana seems to suggest a different view. According to it. Kali is distinct from Durga. A comparison between the Vedic Goddesses and the Puranic Goddesses cannot be avoided by a student whose business it is not merely to write history but to interpret history. On one point there is a striking contrast, between the two. The worship of the Vedic Goddesses was worship by *courtesy*. They were worshipped only because they were the wives of Gods. The worship of the Puranic Goddesses stand on a different footing.

They claim worship in their own right and not because they are wives of Gods. This difference arises because the Vedic Goddesses never went to the battle-field and never performed any heroic deed. The Puranic Goddesses on the other hand went to the battlefield and performed great heroic deeds. Their worship was not by courtesy. It was based upon their heroic and thundering deeds.

There was agreat battle, it is said, between Durga and the two *asuras* which brought renown to Durga. The story is told in the Markandeya Purana in full details. It says: At the close of the Treta Age, two giants, named Sumbha and Nishumbha performed religious austerities for 10,000 years, the merit of which brought Shiva from heaven, who discovered that by this extraordinary devotion, they sought to obtain the blessing of immortality. He reasoned long with them, and vainly endeavoured to persuade them to ask for any other gift. Being denied what they specially wanted, they entered upon still more severe austerities for another thousand years, when Shiva again appeared, but still refused to grant what they asked. They now suspended themselves with their heads downwards over a slow fire, till the blood streamed from their necks; they continued thus for 800 years. The Gods began to tremble, lest, by performing such rigid act of holiness, these demons should supplant them on their thrones. The king of the Gods thereupon called a council, and imparted to them his fears. They admitted that there was ground for anxiety, but asked what was the remedy.

Acting upon the advice of Indra, Kandarpa (the God of love), with Rambha and Tilotama, the most beautiful of the celestial nymphs, were sent to fill the minds of the giants with sensual desires. Kandarpa with his arrow wounded both; upon which, awaking from their absorption, and seeing two beautiful women, they were taken in the snare, and abandoned their devotions. With these women they lived for 5000 years; after which they saw the folly of renouncing their hopes of immortality for the sake of sensual gratifications. They suspected this snare must have been a contrivance of Indra; so, driving back the nymphs to heaven, they renewed their devotions, cutting the flesh off their bones, and making burnt offerings of it to Shiva. They continued in this way for 1000 years till at last they became mere skeletons; Shiva again appeared and bestowed upon them his blessing—that in riches and strength they should excel the Gods. Being exalted above the Gods, they began to make war upon them. Aftervarious successes on both sides, the giants became everywhere victorious; when Indra and the Gods, reduced to a most deplorable state of wretchedness, solicited the interference of Brahma and Vishnu. They referred them to Shiva, who declared that he could do nothing for them. When, however, they reminded him that it was through his blessing they had been ruined, he advised them to perform religious austerities to Durga. They did so: and after some time the goddess; appeared, and gave them her blessing;

then disguising herself as a common female carrying a pitcher of water, she passed through the assembly of the gods. She, then assumed her proper form, and said, 'They are celebrating my praise '. 'This new goddess now ascended Mount Himalaya where Chanda and Manda, two of Sumbha and Nisumbha's messangers resided. As these demons wandered over the mountain, they saw the goddess; and being exceedingly struck with her charms, which they described to their masters, advised them to engage her affections, even if they gave her all the glorious things which they had obtained in plundering the heavens of the gods.

Sumbha sent Sugriva as messenger to the goddess, to inform her that the riches of the three worlds were in his palace; that all the offerings which used to be presented to the gods were now offered to him; and that all these offerings, riches, etc., would be hers, if she would come to him. The goddess replied that the offer was very liberal, but that she had resolved that the person she married must first conquer her in war, and destroy her pride. Sugriva, unwilling, to return unsuccessful, pressed for a favourable answer, promising that he would conquer her in war, and subdue her pride; and asked in an authoritative strain; ' Did she know his master, before whom none of the inhabitants of the worlds had been able to stand, whether gods, demons, or men? How then could she, a female think of resisting his offers? If his master had ordered him, he would have compelled her to go into his presence immediately. She agreed that this was very correct, but that she had taken her resolution, and exhorted him, therefore to persuade his master to come and try his strength with her.

The messenger went and related what he had heard. On hearing his account, Sumbha was filled with rage, and, without making any reply, called for Dhumlochana his commander-in-chief and gave him orders to go to Himalaya and seize the goddess and bring her to him and, if any attempted a rescue, utterly to destroy them. The commander went to Himalaya, and acquainted the goddess with his master's orders. She, smiling, invited him to execute them. On the approach of this hero, she set up a dreadful roar, by which he was reduced to ashes. After which she destroyed the army of the giant leaving only a few fugitives to communicate the tidings. Sumbha and Nisumbha, infuriated, sent

Chanda and Manda, who on ascending the mountain, perceived afemale sitting on an ass, laughing. On seeing them she became enraged, and drew to her ten, twenty, or thirty of their army at a time, devouring them like fruit. She next seized Manda by the hair, cut off his head and holding it over her mouth, drank the blood. Chanda, on seeing the other commander slain in this manner, himself came to close quarters with the goddess. But she, mounted on a lion, sprang on him, and, despatching him as she had done Manda, devoured part of his army, and drank the blood of the slain.

The giants no sooner heard this alarming news than they resolved to go themselves, and collecting their forces, an infinite number of giants, marched to Himalaya. The gods looked down with astonishment on this vast army, and the goddesses descended to help Maharnaya (Durga), who, however, soon destroyed her foes, Raktavija, the principal commander under Sumbha and Nishumbha, seeing all his men destroyed encountered the goddess in person. But though she covered him with wounds, from every drop of blood which fell to the ground a thousand giants, arose equal in strength to Raktavija himself. Hence innumerable enemies surrounded Durga, and the gods were filled with alarm at the amazing sight. At length Chandi, a goddess, who had assisted Kali (Durga) in the engagement, promised that if she would drink the giant's blood before it fell to the ground, she (Chandi) would engage him and destroy the whole of his strangely formed offspring.

Kali consented, and the commander and his army were soon despatched. Sumbha and Nishumbha, in a state of desperation, next engaged the goddess in single combat, Sumbha making the first onset. The battle was inconceivably dreadful on both sides, till at last both the giants were slain, and Kali sat down to feed on the carnage she had made. The gods and the goddesses chanted the praises of the celestial heroine, who in return bestowed a blessing on each." The Markandeya Purana also gives a short account of the valorous deeds of Durga done in the various forms it took. It says: " As Durga she received the message of the giants; As Dasabhuja (the ten-armed) she slew part of their army; As Singhavahini (seated on a lion) she fought with Raktavija; As

Mahishamardini (destroyer of a buffalo) she slew Sumbha in the form of a buffalo; As Jagaddhatri (the mother of the world) she overcame the army of the giants; As Kali (the black woman) she slew Raktavija; As Muktakesi (with flowing hair) she overcame another of the armies of the giants; As Tara (the saviour) she slew Sumbha in his own proper shape; As Chinnamastaka (the headless) she killed Nisumbha; As Jagadgauri (the golden-coloured lady renowned through the world) she received the praises and thanks of the gods." A comparison between the Vedic and Puranic Goddesses raises some interesting questions. One of them is quite obvious. Vedic literature is full of references to wars against the Asuras. The literature known as Brahmanas replete with them. But all these wars against the Asuras are fought by the Vedic Gods. The Vedic Goddesses never took part in them. With the Puranic Goddesses the situation has undergone a complete change. In the Puranic times there are wars with the Asuras as there were in the Vedic times.

The difference is that while in the Vedic times the wars with the Asuras are left to be fought by the Gods in the Puranic times they are left to be fought by the Goddess. Why is that Puranic Goddesses had to do what the Gods in Vedic times did? It cannot be that there were no Gods in Puranic times. There were Brahma, Vishnu and Shiva gods who ruled in the Puranic times. When they were there to fight the Asuras why were the Goddesses enrolled for this purpose. This is a riddle which requires explanation. The second question is what is the source of this power which the Puranic Goddesses possessed and which the Vedic Goddesses never had? The answer given by the Puranic writers is that this power was the power of the Gods which dwelt in the Goddesses. The general theory was that every God had energy or power which was technically called *Shakti* and that the *Shakti* of every God resided in his wife the Goddess. This had become such an accepted doctrine that every goddess is called a *Shakti* and those who worship the Goddess only are called *Saktas*. With regard to this doctrine there are one or. two questions that call for a reply.

First is this. We may now take it that notwithstanding the many names of the Goddesses as we find in the Puranas we have really five Puranic Goddesses before us—namely, *Sarasvati, Lakshmi, Parvati, Durga* and *Kali.* Sarasvati and Lakshmi are the wives of Brahma and Vishnu who along with Shiva are recognized as the Puranic Gods. Parvati, Durga and Kali are the wives of Shiva. Now *Sarasvati* and *Lakshmi* have killed no Asura and have in fact done no deed of valour. Question is why? Brahma and Vishnu had *Shakti* which in conformity with the theory must have dwelt in their wives. Why then did *Sarasvati* and *Lakshmi* not take part in the battle with the Asuras? This part is only reserved for the wives of Shiva. Even here Parvati's role is quite different from that of Durga. Parvati is represented as a simple woman. She has no heroic deeds to her credit like the ones claimed for Durga. Like Durga, Parvati is also the Shakti of Shiva. Why was Shiva's Shakti dwelling in Parvati so dull, so dormant, and so inactive as to be non-existent?

The second point is that though this doctrine may be a good justification for starting the worship of Goddesses independently of Gods, it is difficult to accept either the logical or historical basis of the doctrine. Looking at it purely from the point of view of logic if every God has *Shakti* then even the Vedic Gods must have had it. Why then was this doctrine not applied to the wives of the Vedic Gods? Looking at it from the point of view of history, there is no justification for saying that the Puranic Gods had *Shakti* in them.

Further the Brahmins do not seem to have realized that by making Durga the heroine who alone was capable of destroying the Asuras, they were making their own Gods a set of miserable cowards. It seems that the Gods could not defend themselves against the Asuras and had to beg of their wives to come to their rescue. One illustration from the Markandeya Purana is enough to prove how imbecile the Puranic Gods were shown by the Brahmins against the Asuras. Says the Markandeya Purana.: "Mahisha, king of the giants at one time overcame the gods in war and reduced them to such a state of want that they wandered through the earth as beggars. Indra first conducted them to Brahma, and then to Shiva; but as these gods could render no assistance, they turned to Vishnu, who was so grieved at the sight of their wretchedness, that streams of glory issued from his face. whence came a female figure named Mahamaya (another name of Durga). Streams of glory issued from the faces of the other gods also which in like manner entered Mahamaya: in consequence of which she became a body of glory, like a mountain of fire. The gods then handed their weapons to this dreadful being, who with a frightful scream ascended into the air, slew the giant and gave redress to the gods."

How can such cowardly Gods have any prowess? If they had none, how can they give it to their wives. To say that Goddesses must be worshipped because they have *Shakti* is not merely a riddle but an absurdity. It requires explanation why this doctrine of Shakti was invented. Was it to put it a new commodity on the market that the Brahmins started the worship of the Goddesses and degraded the Gods?.

7 Hindus and Want of Public Conscience

HINDUS AND THEIR WANT OF SOCIAL CONSCIENCE

Everyone who feels moved by the deplorable condition of the Untouchables begins by saying: "We must do something for the Untouchables". One seldom hears any of the persons interested in the problem saying: "Let us do something to change the Hindu." It is invariably assumed that the object to the reclaimed is the Untouchables as though untouchability was due to his depravity and that he alone is responsible for his condition. If there is to be a Mission, it must be to the Untouchables. Nothing requires to be done to the Hindu. He is sound in mind, manners and morals. He is whole, there is nothing wrong with him. He is not the Sinner. What is the real state of affairs? This argument that there is nothing wrong with the Hindus and that the Untouchable is responsible for whatever wrong he suffers is very much the argument that is used by the Christians for defending themselves against the inhuman treatment accorded by them to the Jews.

A very crushing reply has been given by Mr. Louis Goulding to the Christians on behalf of the suffering Jews. In discussing the source of the Jewish Problem Mr. Louis Goulding says: "I beg leave to give a very homely instance of the sense in which I consider the Jewish Problem in essence a Gentile Problem. A close acquaintance of mine is a certain Irish Terrier of mixed pedigree, the dog Paddy, who is to my friend John Smith as the apple of both his eyes. Paddy dislikes Scotch terriers; it is enough for one to pass within twenty yards of Paddy to deafen the neighbourhood with challenges and insults. It is a practice which John Smith deplores, which, therefore, he does his best to check—all the more as the object of Paddy's detestation are often inoffensive creatures, who seldom speak first. Despite all his affection for Paddy, he considers, as I do, that Paddy's unmannerly behaviour is due to some measure of original sin in Paddy. It has not yet been suggested to us that what is here involved is a Scotch Terrier Problem and that when Paddy attacks a neighbour who is peacefully engaged in inspecting the evening smells it is the neighbour who should be arraigned for inciting to attack by the fact of his existence." If we equate Paddy to the Hindu and Scotch Terrior to the Untouchable the argument of Goulding will apply to the Hindus no less than it does to the Christians.

If for the reasons given by Mr. Goulding the Jewish Problem is in reality a Christian Problem then the Problem of the Untouchables is primarily a Hindu Problem. Are the Hindus conscious, do they recognise that the Untouchables are a problem to them? Are they worried about it? Is it weighing on their minds? Certain obvious tests may be applied in order to ascertain the truth. One test is the volume of literature on the subject. One can take the volume of literature issued on the Negroes of America as a standard measure. One is amazed at the huge amount of printed material that exists in the United States on the subject of the Negroes. It is said that a really complete bibliography on the Negro Problem would run up to several hundred thousand titles. The literature is really immeasurable. This proves as nothing else can, how much it is a problem to the Whites. It has disturbed through several generations all classes of people in America, the religious moralists, the political philosophers, the Statesmen, the philanthropists, the social scientists, the politicians, the businessmen and the plain ordinary citizen as well.

What is the amount of literature on the Untouchables that exists in India? Not more than half a dozen pamphlets! Another test would be the test of social behaviour. I give below two cases reported in the papers. One is from the '*Pratap*' of 5th March 1926. It gives the following news: "On the 23rd of February at about 11 O'clock in the day, a group of about 12 or 13 were digging earth in Begumganj, Lucknow when the quarry collapsed and they were all buried under heaps of earth. One boy and six women were rescued after the earth had been removed out of whom only one woman turned out to be alive, who belonged to Mirpur. She had received grievous injuries and her condition was very critical.

The Hindu inhabitants of Begumganj however refused to give a bed to lay that woman on. At last a Muslim offered a bed; now there was no Hindu prepared to help to carry the poor woman as far as her house. At last, a sweeper was called and he undertook to carry the woman to her home as she lay on the bed."

The best illustration of the absence of conscience in the Hindu towards the Untouchables is to be found in the following incident which is reported by the Correspondent of the *'Sangram'* and published in its issue of 10th July 1946. The correspondent says: "A woman died on the 8th of July 1946 in the Anath Ashram (Beggars Home) called Azil situated in a village called Mhapse (in Goa) and maintained by Christians. The woman was believed to be a Hindu. She was alone and had no relations. Seeing that there was no one to dispose of the dead body and to perform funeral rites, the Hindus of the village came together and raised a subscription for the purpose. They brought the dead body out of the Beggars' Home. Just about that time some Untouchables, who knew the woman came there and recognized the dead body. The moment the Hindus came to know that the woman belonged to the Untouchables the Hindus who had gathered there deserted the dead body and started walking away. The Untouchables who had come requested the Hindus to give them the amount they had collected for buying the coffin and the shroud. The Hindus refused to part with the money saying that the money was collected from the subscribers on the representation that the deceased woman was a Hindu woman. As she is not a Hindu but an Untouchable, they can't spend the money on her funeral. The Untouchables had to do their best to dispose of their dead body. The Untouchables had good evidence of the love and affection the Hindus bear towards them.

The following is from the *'Milap'* of 2nd October 1925. Its correspondent reports: "News has been received from Ruddurprayag that one evening in the first week of September a Harijan came to the Dharmashala (or monastery) of Ruddurprayag. When he learnt that a tiger came there every night, he requested the pastor of the Dharmashala to let him lie hidden in some corner of the Dharmashala for the night, so that he may remain safe from the tiger. The callous pastor, however, paid no heed to the request and closed the gates of the

Dharmashala. The ill-starred Harijan laid himself down outside in one corner, full of apprehensions of the tiger. Towards the end of the night the tiger came and attacked the Harijan. As the man was quite strong and healthy and despair made him fearless, he caught hold of the tiger's neck and shouted 'I have grabbed the tiger. Come and kill him'. But the high caste pastor did not open the door, nor did he offer any sort of help, so that very soon the grip of the Harijan loosened and the tiger also ran away. At present the man is lying wounded in Shrinagar (Garhwal) where he is getting himself treated. His condition is said to be critical."

The heartlessness disclosed by these instances shows that the Hindu does not bother about what he does to the Untouchables or about what happens to the Untouchables. A third test would be the test of service and sacrifice for the uplift of the Untouchables. Here again, one may adopt the service and sacrifice of the Americans for raising the Negroes as our standard measure. Here are some figures.

Consider the requests made by the Whites for the benefit of the Negro education.

Testator	Amount (in Dollars)	Testator	Amount (in Dollars)
Kane	50.000	Mason	1.00.000
Harton	5.000	Naunbert	40.000
Troughton	1.60.600	Harrison	2.30.000
Ottinger	500	Munger	75.000
Gambrille	35.000	Corliss	45.000
Jarepki	1.000	Rosenbanin	1.000
Strock	500	Burton	1.000
Kidder	5.000	Conroy	1.00.000
Clodin	10.000	Kent	10.000
Wood	500	Duke	1.40.000
Harkness	12.50.000	Marciliat	5.000
Beatie	2.90,000	Masey	25.000
Marquant	5.000	Nicholas	20.000
Newton	5.000	Garretson	15.00.000
Hummington	25,000	Hatcher	20.000
Phelps-Stokes	2.80.000	Wright	10.000
Butler	30.000		

These figures relate to the period before 1930. They do not take account of residuary bequests. Compare the Educational funds that exist for the advancement of education among the Negroes. They are:

(i) The Avery Fund.

(ii) The Vilas Bequest.

(iii) The African Fund.

(iv) The Buckingham Fund.

(v) The George Washington Educational Fund.

(vi) The Miner Fund.

(vii) The Steward Missionary Foundation.

(viii) The Daniel Hand Fund.

(ix) The John Slater Fund.

(x) The Phelps-Stokes Fund.

In addition to this, there are general Funds such as the Carnegie Corporation Julius Rosenwald Fund and the Rockfeller Foundation which also help the Negroes. The amounts distributed by these funds is not known. But they must be amounting to millions. Compare the amount spent by Religious organizations on the education of the Negroes. Here are some interesting figures.

It is estimated that the total amount spent for the religious and philanthropic organizations between 1865 and 1930 comes to 135,000,000 dollars on the advancement of the Negroes. Of this amount, 85,000,000 dollars have been contributed by the Whites. What is the measure of service and sacrifice of the Hindus for the elevation of the Untouchables. The only organization the Hindus can boast of is the Harijan Sevak Sangh. Its capital fund does not probably go beyond 10 lakhs. Its annual expenditure does not go beyond a few thousand rupees on petty and insignificant and insubstantial purposes. The Fund is not a welfare fund. It is essentially a Political Fund intended to make the Untouchables vote with the Hindus. Why is this difference?

Why do the Americans exert so much in service and sacrifice for the elevation of the Negroes and why have the Hindus cared to do nothing for the elevation of the Untouchables? The answer is that the Americans have a social conscience while the Hindus have none. It is not that the Hindus have no sense of right and wrong, good and bad, moral and immoral. What is wrong with the Hindu is that his sense of moral obligation towards others is restricted to a limited class of people, namely, the members of his caste. As Mr. H. J. Paton says" Clearly a man may be a good member of a limited society without being a morally good man. There seem indeed to be already shadows or anticipations of moral excellence even in the man who carries out coherently an individual policy of life; and we begin to find something which we may almost mistake for virtue itself, when we consider the man who is a loyal member of any society, even of a gang of thieves.

Yet although there must be honour among thieves, a thief is not therefore an honourable man. The morally good man seems to be the man who is good as a member not of a limited society but of an unlimited society—of a society of societies whose purpose includes all purposes, and beyond which there is no other society to be a source of conflicting claims ot duties." The Untouchable does not belong to the society of the Hindus and the Hindu does not feel that he and the Untouchables belong to one society. This is the reason why the conduct of the Hindu is marked by a moralistic unconcernedness. Not having conscience, the Hindu has no such thing in him as righteous indignation against the inequities and injustices from which the Untouchable has been suffering. He sees no wrong in these inequities and injustices and refuses to budge. By his absence of conscience the Hindu is a great obstacle in the path of the removal of untouchability.

HINDU SOCIAL REFORMERS

Among the Hindu social reformers there is a moderate section. This section holds that untouchability is separate from the caste system. Following this ideology they hold that it is possible to remove untouchability without attacking the caste system. The religious minded Hindu is as opposed to the removal of untouchability as he is to the removal of the caste system. He is as opposed to dealing with social reform in two stages as he is in dealing with it in one stage. But the politically minded Hindu is tremendously fond of the idea. That is obviously for two reasons.

In the first place, it gives the Hindu the chance of showing himself in international world as a better specimen of democracy than he really is. Secondly, by leaving caste alone there is no risk of the caste Hindus forsaking the Congress.

In the verse, Manu says that there are only four varnas and that there is no fifth varna. This verse is interpreted to mean that the untouchables are included in the fourth varna, that they are part of the Sudras and as there is no objection to touching the Sudras there could be no objection to touching the Untouchables. However pleasing this construction may be to the politically minded Hindu, it does accord with the intention of what Manu wanted to convey. The verse is open to another construction. It may mean that Manu was not prepared to enlarge the Chaturvarnya and make it a Panchavarnya by recognising these communities which were outside the four varnas as constituting the fifth varna. In saying that there is no fifth varna what he means to suggest is that he did not want to incorporate those outside the four varnas into the Hindu society by making the Hindu society consist of five varnas instead of four.

That he wanted to convey the latter intention is abundantly clear by speaking of a category of people as Bahyas or Varna Bahyas which means those outside the varna system. If Manu wanted to include all persons within the four varnas there was no reason for speaking of some people as varna Bahyas. Indeed, he recognises two sub-divisions within the class of Varna Bahyas. He calls them Hinas and Antayevasins . Given these facts, it is obvious that the construction sought to be placed in the verse in the Manusmriti will not deceive the orthodox Hindu into accepting that the maintenance of untouchability is contrary to the Manusmriti and that its abolition is not therefore contrary to the tenets of the Hindu religion. The argument based on the interpretation of Manu's text is too intellectual for the ordinary uneducated Hindu. He knows only two things. One thing he knows is that there are three barriers in the matter of social intercourse which he must observe. They are:

(1) prohibition against inter-dining,

(2) prohibition against inter-marriage, while in untouchability there is third barrier added and

(3) prohibition against physically touching certain class of people.

The first two barriers make up the caste. The third forms untouchability. The caste Hindu does not bother about the number of barriers. He is particular about the observance of the barrier. When he is asked not to observe, he turns round and asks why not? His argument is that, if I am free to observe the first two barriers, what is wrong if I observe the third? Psychologically, caste and untouchability are one integral system based on one and the same principle. If the caste Hindus observe untouchability it is because they believe in caste. Looked at from this point of view, the idea of hoping to remove untouchability without destroying the caste system is an utter futility. The underlying idea that caste and untouchability are two different things is founded on a fallacy. The two are one and are inseparable. Untouchability is only an extension of the caste system. There can be no severance between the two.

The two stand together and will fall together. There is another reason why untouchability cannot disappear by a stratagem, legal or rational. As has already been pointed out, the Hindu social order is based on the principle of graded inequality. It may not bean exaggeration to say that not many people understand the significance of this principle. The social system based on inequality stands on a different footing from a social system based on graded, inequality. The former is a weak system which is not capable of self-I preservation. The latter on the other hand, is capable of self-preservation. In a social system based on inequality, the low orders can combine to overthrow the system. None of them have any interest to preserve it. In a social system based on graded inequality the possibility of a general common attack by the aggrieved parties is nonexistent. In a system of graded inequality, the aggrieved parties are not on a common level. This can happen only when they are only high and low.

In the system of graded inequality there are the highest (the Brahmins). Below the highest are the higher (the Kshatriyas). Below the higher are those who are high (Vaishya). Below the high are the low (Sudra) and below the low are those who are lower (the Untouchables). All have a grievance against the highest and would like to bring about their down fall. But they will not combine. The higher is anxious to get rid of the highest but does not wish to combine with the high, the low and the lower lest they should reach his level and be his equal. The high wants to overthrow the higher who is above him but does not want to join hands with the low and the lower, lest they should rise to his status and become equal to him in rank. The low is anxious to pull down the highest, the higher and the high but he would not make a common cause with the lower for fear of the lower gaining a higher status and becoming his equal in the system of graded inequality there is no such class as completely unprivileged class except the one which is at the base of the social pyramid. The privileges of the rest are graded. Even the low is a privileged class as compared with the lower. Each class being privileged, every class is interested in maintaining the social system.

Untouchability may be a misfortune to the Untouchables. But there is no doubt that it is a good fortune to the Hindus. It gives them a class which they can look down upon. The Hindus do not want a system in which nobody will be anybody. They also do not want a system in which everybody may be somebody. They want a system in which they will be some bodies and others will be nobodies. The Untouchables are nobodies. This makes the Hindus some bodies. The system of untouchability sustains the natural pride of the Hindus and make them feel as well as look big. This is an additional reason why the Hindus are not likely to give up untouchability particularly those large majority who are small men.

Untouchability will vanish only when the whole of the Hindu Social Order, particularly the caste system will be dissolved. Is this possible? Every institution is sustained by some sort of a sanction. There are three kinds of sanction, which supply life force to an institution. They are legal, social and religious. The vitality of the institution depends upon the nature of the sanction. What is the nature of the sanction behind the caste system? Unfortunately, the sanction behind the caste system is the religious sanction, for, the caste as a new form of the Varna system derives its sanction from the Vedas which form the sacred book of the Hindu religion and which are infallible. I say unfortunately because anything which has a religious sanction becomes by virtue of it sacred and eternal. To the Hindu, caste is sacred and caste is eternal. If caste cannot vanish what hope is there for untouchability to disappear?

VIOLENCE AGAINST THE UNTOUCHABLES

The cases in which the Hindus have indulged in violence against the Untouchables are cases of fight for equal freedom to all. If the Untouchables want to go in procession, they have no objection to the Hindus doing the same. If the Untouchables want to wear gold and silver ornaments, they do not object to the Hindus having the same right. If the Untouchables want to send their children to schools, they are not against the children of the Hindus having full freedom for education. If the Untouchables wish to draw water from the well, they have no objection to the Hindus exercising their right to take water. One can go on *ad infinitum*. But it is unnecessary. The point is easy and simple to grasp. It is that whatever freedom the Untouchables claim is not exclusive to them and is not inconsistent with the right of the Hindus to equal freedom. Why then does the Hindus use violence to put down such innocent and perfectly lawful acts? Why does he regard his lawlessness as lawful? Who cannot see that the acts and omissions of the Hindus in his dealings with the Untouchables cannot be called by any other name except that of social wrongs. The acts and omissions are not mere inequities; they are not mere indignities.

They are gross instances of man's inhumanity to man. For a doctor not to treat a patient because the patient is an Untouchable, for a body of Hindu villages to burn the houses of the Untouchables, to throw human excreta in their well if these are not acts of inhumanity, I wonder what can be? The question is why has the Hindu no conscience? There is only one answer to these questions. The class composition in other countries were based on economic and social considerations. Slavery and serfdom had no foundation in religion. Untouchability though it can give and does economic advantages to the Hindus, is primarily based on religion. There is nothing sacrosanct in economic and social interests. They yield to time and circumstances. This is the broad explanation why slavery and serfdom have vanished and why untouchability has not. The same is the answer to the two other questions. If the Hindu observes untouchability it is because his religion enjoins him to do so. If he is ruthless and lawless in putting down the Untouchables rising against his Established Order, it is because his religion not only tells him that the Established Order is divine and therefore sacrosanct but also imposes upon him a duty to see that this Established Order is maintained by all means possible.

If he does not listen to the call of humanity, it is because his religion does not enjoin him to regard the Untouchables as human beings. If he does not feel any qualms of conscience in assaulting, looting, burning and other acts of atrocities against the Untouchables, it is because his religion tells him that nothing is sin, which is done in defence of the social order. Many Hindus would regard this as a travesty of their religion. The best way to meet the charge is to quote Chapter and verse from Manu who is the architect of Hindu Society. Let anyone, who denies what I have said, read the following Commands of Manu regarding untouchability. Untouchables and the duties of the Hindus in regard to them:

1. All those tribes in this world, which are excluded from (the community of) those born from the mouth, the arms, the thighs, and the feet (of Brahman), are called Dasyus, whether they speak the language of the Mlenchhas (barbarians) or that of the Aryans.
2. Near well known trees and burial ground, on mountains and in groves, let these (tribes) dwell, known (by certain marks), and subsisting by their peculiar occupations.
3. But the dwellings of the Chandalas and Shwapakas shall be outside the village, they must be made Apatras and their wealth (shall be) dogs and donkeys.
4. Their dress (shall be) the garments of the dead, (they shall eat) their food from broken dishes, black iron (shall be) their ornaments, they must always wander from place to place.
5. A man who fulfils a religious duty shall not seek intercourse with them; their transactions (shall be) among themselves, and their marriages with their equals.

6. Their food shall be given to them by others (than an Aryan giver) in a broken dish; at night they shall not walk about in villages and in towns.
7. By day they must go about for the purpose of their work, distinguished by marks at the king's command, and they shall carry out the corpses (of persons) who have no relatives, that is a settled rule.
8. By the king's order, they shall always execute the criminals in accordance with the law, and they shall take for themselves the clothes, the beds and the ornaments of (such) criminals.
9. He who has had connection with a woman of one of the lowest castes shall be put to death.
10. If one who (being a member of the Chandalas, or some other low caste) must not be touched, intentionally defiles by his touch one who (as a member of a twice born caste) may be touched (by the other twice born persons only) he shall be put to death." Can anybody, who reads these Commandments of Manu deny that it is Hindu religion, which is responsible for the perpetuation of untouchability and for the lawlessness and want of conscience on the part of the Hindus towards the Untouchables? Indeed, if the acts of omission and commission which have been detailed in the this books of this book were correlated to these ten Commandments, it will be found that the Hindus in committing these acts are merely following the Commandments of Manu. If the Hindu will not touch an Untouchable and regards it as an offence if an Untouchable touches him, it is because of the Commandments Nos. 5 and 10. If the Hindus insist upon the segregation of the Untouchables, it is because of Commandment No. 3. If the Hindu will not allow the Untouchable to wear clean clothes, gold ornaments, he is only following Commandment No. 8. If the Hindu will not tolerate an Untouchable acquiring property and wealth, he is only following Commandment No. 3.

It is really unnecessary to labour the matter further. It is incontrovertible that the main cause which is responsible for the fate of the Untouchables is the Hindu religion and its teachings. A comparison between Paganism and Christianity in relation to slavery and Hinduism in relation to untouchability reveals how different has been the influence of the two religions on human institutions, how elevating has been the influence of the former and how degrading that of the latter. Those who are fond of comparing slavery with Untouchability do not realize that they are facing a paradox. Legally the slave was not a freeman. Yet, socially he had all the freedom necessary for the growth of his personality. Legally the Untouchable is a freeman. Yet, socially he has no freedom for the growth of his personality. This is indeed a very glaring paradox. What is the explanation of this paradox?

There is only one explanation of this paradox. It is that while religion was on the side of the slave, religion has been against the Untouchables. The Roman law declared that the slave was not a person. But the religion of Rome refused to accept that principle, at any rate, refused to extend that principle to social field. It treated him I as a human being fit for comradeship. The Hindu Law declared that the Untouchable was not a person. Contrary to Paganism, the Hindu religion not only accepted the principle but also extended it to the social field. As the Hindu Law did not regard the Untouchable a person, Hinduism refused to regard him as a human being fit for comradeship.

That the Roman religion saved the slave from the social degradation consequent upon his legal degradation is beyond question. It saved him from such degradation in three different ways. One way by which the Roman religion saved the slave was to keep the most sacred place open for the slave to occupy. As has been observed: "Roman religion was never hostile to the slave. It did not close the temple doors against him; it did not banish him from its festivals. If slaves were excluded from certain ceremonies the same may be said of freemen and women—men being excluded from the rites of Bona Dea, Vesta and Ceras, women from those of Hercules at the Ara Maxima. In the days when the old Roman divinities counted for something, the slave came to be informally included in the family, and could consider himself under the protection of the Gods of the household..... Augustus ordered that freed women should be eligible as priestesses of Vesta. The law insisted that a slave's grave should be regarded as sacred and for his soul Roman Mythology provided no special heaven and no particular hell. Even Juvenal agrees that the slave's soul and body, is made of the same stuff as his master." The second way in which the Roman religion helped the slave was equivalent to lodging a complaint before the City Prefect whose duty it became to hear cases of wrong done to slaves by their masters.

This was a secular remedy. But the Roman religion had provided another and a better remedy. According to it, the slave was entitled to throw himself before the altar and demand that he should be sold to a kinder master. The third way in which the Roman religion saved the slave by preventing the Roman Law from destroying the sanctity of his personality as a human being. It did not make him unfit for human association and comradeship. For the Roman slave this was the greatest saving grace. Suppose Roman society had an objection to buy vegetables, milk, butter or take water or wine from the hands of the slave; suppose Roman society had an objection to allow slaves to touch them, to enter their houses, travel with them in cars, etc., would it have been possible for the master to train his slave to raise him from semi-barbarism to a cultured state? Obviously not; it is because the slave was not held to be an Untouchable that the master could train him and raise him. We again come back therefore to the same conclusion, namely, that What has saved the slave is that his personality was recognised by society and what has ruined the Untouchable is that Hindu society did not recognise his personality, treated him as one whose personality was unclean which rendered him as unfit for human association and common dealing.

There was no gulf, social or religious, which separated the slave from the rest of the society. In outward appearance he did not differ from the freeman; neither colour nor clothing revealed his condition; he witnessed the same games as the freeman; he shared in the life of the Municipal towns and got employed in the State service, engaged himself in trade and commerce as all freemen did. Often apparent equality in outward things counts far more to the individual than actual identity of rights before the law.

Between the slave and the freed there seems often to have been little social barrier, Marriage between the slave and freed and even freed and slave was very common. The slave status carried no stigma on the man in the slave. He was Touchable and even respectable. All this was due to the attitude of the Roman religion towards the slave. There is no space to describe at length the attitude of Christianity to slavery.

But it was different from Paganism. It is not known to many that during the period of slavery in America, Christian priests were not prepared to convert Negro slaves to Christianity because of their view that it would degrade Christianity if the convert remained a slave. In their opinion, one Christian could not hold another Christian as a slave. He was bound to offer him fellowship. To sum up. Law and Religion are two forces which govern the i conduct of men. At times, they act as handmaids to each other. At other times, they act as check and counter-check. Of the two forces, Law is personal while religion is impersonal. Law being personal it is Capable of being unjust and iniquitous. But religion being impersonal, it can be impartial. If religion remains impartial, it is capable of defeating the inequity committed by law. This is exactly what happened in Rome in regard to the slave. That is why religion is believed to ennoble man and not to degrade him. Hinduism is an exception. It has made the Untouchable sub-human. It has made the Hindu inhuman. There is no escape to either from the established order of the sub-human and the inhuman.

8 The House the Hindus have Built

SOCIAL ORGANISATION OF THE HINDUS

Is there any thing peculiar in the social organisation of the Hindus? An unsophisticated Hindu who is unaware of investigations conducted by scholars will say that there is nothing peculiar, abnormal or unnatural in the organisation of the society to which he belongs. This is quite natural. People who live their lives in isolation are seldom conscious of the peculiarities of their ways and manners. People have gone on from generation to generation without stopping to give themselves a name. But how does the social organisation of the Hindu strike the outsiders, non-Hindus? Did it appear to them as normal and natural? Megasthenese who came to India as the ambassador of the Greek King Seleukos Nickator to the Court of Chandragupta Maurya some time about the year 305 B.C. did feel that the social organisation of the Hindus was of a very strange sort. Otherwise he would not have taken such particular care to describe the peculiar features of the Hindu social organisation.

He has recorded: "The population of India is divided into seven parts. The philosophers are first in rank, but form the smallest class in point of number. Their services are employed privately by persons who wish to offer sacrifices or perform other sacred rites, and also publicly by the kings at what is called the Great Synod, wherein at the beginning of the new year all the philosophers are gathered together before the King at the gates, when any philosopher who may have committed any useful suggestion to writing, or observed any means for improving the crops and the cattle, or for promoting the public interests, declares it publicly. If any one is detected giving false information thrice, the law condemns him to be silent for the rest of his life, but he who gives sound advice is exempted from paying any taxes or contributions. The second caste consists of the husbandmen, who form the bulk of the population, and are in disposition most mild and gentle.

They are exempted from military service, and cultivate their lands undisturbed by fear. They never go to town, either to take part in its tumults, or for any other purpose. It therefore not infrequently happens that at the same time, and in the same part of the country, men maybe seen drawn up in array of battle, and fighting at risk of their lives, while other men close at hand are ploughing and digging in perfect security, having these soldiers to protect them. The whole of the land is the property of the King, and the husbandmen till it on condition of receiving one-fourth of the produce. The third caste consists of herdsmen and hunters, who alone are allowed to hunt, and to keep cattle, and to sell draught animals or let them out on hire. In return for clearing the land of wild beasts and fowls which devour the seeds sown in the fields, they receive an allowance of grain from the king. They lead a wandering life and live under tents. The fourth class, after herdsmen and hunters, consists of those who work at trades, of those who vend wares, and of those who are employed in bodily labour.

Some of these pay tribute, and render to the State certain prescribed services. But the armour-makers and shipbuilders receive wages and their victuals from the king, for whom alone they work. The general in command of the army supplies the soldiers with weapons, and the admiral of the fleet lets out ships on hire for the transport both of passengers and merchandise. The fifth class consists of fighting men, who when not engaged in active service, pass their time in idleness and drinking. They are maintained at the King's expense, and hence they are always ready, when occasion calls, to take the field, for they carry nothing of their own with them but their own bodies. The sixth class consists of the overseers, to whom is assigned the duty of watching all that goes on, and making reports secretly to the King. Some are entrusted with the inspection of the city, and others with that of the army.

The former employs as their coadjutors the courtesans of the city, and the latter the courtesans of the camp. The ablest and most trustworthy men are appointed to fill these offices. The seventh class consists of the councillors and assessors of the king. To them belong the highest posts of government, the tribunals of justice, and the general administration of public affairs. No one is allowed to marry out of his own caste, or to exchange one profession or trade for another, or to follow more than one business. An exception is made in favour of the philosopher, who for his virtue is allowed this privilege. Alberuni who wrote an account of his travels in India some time about 1030 A.D. must have been struck by the peculiarity of the Hindu Social Organisation. For he too has not omitted to make a note of it. He observed: The Hindus call their castes varna, *i.e.* colours, and from a genealogical point of view they call them jataka, *i.e.* births. These castes are from the very beginning only four.

I. The highest caste is the Brahmana, of whom the books of the Hindus tell that they were created from the head of Brahman. And a Brahman is only another name for the force called nature, and the head is the highest part of the animal body, the Brahmana are the choice part of the whole genus. Therefore the Hindus consider them as the very best mankind.

II. The next caste are the Kshatriya, who were created, as they say, from the shoulders and hands of Brahman. Their degree is not much below that of the Brahmana.

III. After them follow the Vaisya, who were created from the thigh of Brahman.

IV. The Sudra, who were created from his feet, "Between the latter two classes there is no very great distance. Much, however, as these classes differ from each other, they live together in the same towns and villages, mixed together in the same houses and lodgings.

After the Sudra follow the people called Antyaja, who render various kinds of services, who are not reckoned amongst any caste, but only as members of a certain craft or profession. There are eight classes of them who freely intermarry with each other, except the fuller, shoemaker and weaver, for no others would condescend to have anything to do with them. These eight guilds are the fuller, shoemaker, juggler, the basket and shield maker, the sailor, fisherman, the hunter of wild animals and of birds, and the weaver. The four castes do not live together with them in one and the same place. These guilds live near the villages and towns of the four castes, but outside them.

The people called Hadi, Doma (Domba), Candala and Badhatau (sic) are not reckoned amongst any caste or guild. They are occupied with dirty work, like the cleansing of the villages and other services. They are considered as one sole class, and distinguished only by their occupations. In fact, they are considered like illegitimate children; for according to general opinion they descend from a Sudra father and a Brahmani mother as the children of fornication; therefore they are degraded outcaste. The Hindus give to every single man of the four castes characteristic names, according to their occupations and modes of life, *e.g.* the Brahman is in general called by this name as long as he does his work staying at home. When he is busy with the service of one fire, he is called Ishtin; if he serves three fires, he is called Agnihotrin; if he besides offers an offering to the fire, he is called Dikshita.

And as it is with the Brahmana, so is it also with the other castes. Of the classes beneath the castes, the Hadi are the best spoken of, because they keep themselves free from everything unclean. Next follow the Doma, who play on the lute and sing. The still lower classes practise as a trade killing and the inflicting of judicial punishments. The worst of all are the Badhatau, who not only devour the flesh of dead animals, but even of dogs and other beasts. Each of the four castes, when eating together, must form a group of themselves, one group not being allowed to comprise two men of different castes. If, further, in the group of the Brahmana there are two men who live at enmity with each other, and the seat of the one is by the side of the other, they make a barrier between the two seats by placing a board between them, or by spreading a piece of dress, or in some other way; and if there is only a line drawn between them, they are considered as separated.

Since it is forbidden to eat the remains of a meal, every single man must have his own food for himself; for if any one of the party who are eating should take of the food from one and the same plate, that which remains in the plate becomes, after the first eater has taken part, to him who wants to take as the second, the remains of the meal, and such is forbidden. Alberuni did not merely content himself with recording what struck him as peculiar in the Hindu Social organisation. He went on to say: "Among the Hindus institutions of this kind abound. We Muslims, of course, stand entirely on the other side of the question, considering all men as equal, except in piety; and this is the greatest obstacle which prevents any approach or understanding between Hindus and Muslims."

Duarte Barbosa who was Portuguese official in the service of the Portuguese Government in India from 1500 to 1517 has left a record of his impressions of Hindu Society. This is what struck him: "And before this kingdom of Guzerate fell into the hands of the Moors, a certain race of Heathen whom the Moors called Resbutos dwelt therein, who in those days were the knights and wardens of the land, and made war where so ever it was needful. These men kill and eat sheep and fish and all other kinds of food; in the mountains there are yet many of them, where they have great villages and obey not the king of Guzerate, but rather wage daily war against him: who, do what he may, is yet not able to prevail against them, nor will do so, for they are very fine horsemen, and good archers, and have besides divers other weapons to defend themselves withal against the Moors, on whom they make war without ceasing; yet have they no king nor lord over them."

And in this kingdom there is another sort of Heathen whom they call Baneanes, who are great merchants and traders. They dwell among the Moors with whom they carry on all their trade. This people eat neither flesh nor fish, nor anything subject to death; they slay nothing, nor are they willing even to see the slaughter of any animal; and thus they maintain their idolatry and hold it so firmly that it is a terrible thing. For often it is so that the Moors take to them live insects or small birds, and make as though to kill them in their presence, and the Baneanes buy these and ransom them, paying much more than they are worth, so that they may save their lives and let them go. And if the King or a Governor of the land has any man condemned to death, for any crime, which he has committed, they gather themselves together and buy him from justice, if they are willing to sell him, that he may not die. And divers Moorish mendicants as well, when they wish to obtain alms from this people, take great stones wherewith they beat upon their shoulders and bellies as though they would slay themselves before them, to hinder which they give them great alms that they may depart in peace.

Others carry knives with which they slash their arms and legs, and to these too they give large alms that they may not kill themselves. Others go to their doors seeking to kill rats and snakes for them, and to them also they give much money that they may not do so. Thus they are much esteemed by the Moors! When these Baneanes meet with a swarm of ants on the road they shrink back and seek for some way to pass without crushing them. And in their houses they sup by daylight, for neither by night nor by day will they light a lamp, by reason of certain little flies which perish in the flame thereof; and if there is any great need of a light by night they have a lantern of varnished paper or cloth, so that no living thing may find its way in, and die in the flame. And if these men breed many lice they kill them not, but when they trouble them too much they send for certain men, also Heathen, who live among them and whom they hold to be men of a holy life; they are like hermits living with great abstinence through devotion to their gods. These men louse them, and as many lice as they catch they place on their own heads and breed them on their own flesh, by which they say they do great service to their Idol. Thus one and all they maintain with great self-restraint their law of not killing. On the other hand they are great usurers, falsifiers of weights and measures and many other goods and of coins; and great liars. These heathen are tawny men, tall and well looking, gaily attired, delicate and moderate in their food. Their diet is of milk, butter, sugar and rice, and many conserves of divers sorts.

They make much use of dishes of fruit and vegetables and potherbs in their food. Where so ever they dwell they have orchards and fruit gardens and many water tanks wherein they bathe twice a day, both men and women; and they say when they have finished bathing that they are clear of as many sins as they have committed up to that hour. These Baneanes grow very long hair, as women do with us, and wear it twisted up on the head and made into a knot, and over it a turban, that they may keep it always held together; and in their hair they put flowers and other sweet scented things. They use to anoint themselves with white sandalwood mixed with saffron and other scents. They are very amorous people. They are clad in long cotton and silken shirts and are shod with pointed shoes of richly wrought cordwain; some of them wear short coats of silk and brocade. They carry no arms except certain very small knives ornamented with gold and silver, and this for two reasons: First, because they are men who make but little use of weapons; and secondly, because the Moors defend them.

Bramenes

And there is here another class of Heathen whom they call Bramenes, who are priests among them, and persons who manage and rule their houses of prayers and idol-worship, which are of great size and have great revenues; and many of them also are maintained by alms. In these houses are great numbers of wooden Idols, and others of stone and copper and in these houses or monasteries they celebrate great ceremonies in honour of these idols, entertaining them with great store of candles and oil lamps, and with bells after our fashion. These Bramenes and Heathen have in their creed many resemblance to the Holy Trinity, and hold in great honour the relation of the Triune Three, and always make their prayers to God, whom they confess and adore as the true God, Creator and maker of all things, who is three persons and one God and they say that there are many other gods who are rulers under him, in whom also they believe. These Bramenes and heathen wheresoever they find our churches enter them and make prayers and adoration to our Images, always asking for Santa Maria, like men who have some knowledge and understanding of these matters; and they honour the Church as is our manner, saying that between them and us there is little difference. These men never eat anything subject to death, nor do they slay anything.

Bathing they hold to be a great ceremony and they say that by it they are saved. There is also in this same Kingdom of Calicut a caste of people called Bramenes who are priests among them (as are the clergy among us) of whom I have spoken in another place. These all speak the same tongue, nor can any be a Bramene except he be the son of a Bramene. When they are seven years of age they put over their shoulder a strip of two fingers in breadth of untanned skin with the hair on it of a certain wild beast, which they call Cryvamergam, which resembles a wild ass. Then for seven years he must not eat betel for which time he continues to wear this strap. When he is fourteen years old they make him a Bramene, and taking off their leather strap they invest him with the cord of three strands which he wears for the rest of his life as a token that he is a Bramene. And this they do with great ceremonial and rejoicings, as we do here for a cleric when he sings his first mass. Thereafter he may eat betel, but not flesh or fish. They have great honour among the Indians and as I have already said, they suffer death for no cause whatsoever, their own headman gives them a mild chastisement. They marry once only in our manner, and only the eldest son marries, he is treated like the head of an entailed estate.

The other brothers remain single all their lives. These Bramenes keep their wives well guarded, and greatly honoured, so that no other men may sleep with them; if any of them die, they do not marry again, but if a woman wrongs her husband she is slain by poison. The brothers who remain bachelors sleep with the Nayre women, they hold it to be a great honour, and as they are Bramenes no woman refuses herself to them, yet they may not sleep with any woman older than themselves. They dwell in their own houses and cities, and serve as clergy in the houses of worship, whither they go to pray at certain hours of the day, performing their rituals and idolatries. Some of these Bramenes serve the Kings in every manner except in arms.

No man may prepare any food for the King except a Bramene or his own kin; they also serve as couriers to other countries with letters, money or merchandise, passing wherever they wish to go in safety, and none does them any ill, even when the Kings are at war. These Bramenes are learned in their idolatry, and possess many books thereof. The Kings hold them in high esteem. I have already spoken many times of the Nayres, and yet I have not hitherto told you what manner of men they are. You are to know that in this land of Malbar there is another caste of people, called Nayres, and among them are noble men who have no other duty than to serve in war, and they always carry their arms whither so ever they go, some swords and shields, others bows and arrows, and yet others spears. They all live with the King, and the other great Lords; nevertheless all receive stipends from the King or from the great Lords with whom they dwell. None may become a Nayre, save only he who is of Nayre lineage. They are very free from stain in their nobility. They will not touch any one of low caste, nor eat, nor drink save in the house of a Nayre.

These men are not married, their nephews (sisters' sons) are their heirs. The Nayre women of good birth are very independent, and dispose of themselves as they please with Bramenes and Nayres, but they do not sleep with men of caste lower than their own under pain of death. When they reach the age of twelve years their mothers hold a great ceremony.

When a mother perceives that her daughter has attained that age, she asks her kinsfolk and friends to make ready to honour her daughter, then she asks of the kindred and especially of one particular kinsman or great friend to marry her daughter; this he willingly promises and then he has a small jewel made, which would contain a half ducat of gold, long like a ribbon, with a hole through the middle which comes out on the other side, string on thread of white silk.

The mother then on a fixed day is present with her daughter gaily decked with many rich jewels, making great rejoicing with music and singing, and a great assembly of people. Then the Kinsman or friend comes bringing that jewel, and going through certain forms, throws it over the girl's neck. She wears it as a token all the rest of her life, and may then dispose of herself, as she will. The man departs without sleeping with her inasmuch as he is her kinsman; if he is not, he may sleep with her, but is not obliged to do so. Thenceforward the mother goes about searching and asking some young man to take her daughter's virginity; they must be Nayres and they regard it among themselves as a disgrace and a foul thing to take a woman's virginity. And when any one has once slept with her, she is fit for association with men.

Then the mother again goes about enquiring among other young Nayres if they wish to support her daughter, and take her as a Mistress so that three or four Nayres agree with her to keep her, and sleep with her, each paying her so much a day; the more lovers she has the greater is her honour. Each one of them passes a day with her from midday on one day, till midday on the next day and so they continue living quietly without any disturbance nor quarrels among them. If any of them wishes to leave her, he leaves her, and takes another, and she also if she is weary of a man, she tells him to go, and he does so, or makes terms with her.

Any children they may have stay with the mother who has to bring them up, for they hold them not to be the children of any man, even if they bear his likeness, and they do not consider them their children, nor are they heirs to their estates, for as I have already stated their heirs are their nephews, sons of their sisters, (which rule whosoever will consider inwardly in his mind will find that it was established with a greater and deeper meaning than the common folk think) for they say that the Kings of the Nayres instituted it in order that the Nayres should not be held back from their service by the burden and labour of rearing children.

In this Kingdom of Malabar there is also another caste of people whom they call Biabares, Indian Merchants, natives of the land. They were there ere foreign nations had sailed to India. They deal in goods of every kind both in the seaports and inland, where so ever their trade is of most profit. They gather to themselves all the pepper and ginger from the Nayres and husbandmen, and offtimes they buy the new crops beforehand in exchange for cotton clothes and other goods which they keep at the seaports. Afterwards they sell them again and gain much money thereby. Their privileges are such that the King of the country in which they dwell cannot execute them by legal process.

There is in this land yet another caste of folk known as Cuiavern. They do not differ from the Nayres, yet by reason of a fault which they committed, they remain separate from them. Their business is to make pottery and bricks for roofing the houses of the Kings and idols, which are roofed with bricks instead of tiles; only these, for as I have already said, other houses are thatched with branches. They have their own sort of idolatry, and their separate idols. There is another Heathen caste which they call Mainatos, whose occupation is to wash clothes for the Kings, Bramenes and Nayres. By this they live, and may not take up any other.

There is another lower caste than these which they call Caletis, who are weavers who have no other way of earning save by weaving of cotton and silk cloths, but they are low caste folk and have but little money, so that they clothe the lower races. They are apart by themselves and have their own idolatry. Besides the castes mentioned above, there are eleven others lower than they within whom the others do not associate, nor do they touch them under pain of death; and there are great distinctions between one and another of them, preserving them from mixture with one another. The purest of all these low, simple folk they call Tuias. Their work is mainly that of tending the palm-groves, and gathering the fruit thereof, and carrying it away for wages on their backs, for there are no beasts of burden in the land. There is another caste still lower than these whom they call Manen (Mancu in the printed text) who neither associate with others nor touch them, nor do the others touch them.

They are washermen for the common people, and makers of sleeping mats, from which occupations all but they are barred; their sons must perforce follow the same trade; they have their own separate idolatry. There is another caste in this land still lower whom they call Canaqus. Their trade is making buckles and umbrellas.

They learn letters for purposes of astronomy, they are great astrologers, and foretell with great truth things that are to come; there are some lords who maintain them for this cause. There is also another lower caste, also Heathens, called Ageres. They are masons, carpenters, smiths, metal workers and some are goldsmiths, all of whom are of a common descent, and a separate caste, and have their idols apart from other folk. They marry, and their sons inherit their property, and learn their fathers' trade. There is another caste still lower in this country called Mogeres, they are almost the same as the Tuias, but they do not touch one another.

They work as carriers of things belonging to the Royal State when it moves from one place to another, but there are very few of them in this land; they are a separate caste; they have no marriage law; the most of them gain their living on the sea, they are sailors, and some of them fishers; they have no idols. They are as well slaves of the Nayres. There is another caste yet lower whom they call Monger, fishers who have no other work than fishing, yet some sail in the Moors' ships and in those of other heathens, and they are very expert seamen. This race is very rude. They are shameless thieves; they marry and their sons succeed them, their women are of loose character, they sleep with any one-so ever, and it is held no evil. They have their own idolatry. In this land of Malabar there is another caste of Heathen even lower than these, whom they call Betunes. Their business is salt making and rice growing, they have no other livelihood. They dwell in houses standing by themselves in the fields away from the roads, whither the gentlefolk do not walk.

They have their own idolatry. They are slaves of the Kings and Nayres and pass their lives in poverty. The Nayres make them walk far away from them and speak to them from afar off. They hold no intercourse with any other caste. There is another caste of Heathen, even lower and ruder, whom they call Paneens, who are great sorcerers, and live by no other means. There is another caste lower and ruder than they, named Revoleens, a very poor folk, who live by carrying firewood and grass to the towns, they may touch none, nor may any touch them under pain of death. They go naked, covering only their private parts with scant and filthy rags, the more part of them indeed with leaves of certain trees. Their women wear many brass rings in their ears; and on their necks, arms and legs necklaces and bracelets of heads. And there is yet another caste of Heathens lower than these whom they call Poleas, who among all the rest are held to be accursed and excommunicate; they dwell in the fields and open campaigns in secret lurking places, whither folk of good caste never go save by mischance, and live in huts very strait and mean.

They are tillers of rice with buffaloes and oxen. They never speak to the Nayres save from off, shouting so that they may hear them, and when they go along the roads they utter loud cries, that they may be let past, and whosoever hears them leaves the road, and stands in the wood till they have passed by: and if any one, whether man or woman, touches them his kinsfolk slay them forthwith, and in vengeance therefore they slay Poleas until they are weary without suffering any punishment. Yet another caste there is even lower and baser called Pareens, who dwell in the most desert places away from all other castes.

They have no intercourse with any person nor any one with them they are held to be worse than devils, and to be damned. Even to see them is to be unclean and out-caste. They eat yams and other roots of wild plants. They cover their middles with leaves, they also eat the flesh of wild beasts. With these end the distinctions between the castes of the Heathen, which are eighteen in all, each one separate and unable to touch others or marry with them; and besides these eighteen castes of the Heathen who are natives of Malabar, which I have now related to you, there are others of outlandish folk, merchants and traders in the land, where they possess houses and estates, living like the natives, yet with customs of their own.

These foreigners were not able to give a full and detailed picture of caste. This is understandable. For to every foreigner the private life of the Hindu is veiled and it is not possible for him to penetrate it. The social organism of India, the play of its motive forces, is moreover, regulated infinitely more by custom, varying according to locality and baffling in its complexity, than by any legal formula which can be picked out of a legal text book. But there is no doubt that caste did appear to the foreigners as the most singular and therefore the most distinguishing feature of Hindu Society. Otherwise they would not have noted its existence in the record they made of what they observed when they came to India.

Caste therefore is something special in the Hindu Social organization and marks off the Hindus from other peoples. Caste has been a growing institution. It has never been the same at all time. The shape and form of caste as it existed when Magasthenes wrote his account was very different from what the shape and form it has taken when Alberuni came and the appearance it gave to the Portuguese was different from what it was in the time of

Alberuni. But to understand caste one must have more exact idea of its nature than these foreigners are able to give.

To follow the discussion of the subject of caste it is necessary to familiarise the readers with some basic conceptions, which underlie the Hindu Social organisation. The basic conception of social organisation which prevails among the Hindus starts with the rise of our classes or varnas into which Hindu society is believed to have become divided. These four classes were named: (1) Brahmins, the priestly and the educated class, (2) The Kshatriyas, the Military Class, (3) The Vaishyas, the trading class and, (4) The Sudras, the servant class. For a time these were merely classes. After a time what were only Classes (Varnas) became Castes (Jatis) and the four castes became four thousand. In this way the modern Caste System was only the evolution of the ancient Varna System. No doubt the caste system is an evolution of the Varna System. But one can get no idea of the caste system by a study of the Varna System. Caste must be studied apart from Varna. An old agnostic is said to have summed up his philosophy in the following words: "The only thing I know is that I know nothing; and I am not quite sure that I know that."

Sir Denzil Ibbetson undertaking to write about caste in the Punjab said that the words of these agnostic about his philosophy expressed very exactly his own feelings regarding caste. It is no doubt true that owing to local circumstances there does appear a certain diversity about caste matters and that it is very difficult to make any statement regarding any one of the castes absolutely true as it may be as regards one locality which will not be contradicted with equal truth as regards the same caste in some other area.

Although this may be true yet it cannot be difficult to separate the essential and fundamental features of caste from its nonessential superficial features. For easy approach to this to ascertain by asking what are the matters for which a person is liable to be excluded from caste. Mr. Bhattacharya has stated the following as causes for expulsion from caste: (1) Embracing Christianity or Islam, (2) Going to Europe or America, (3) Marrying a widow, (4) Publicly throwing the sacred thread, (5) Publicly eating beef, pork or foul, (6) Publicly eating *Kaccha* food prepared by a

Mahomedan, Christian or low caste Hindu, (7) Officiating at the house of a very low caste Sudra, (8) By a female going away from home for immoral purposes and (9) By a widow becoming pregnant. This list is not exhaustive and omits the two most important causes which entail expulsion from caste. They are (10) intermarrying outside caste, (11) Interdining with persons of another caste, (12) Change of occupation. The second defect in the statement of Mr. Bhattacharya is that it does not make any distinction between essentials and (un) essentials. Of course when a person is expelled from his caste the penalty is uniform. His friends, relatives, and fellow men refuse to partake of his hospitality. He is not invited to entertainment in their houses. He cannot obtain brides or bridegrooms for his children. Even his married daughters cannot visit him without running the risk of being excluded from caste. His priest, his barber and washer man refuses to serve him. His fellow caste men sever their connection with him so completely that they refuse to assist him even at the funeral of a member of his household. In some cases the man excluded from caste is debarred access to public temples and to the cremation or burial ground.

These reasons for expulsion from caste indirectly show the rules and regulations of the caste. But all regulations are not fundamental. There are many which are unessential. Caste can exist even without them. The essential and unessential can be distinguished by asking another question. When can a Hindu who has lost caste regain his caste. The Hindus have a system of *Prayaschitas* which are penances and which a man who has been expelled from caste must perform before he can be admitted to cast fellowship. With regard to these *Prayaschitas* or Penances certain points must be remembered. In the first place there are caste offences for which there is no *Prayaschita.* In the second place the *Prayaschitas* vary according to the offence. In some cases the *Prayaschita* involves a very small penalty. In other cases the penalty involved is a very severe one.

The existing of a *Prayaschita* and its absence have a significance which must be clearly understood. The absence of *Prayaschita* does not mean that any one may commit the offence with impunity. On the contrary it means that the offence is of an immeasurable magnitude and the offender once expelled is beyond reclamation. There is no re-entry for him in the caste from which he is expelled. The existence of a *Prayaschita* means that the offence is compoundable. The offender can take the prescribed *Prayaschita* and obtain admission in the caste from which he is expelled. There are two offences for which there is no penance. These are (1) change from Hindu Religion to another religion, (2) Marriage with a person of another caste or another religion. It is obvious if a man loses. Caste for these offences he loses it permanently. Of the other offences the *Prayaschitas* prescribed are of the severest kind are two: (1) Interdining with a person of another caste or a non-Hindu and (2) Taking to occupations which is not the occupation of the caste. In the case of the other offences the penalty is a light one almost nominal.

The surest clue to find out what are the fundamental rules of caste and what caste consists in is furnished by the rules regarding *Prayaschitas*. Those for the infringement of which there is no *Prayaschita* constitute the very soul of caste and those for the infringement of which the *Prayaschita* is of the severest kind make up the body of caste. It may therefore be said without any hesitation that there are four fundamental rules of caste. A caste may be defined as a social group having (a) belief in Hindu Religion and bound by certain regulations as to, (b) marriage, (c) food and (d) occupation. To this one more characteristic may be added namely a social group having a common name by which it is recognised. In the matter of marriage the regulation lays down that the caste must be endogamous. There can be no intermarriage between members of different castes. This is the first and the most fundamental idea on which the whole fabric of the caste is built up.

In the matter of food the rule is that a person cannot take food from and dine with any person who does not belong to his caste. This means that only those who can intermarry can also interdine. Those who cannot intermarry cannot interdine. In other words caste is an endogamous unit and also a communal unit. In the matter of occupation the regulation is that a person must follow the occupation which is the traditional occupation of his caste and if the caste has no occupation then he should follow the occupation of his father. In the matter of status of a person it is fixed and is hereditary.

It is fixed because a person's status is determined by the status of the caste to which he belongs. It is hereditary because a Hindu is stamped with the caste to which his parents belonged, a Hindu cannot change his status because he cannot change his caste. A Hindu is born in a caste and he dies a member of the caste in which he is born. A Hindu may lose his status if he loses caste. But he cannot acquire a new or a better or different status. What is the significance of a common name for a caste? The significance of this will be clear if we ask two questions, which are very relevant, and a correct answer to each is necessary for a complete idea of this institution of caste. Social groups are either organised or unorganised. When the membership of the group and the process of joining and leaving the groups, are the subject of definite social regulations and involve certain duties and privileges in relation to other members of the group then the group is an organised group. A group is a voluntary group in which members enter with a full knowledge of what they are doing and the aims which the association is designed to fulfil. On the other hand there are groups of which an individual person becomes a member without any act of volition, and becomes subject to social regulation and traditions over which he has no control of any kind.

Now it is hardly necessary to say that caste is a highly organised social grouping. It is not a loose or a floating body. Similarly it is not necessary to say that caste is an involuntary grouping. A Hindu is born in a caste and he dies as a member of that caste. There is no Hindu without caste, cannot escape caste and being bounded by caste from birth to death he becomes subject to social regulations and traditions of the caste over which he has no control. The significance of a separate name for a caste lies in this, namely it makes caste an organised and an involuntary grouping.

A separate and a distinctive name for a caste make caste asking to a corporation with a perpetual existence and a seal of separate entity. The significance of separate names for separate castes has not been sufficiently realised by writers on caste. In doing that they have lost sight of a most distinctive feature of caste social groups there are and there are bound to be in every society.

Many social groups in many countries can be equated to various castes in India and may be regarded as their equivalent. Potters, Washermen, Intellectuals, as social groups are every where. But in other countries they have remained as unorganised and voluntary groups while in India they have become organised and involuntary *i.e.* they have become castes is because in other countries the social groups were not given name while in India they did. It is the name which the caste bears which gives it fixate and continuity and individuality. It is the name which defines who are its members and in most cases a person born in a caste carries the name of the caste as apart of his surname. Again it is the name which makes it easy for the caste to enforce its rules and regulations. It makes it easy in two ways. In the first place, the name of the caste forming a surname of the individual prevents the offender in passing off as a person belonging to another caste and thus escape the jurisdiction of the caste. Secondly, it helps to identify the offending individual and the caste to whose jurisdiction he is subject so that he is easily handed up and punished for any breach of the caste rules.

This is what caste means. Now as to the caste system. This involves the study of the mutual relations between different castes. Looked at as a collection of caste the caste system presents several features, which at once strike the observer. In the first place there is no inter-connection between the various castes, which form a systems each caste is separate and distinct. It is independent and sovereign in the disposal of its internal affairs and the endorsement of caste Regulations. The castes touch but they do not interpenetrate. The second feature relates to the order in which one caste stands in relation to the other castes in the system. That order is vertical and not horizontal.

In other words castes are not equal in status. Their order is based on inequality. One caste is higher or lower in relation to another. Castes form an hierarchy in which one caste is at the top and is the highest, another at the bottom and it is the lowest and in between there are castes every one of which is at once above some caste and below some caste, The caste system is a system of gradation in which every caste except the highest and the lowest has a priority and precedence over some other caste: How is this precedence or this superiority determined? This order of superiority and inferiority or this insubordination is determined by Rules (1) which are connected with religious rites and (2) which are connected with commonality. Religion as a basis of Rules of precedence manifests itself in three ways.

Firstly through religious ceremonies, secondly through incantations that accompany the religious ceremonies and thirdly through the position of the priest. Beginning with the ceremonies as a source of rules of precedence it should be noted that the Hindu Scriptures prescribe sixteen religious ceremonies. Although those are Hindu ceremonies every Hindu Caste cannot by right claim to perform all the sixteen ceremonies. Few can claim the right to perform all. Some are allowed to perform certain ceremonies, some are not allowed to perform certain of the ceremonies. For instance take the ceremony of Upanayan, wearing the sacred thread. Some castes can't. Precedence follows this distinction in the matters of right to perform the ceremonies. A caste which can claim to perform all the ceremonies is higher in status than the caste which has a right to perform a few.

Turning to the Mantras it is another source for rules of precedence. According to the Hindu Religion the same ceremony can be performed in three different ways: (1) Vedokta, (2) Shastrokta and (3) Puranokta. In the Vedokta form the ceremony is performed with Mantras (incantations) from the Vedas. In the Shastrokta form the ceremony is performed with Mantras (incantations) from the Shastras. In the Puranokta form the ceremony is performed with Mantras (incantations) from the Puranas. Hindu Religious Scriptures fall into three distinct categories: (1) The Vedas which are four, (2) The Shastras which are six and (3) The Puranas which are eighteen. Although they are all respected as scriptures they do not all have the same sanctity. The Vedas have the highest sanctity. The Shastras stand next in order of sanctity and the Puranas have the lowest sanctity. The way the Mantras give rise to social precedence will be obvious if it is borne in mind that not every caste is entitled to have the ceremony performed in the Vedokta form. Three castes may well claim the right to the performance of one of the sixteen ceremonies. But it well be that one of it is entitled to perform it in the Vedokta form, another in the Shastrokta form and the third only in the Puranokta form. Precedence goes with the kind of Mantra that a caste is entitled to use in the performance of a religious ceremony.

A caste which is entitled to use Vedic Mantra is superior to a caste which is entitled to use Shastrik Mantra and a caste which is entitled to use Shastrik Mantras is higher than a caste which is entitled to use only Puranokta Mantras. Taking the priest as third source of precedence connected with Religion Hinduism requires the instrumentality of a priest for the derivation of the full benefit from the performance of a religious ceremony. The priest appointed by the scriptures is the Brahmin. A Brahmin therefore is indispensable. But the scriptures do not require that a Brahmin shall accept the invitation of any and every Hindu irrespective of his caste to officiate at a religious ceremony. The invitation of which caste he will accept and of which he will refuse is a matter left to the wishes of the Brahmin. By long and well-established custom it is now settled at which caste he will officiate and at which caste he will not. This fact has become the basis of precedence as between castes. The caste at which a Brahmin will officiate is held as superior to a caste at whose religious functions a Brahmin will not officiate.

The second source for rules of precedence is commonality. It will be noticed that rules of marriage have not given rise to rules of precedence as rules of commonality have. The reason lies in the distinction between the rules prohibiting intermarriage and interdining. That difference is obvious. The prohibition on intermarriage is such that it can not only be respected but it can be carried out quite strictly. But the prohibition of interdining creates difficulties. It cannot be carried out quite strictly in all places and under all circumstances. Man migrates and must migrate from place to place. In every place he happens to go he may not find his castemen. He may find himself landed in the midst of strangers. Marriage is not a matter of urgency but food is. He can wait for getting himself married till he returns to the society of his castemen.

But he cannot wait for his food. He must find it from somewhere and from someone. Question arises from which caste he can take food if he has to. The rule is that he will take food from a caste above his but will not take food from a caste, which is below his. There is no way of finding how it came to be decided that a Hindu can take food from one caste and not from another. By long series of precedent every Hindu knows from what caste he can take food and from what caste he cannot. This is determined chiefly by the rule followed by the Brahmin. A caste is higher or lower according as the Brahmin takes from it food or not.

In this connection the Brahmin has a very elaborate set of rules in the matter of food and water. (1) He will take only water from some and not from others. (2) A Brahmin will not take food cooked in water by any caste. (3) He will take only food cooked in oil from some castes. Again he has as a set of rules in the matter of the vessel, in which he will accept food and water. He will take food or water in an earthen vessel from some caste, only in metallic vessel from some and only in glass vessel from others. This goes to determine the level of the caste. If he takes food cooked in oil from a caste its status is higher than the caste from which he will not. If he takes water from a caste it is higher than the caste from which he will not. If he takes water in a metallic vessel that caste is higher than the caste from which he will take water in an earthen vessel and the caste from which he will take water in an earthen vessel is higher than the caste from which he will take water in a glass vessel. Glass is a substance which is called *Nirlep* (which conserves no stain) therefore a Brahmin can take water in it even from the lowest. But other metals do conserve stains. Contaminating character of the stain depends upon the status of the person who has used it. That status depends upon the Brahmin's will to accept water in that vessel. These are some of the factors which determine the place and status of a caste in this Hindu hierarchical system of castes.

Such is caste and such is caste system. Question is, is this enough to know the Hindu Social Organisation. For a static conception of the Hindu Social Organisation an idea of the caste and the caste system is enough. One need not trouble to remember more than the facts that the Hindus are divided into castes and that the castes form a system in which all hang on a thread which runs through the system in such a way that while encircling and separating one caste from another it holds them all as though as it was a string of tennis balls hanging one above the other. But this will not be enough to understand caste as a dynamic phenomenon. To follow the workings of caste in action it is necessary to note one other feature of caste besides the caste system, namely class-caste system.

RELATIONSHIP BETWEEN THE IDEAS OF CASTE AND CLASS

The relationship between the ideas of caste and class has been a matter of lively controversy. Some say that caste is analogous to class. Others hold that the idea of caste is analogous to class and that there is no difference between the two. Others hold that the idea of caste is fundamentally opposed to that of class. This is an aspect of the subject of caste about which more will be said hereafter.

For the present it is necessary to emphasis one feature of the caste system which has not been referred to here in before. It is this. Although caste is different from and opposed to the notion of class yet the caste-system as distinguished from caste recognises a class system which is somewhat different from the graded status referred to above. Just as the Hindus are divided into so many castes, castes are divided into different classes of castes. The Hindu is caste conscious. He is also class conscious. Whether he is caste conscious or class conscious depends upon the caste with which he comes in conflict.

If the caste with which he comes in conflict is a caste within the class to which he belongs he is caste conscious. If the caste is outside the class to which he belongs he is class conscious. Any one who needs any evidence on this point may study the Non-Brahmin Movement in the Madras and Bombay Presidency. Such a study will leave no doubt that to a Hindu caste periphery is as real as class periphery and caste consciousness is as real as class-consciousness. Caste, it is said, is an evolution of the Varna System. I will show later on that this is nonsense. Caste is a perversion of Varna, at any rate it is an evolution in the opposite direction. But while Caste has completely perverted the Varna System it has borrowed the class system from the Varna System. Indeed the Class-Caste System follows closely the class cleavages of the Varna

System. Looking at the caste system from this point of view one comes across several lines of class cleavage which run through this pyramid of castes dividing the pyramid into blocks of castes.

The first line of cleavage follows the line of division noticeable in the ancient Chaturvarna system. The old system of Chaturvarna made a distinction between the first three Varnas, the Brahmins, Kshatriyas, Vaishyas, and the forth Varna namely the Sudras. The three former were classes as the Regenerate classes. The Sudra was held as the unregenerate class. This distinction was based upon the fact that the former were entitled to wear the sacred thread and study the Vedas. The Sudra was entitled to neither and that is why he was regarded as the unregenerate class. This line of cleavage is still in existence and forms the basis of the present day class division separating the castes which have grown out of the vast class of Sudras from those which have grown out of the three classes of Brahmins, the Kashatriyas and Vaishyas. This line of class cleavage is the one which is expressed by the terms High Castes and Low Castes and which are short forms for High Class Castes and Low Class Castes.

Next after this line of cleavage there runs through the pyramid a second line of class cleavage. It runs just below the Low Class Castes. It sets above all the castes born out of the four Varnas *i.e.* The High Castes as well as the Low Castes above the remaining Castes, which I will merely describe as the 'rest'. This line of class cleavage is again a real one and follows the well defined distinction which was a fundamental principle of the Chaturvarna System. The Chaturvarna System as is pointed out made a distinction between the four Varnas putting the three Varnas above the fourth. But it also made an equally clear distinction between those within the Chaturvarna and those outside the Chaturvarna. It had a terminology to express this distinction. Those within the Chaturvarna high or low. Brahmins or Sudras were called *Savarna* *i.e.* those with the stamp of the Varna. That outside the Chaturvarna were called Avarna *i.e.* those without the stamp of Varna. All the Castes, which have evolved out of the four Varnas, are called Savarna Hindus—which is rendered in English by the term caste Hindus. The 'rest' are the *Avarnas* who in present parlance spoken of by Europeans as Non-Caste Hindus *i.e.* those who are outside the 4 original castes or Varnas. Much that is written about the Caste System has reference mostly to the Caste-System, among the Savarna Hindus. Very little is known about the Avarna Hindus. Who are these Avarna Hindus, what is their position in Hindu Society, how are they related to the Savarna Hindus, are questions to which no attention has so far been paid. I am sure that without considering these questions no one can get a true picture of the social structure the Hindus have built. To leave out the Class cleavage between the Savarna Hindus and the Avarna Hindus is to relate Grimm's Fairy Tale which leaves out the witches, the goblins and the ogres.

The Avarna Hindus comprise three divisions: (1) Primitive Castes, (2) Criminal Castes and (3) The Untouchable Castes. The total population of persons comprising these three classes is by no means small. The population of the Primitive Tribes in India according to the Census of 1931 is stated to be about 25 millions. The total population of persons listed as Criminal is somewhere about 4 1/2 millions. The total population of Untouchables in 1931 was about 50 millions. The grand total of these three comes to 79 1/2 millions.

What is the relation of the Savarna Castes to the Avarna Castes? The cleavage between the Savarna Castes and the Avarna Castes is not uniform in its consequences with the result that the position created is not easy to grasp. The line of the cleavage running between the Savarna Castes and the Avarna Castes produces a relationship between the Savarna Castes and the two Avarna Castes—the Primitive and the Criminal Castes which is different from the relationship which it produces between the Savarna Castes and the last of the Avarna Castes namely the Untouchables. This line of cleavage between the Savarna Castes and the first two of the Avarna Castes is a cleavage between kindred and friends. It does not make intercourse on respectful terms between the two impossible. The cleavage between the Savarna Castes and the Untouchables is of a different kind. It is a cleavage between two non-kindred and hostile groups. There is no possibility of friendly intercourse on respectable terms.

What is the significance of this line of cleavage? On what is it based? Although the cleavage is definite the basis of it has not been defined. But it seems that the basis of cleavage is the same as that which exists between the Dwijas and the Sudras. Like the Sudras the Avarna Castes are composed of unregenerate people. They are not twice born and have no right to wear the sacred thread. This also brings out two facts which otherwise are lost sight of. The first fact is that the difference between the Sudra Castes of the Savarna division of cast's and the Primitive and the Criminal Castes of the Avarna division is very thin. Both are touchable and both are unregenerate. The difference is one of cultural development. But although the cultural difference between the two sections is great—as great as there is between a highly cultured and the unmitigated barbarian—from the point of view of the orthodox Hindu, the difference between them is one of degree. It is to mark this difference in culture that the Hindus invented a new terminology which recognised two classes of Sudras: (1) Sat-Sudras and (2) Sudras. Calling the old body of Sudras as Sat Sudras or cultured Sudras and using the term Sudras to those comprising the Primitive Castes who had come within the pale of Hindu Civilisation. The new terminology did not mean any difference in the rights and duties of Sudras. The distinction pointed out those Sudras who were fit for associated life with the Dwijas and those who were less fitted for it.

What is the relation of Avarna Castes to one another? Do they exist as mere collection of castes or have they any class cleavages? They are certainly mere collection of Castes. There are certainly lines of class cleavages running through this block of Avarna Castes. Whether there is a line of class cleavage running between the Primitive Castes and the Criminal Castes may be a matter of some doubt. Perhaps the line is faint. But there is no doubt that there is a very definite a very broad and a very emphatic line of cleavage between the Primitive Castes and the Criminal Castes and the Untouchables. The former two have a very clear notion that they are the higher classes and the Untouchables are the lower classes within this block of Avarna Castes.

The discussion carried on so far reveals three characteristic features of Hindu Social Organisation: (1) Caste, (2) A hierarchical System of Castes and (3) A Class System cutting into the Caste System. Undoubtedly the structure is a very complicated one and it is perhaps difficult for one who has not been woven into it to form a true mental picture of the same. Perhaps a diagrammatic presentation may be helpful. I give below one such representation which in my judgment is calculated to give the idea of this social structure of the Hindus.

A Caste Hindus : C Caste Hindus		: E	Non-Caste Hindus Avarna Castes '	G Non-caste Hindus
Savarna Castes	Savarna Castes			
Class I	Class II		Class III	Class IV
High Castes Dwijas—Castes evolved out of the three Varnas. Brahmins, Kshatriyas and Vaishas.	Low Caste : Shudras-' Castes evolved out of the 4th Varna namely Shudras.	1	Primitive Castes Criminal Castes	Untouchables

This diagram presents a Class-Caste-System of the Hindus and is so drawn as to give a true and a complete picture of their social organisation. This diagram brings out several of its important features. It shows that there are two divisions of Hindus—

(1) Savarna Hindus and

(2) Avarna Hindus.

It shows that within the first division there are two classes of Castes:

(1) Dwijas and

(2) Sudras and within the second division.

There are two Classes of castes:

(1) Primitive and Criminal Castes and

(2) The Untouchable Castes.

The next thing to note is that each caste is enclosed and separated from the rest a fact which is not shown in the diagram each of the four classes of Castes is grouped together and placed within a class enclosure. This enclosure segregates a class of a Caste and marks it off from another class. A class of Castes is not as organised as a Caste is. But a feeling of Class is there. The third thing to note is the nature of partitions used for the enclosures. They are of various strengths, some are permanent, some are temporary. The partition between the Dwijas Castes and the Sudras Castes is not a partition at all. It is only a curtain. It is not a partition at all.

It is intended to keep them aloof. It is not intended to cut them as under. The line of cleavage between the Sudra Castes and the first two of the Avarna Castes is a regular partition. But it is both thin and small. It can be jumped over.

The partition separates but does not cause severance. But the partition between these three classes and the Untouchables is a real and irremovable partition. It is a barbed wire fence and its intention is to mark a severance. To express the same thing in a different way the first three enclosures are so placed that they are one within the other.

The first partition between the Dwijas and the Sudra Castes may be removed the two become the occupants of one enclosure instead of two separate enclosures. Similarly the second partition may be removed in which case the Castes which are Dwija, Sudra, Primitive and Criminal form one whole—if not a single whole—occupying one single enclosure.

But the third partition can never be removed. Because all three Classes of Castes are united on one issue namely that they shall not be *one (This space is left blank in the typed copy of MS. The word 'one' is introduced by us.*—Ed.) with the Untouchables as one united body of people. There is a bar sinister, which serves the Untouchables from the rest and compels them to be apart and outside. The diagram shows the different Classes of Castes one above the other.

This is done to mark the hierarchy, which is an important feature of the Caste System. I have described the two classes of the Savarna Castes as High Class Castes and Low Class Castes. But I have not described the other two classes of Avarna Castes as lower Class Castes and lowest Class Castes. In a sense this would have been correct.

In general social esteem they are no doubt lower and lowest in status. But in another sense this would not be appropriate. The terminology of high, low, lower and lowest assumes that they are parts of one whole. But are the Avarna Castes and the Savarna Castes parts of one whole? They were not.

The Primitive and the Criminal Castes were not in contemplation when the plan of the Varna System, the parent of the present caste system, was laid. Consequently nothing is said about their status and position in the rules of the Varna System. But that is not the case with ihe Untouchables. They were within the contemplation of the Varna System and the Rule of the Varna System with regard to the Untouchables is very clear and very definite. The rule as laid down by Manu the Hindu Law giver is that there are only four Varnas and that there is not to be a fifth Varna.

The reformers who are friends of Mr. Gandhi in his campaign for removal of Untouchability are endeavouring to give a new meaning to the statement of Manu. They say that Manu has been misunderstood. According to Manu there is no fifth Varna and therefore he intended to include the Untouchables into the 4th Varna namely the Sudras.

But this is an obvious perversion. What Manu meant was there were originally four Varnas and four they must remain. He was not going to admit the Untouchables into the House the ancient Hindus had built by enlarging the Varna System to consist of five Varnas. That is what he meant when he said that there is not to be a fifth Varna. That he wanted the Untouchables to remain out of the Hindu social structure is clear from the name by which he describes the Untouchables. He speaks of them as Varna—Bahyas (those outside the Varna System). That is the difference between the Primitive and Criminal Castes and the Untouchables. There being no positive injunction against their admission in Hindu Society they may in course of time become members of it.

At present they are linked to Hindu Society and hereafter they may become integrated into it and become part of it. But the case of the Untouchables is different. There is positive injunction against their incorporation in Hindu Society. There is no room for reform. They must remain separate and segregated without being a part of the Hindu Society. The Untouchables are not a part of the

Hindu Society. And if they are a part they are a part but not of the whole.

The idea showing the connection between the Hindus and the Untouchables was accurately expressed by Ainapure Shastri the leader of the orthodox Hindus at a Conference held in Bombay. He said that the Untouchables were related to the Hindus as a man is to his shoe. A man wears a shoe. In that sense it is attached to man and may be said to be a part of the man. But it is not part of the whole for two things that can be attached and detached can't be said to form parts of one whole. The analogy though is none the less accurate.

AUTHORITY BEHIND RELIGIOUS SANCTION

The Sacral source of the authority behind religious sanction comes primarily from the individual and only secondarily from the group. That is the noteworthy peculiarity of the social source of religious sanction. It prepares the individual to uphold the religious beliefs. It dispenses with the necessity of the group using its social group.

That is why the sacral source of its authority makes religious sanction of such high order as to supersede all other sanctions indeed to dispense with them. That is why the Religious sanction alone becomes sufficient to maintain the integrity of religious beliefs which even time and circumstances have proved powerless to affect. The way this happens is easy to follow. The Sacred inspires in the individual the sentiment of reverence and deference, which he certainly has not for the profane.

To use the language of Durkheim, "The simple defence inspired by men with high social functions is not different in nature from religious respect (for the sacred). It is expressed by the same movements: a man keeps at a distance from high personage; he approaches him only with precautions; in conversing with him, he used other gestures and language than that used with ordinary mortals." The Sacred creates the sentiment of Reverence.

It also creates the sentiment that it is inviolate. When a belief becomes consecrated as a sacred thing, it is forbidden to touch it, to deny it or to contest it. There is a prohibition of criticism of the

Sacred. The Sacred is 'untouchable and above discussion". When an individual is saturated with these sentiments, when these sentiments become a part of his being, he himself becomes an upholder and protector of what he is taught to regard as something sacred. This is exactly what the Hindus have done in the matter of Caste.

They have given caste a place in the Vedas. Caste has thereby become sacred because the Vedas are Sacred. It would be wrong to say that the Vedas are sacred because they are religious. The position is that they are religious because they are sacred. It might appear that the Hindus have no name for the Veda directly expressing the feeling of sacredness, which the Hindu entertains towards the Vedas.

Veda simply means knowledge. That may be so. But there can be no doubt that they regard the Vedas as sacred. Indeed the term they apply to Vedas expresses a far greater degree of reverence than the word sacred does.

They call the Vedas *Shruti,* which means the word of God heard by (*i.e.* revealed to) man. In the primitive religion the Sacred is what man has made. In the Hindu religion the Sacred is what God has appointed it to be. The Hindus regard the Vedas as the Sacred Book of their religion. They put the Vedas in a class by themselves.

The Hindus hold that there are cycles of creations called *Kalpas.* At the end of every cycle there is a deluge and a new cycle of creation begins. At the end of a Kalpa, the Vedas are destroyed in the deluge. At the beginning of every Kalpa they are revealed by God. Accordingly the *Vedas* were destroyed in the deluge at the end of the last *Kalpa* and that the beginning of the present *Kalpa* commencing with the *Krita Yug,* they were revealed by God to the *Rishis.* The Vedas are regarded by the Hindus as *Nitya* (enternal) *Anadi* (beginningless) and *Apaurusheya* (not made by man), In short the Vedas are the words of God and constitute God's ordinances to man.

Even if the Vedas were not called *Shruti* they would have had the impressiveness of the 'Sacred'. Religions have been variously classified by Prof. Max Muller. Natural as against Revealed is one way of classifying them. Individual as against National is another way. The third way of classifying them is to call them Atheistic, Deistic, Dualistic, Polytheistic, Monotheistic, Henotheistic and Animistic. True and False is also another way of classifying Religions.

Bookless Religions and Religions with books are two classes into which Religion could be grouped. This probably does not exhaust the ways of classifying Religions. For there remains one more distinction to be made, namely Religions which have founders and religions which have no founders. These distinctions have social significance except two.

They are the distinctions between Natural and Revealed and that between Bookless Religion and Book Religion. They differ in their function although that difference is not often noted. The Book religion has a definite advantage over a Bookless religion. A Book religion is a Religion with a written constitution. A Bookless Religion is a Religion without a written constitution. A book religion creates the impression that it is true which a bookless religion cannot.

By comparison with a book religion, a bookless religion wears the inferiority complex of being false. In the language of Max Muller Religions with books are alone "considered as real religions, and though they may contain false doctrines, they are looked upon as a kind of aristocracy to whom much may be forgiven, while the vulgar crowd of bookless or illiterate religions are altogether out of Court". It is easy to understand the superiority accorded to a religion with a book over a bookless religion. When 'black on white' has become synonymous with true, it may seem very natural that a religion which is written, which is something black on white is not false. The Book serves as the voucher for truth. A religion without a book has no voucher.

The social significance of a religion with a book lies in the fact that it controls the mind of the people by giving them the impression that the religion contained in the book is true. It gives Religion authority over people and induces willing obedience in them. But however a Religion may appear to be true by reason of the fact that it is a book religion, such appearance cannot save

Religion from going under, if beliefs and rites empirically erroneous have crept into it. Man may go wrong in theory but his practical instincts will seldom allow him to go after a wrong theory for a long time. Unless therefore the religious beliefs of a social group are true, practically Religion must in the long run give way.

Herein comes the social significance of the distinction between Natural Religion and Revealed Religion. A Revealed Religion has superiority over Natural Religion. Natural Religion is used by several writers to certain historical forms of religion. Something which has grown along with the growth of people as result of the interaction between the needs of the peoples and the environment in which they are placed. A natural religion is made by man. Its sanction is the sense of truth and the voice of conscience that is to be found in man. A Revealed Religion does not rest on the authority of man. It is not man-made, it is God-made. Its sanction is God who is absolute truth and absolute good. The function of Revealed Religion is to make religion sacred therefore inviolate and immune from criticism. The Vedas have the characteristics of both.

They have the advantage, which a Religion with a book has over the Bookless Religion. They have the advantage, which a Revealed Religion has over Natural Religion. This discussion is intended to enforce the conclusion that Caste being preached by the Vedas, it automatically gets the authority of the written book and the sanctity of the divine word. As a scheme propounded by the Veda it is doubly protected. Every one must accept Caste because it is divine truth and no body must attack it as an error without being guilty of sacrilege because it is sacred.

This is the Hindu view of Caste and the average Hindu is not impressed by the modern explanation of it by Risley with his racial theory, by Senart with his occupational theory, by Nesfield with his functional theory. He knows and he believes that Caste must have been created by God, because it is mentioned in the Vedas which is *Shruti* or the word of God. It is therefore eternal and true.

That Caste is divine, that caste is sacred and that caste must therefore remain eternal has been the line of defence adopted by the Brahmins whenever they have been called out to defend 'Caste' against the criticism of its opponents. This view of Caste comes out in its luminous colours in the controversy that once raged on the subject of Caste between Brahmins on the one hand and Buddha and his followers, on the other *i.e.*: If the belief was once established, that not only the simple effusions of the Rishis, but the pointed doctrines of the Brahmanas also, emanated from a divine source and could not therefore be attacked by human reasoning, it is clear that every opposition to the privileges which the Brahmans claimed for themselves, on the sacred authority of the Veda, became heresy; and where the doctrines of the Brahmans were the religion of the people, or rather of the king, such opposition was amenable to the hierarchical laws of the state.

The Brahmans themselves cared much more to see the divine authority of the Sruti as such implicitly acknowledged, than to maintain the doctrines of the Rishis in their original simplicity and purity. In philosophical discussions, they allowed the greatest possible freedom; and, although at first three philosophical systems only were admitted as orthodox (the two Mimansas and the Nyaya), their number was soon raised to six, so as to include the Vaiseshika, Sankhya, and Yoga-schools.

The most conflicting views on points of vital importance were tolerated as long as their advocates succeeded, no matter by what means, in bringing their doctrines into harmony with passages of the Veda, strained and twisted in every possible sense. If it was only admitted that besides the perception of the senses and the induction of reason, revelation also, as contained in the Veda, furnished a true basis for human knowledge, all other points seemed to be of minor importance. Philosophical minds were allowed to exhaust all possible views on the relation between the real and transcendental world, the Creator and the created, the divine and the human nature.

It was not from such lucubrations that danger was likely to accrue to the caste of the Brahmans. Nor was the heresy of Buddha Sakya Muni found so much in his philosophical doctrines, many of which may be traced in the orthodox atheism of Kapila. His real crime lay in his opposition to the exclusive privileges and abuses of the Brahmans. These abuses were sanctioned by the divine authority of the Veda, and particularly of the Brahmans. In attacking the abuses, Buddha attacked the divine authority on which they were founded, and the argument was short: he is a heretic; anathema etc.

Buddha was Kshatriya. He was of principal origin, and belonged to the nobility of the land. He was not the first of his caste who opposed the ambition of the Brahmans. Several centuries before Buddha, Vishvamitra, who, like Buddha, was a member of the royal caste, had to struggle against the exclusiveness of the priests.

At that early time, however, the position of the Brahmans was not yet impregnable; and Vishvamitra, although a Kshatriya, succeeded in gaining for himself and his family the rights for which he struggled, and which the Brahmans had previously withheld from all but their own caste. King Janaka of Videha again, whose story is given in the Brahmanas, refused to submit to the hierarchical pretensions of the Brahmans, and asserted his right of performing sacrifices without the intercession of priests. However great the difference may have been between the personal character of these two men and of Buddha, the first principle of their opposition was the same.

All three were equally struggling against the over-wining pretensions of a selfish priesthood. But while Vishvamitra contented himself with maintaining the rights of his tribe or family, and became reconciled as soon as he was allowed to share in the profits of the priestly power, while King Janaka expressed himself satisfied with the homage paid to him by Yajnavalkya and other Brahmans, while, in short, successive reformers as they appeared were either defeated or gained over to the cause of the Brahmans, the seeds of discontent were growing up in the minds of the people.

There is a dark chapter in the history of India, the reported destruction of all the Kshatriyas by Parsurama. It marks the beginning of the hierarchical supremacy of the Brahmans. Though the Brahmans seem never to have aspired to the royal power, their caste, as far as we know the history and traditions of India, has always been in reality the ruling caste. Their ministry was courted as the only means of winning divine favour, their doctrines were admitted as infallible, their gods were worshipped as the only true gods, and their voice was powerful enough to stamp the simple strains of the Rishis, and the absurd lucubrations of the authors of the Brahmans, with a divine authority. After this last step, however, the triumph of Brahmanism was preparing its fall.

In India, less than in any other country, would people submit to a monopoly of truth; and the same millions who were patiently bearing the yoke of a political despotism threw off the fetters of an intellectual tyranny. In order to overthrow one of the oldest religions of the world, it was sufficient that one man should challenge the authority of the Brahmans, the gods of the earth (Bhudeva), and preach among the scorned and degraded creatures of God the simple truth that salvation was possible without the mediation of priests, and without a belief in books to which these very priests had given the title of revelation. This man was Buddha, a Sakya Muni. Now if we inquire how Buddha's doctrines were met by the Brahmans, it is true that here and there in their philosophical works, they have endeavoured to overthrow some of his metaphysical axioms by an appeal to reason. An attempt of this kind we have, for instance, in Vachaspati Misra's commentary on the Vedanta Sutras.

In commenting on the tenets of Buddha, that "ideas like those of being, and not being, &c., do not admit of discussion", Vachaspati observes that the very fact of speaking of these ideas, includes the possibility of their conception; nay, that to affirm they do not admit of reasoning, involves an actual reasoning on them, and proves that the mind can conceive the idea of being as different from that of not-being. Such, however, were not the usual weapons with which Brahmanism fought against Buddhism. The principal objection has always been, that Buddha's teaching could not be true, because it did not derive its sanction from Sruti or revelation. The Brahmans, as a caste, would readily have allowed being and not being, and the whole of Buddha's philosophy, as they did the Sankhya philosophy, which on the most important points is in open opposition to the Vedanta.

But while Kapila, the founder of the Sankhya school, conformed to the Brahmanic test by openly proclaiming the authority of revelation as paramount to reasoning and experience, Buddha would not submit to this, either for his philosophical (abhidharma), or for his much more important moral and religious doctrines (vinaya). No doubt it would have been easy for him to show how some of his doctrines harmonised with passages of the Veda, as in the Veda all possible shades of the human mind have found their natural reflection.

If he had done so only for some of his precepts, such, for instance, as, "Thou shall not murder", "Thou shall not drink", "Thou shall eat standing", the Brahmans would readily have passed over other doctrines, even such as came into practice after Buddha's death, like "Who longs for heaven, shall worship the holy sepulchre", "He shall pull out his hair", &c. As he refused to do so, the line of argument taken by the Brahmans was simply confined to an appeal to revelation, in disproof of the possibility of the truth of Buddha's doctrines.

There must be something very tempting in this line of argument, for we see that in later times the Buddhists also endeavoured to claim the same divine character for their sacred writings which the Brahmans had established for the Veda. A curious instance of this is given in the following discussion, from Kumarila's Tantra-varttika.

Here the opponent (purva-paksha) observes, that the same arguments which prove that the Veda is not the work of human authors, apply with equal force to Sakya's teaching. His authority, he says, cannot be questioned, because his precepts are clear and intelligible; and as Sakya is not the inventor, but only the teacher of these precepts, and no name of an author is given for Sakya's doctrines, the frailties inherent in human authors affect them as little as the Veda.

Everything, in fact, he concludes, which has been brought forward by the Mimansakas to prove the authority of the Veda, proves in the same way the authority of Buddha's doctrine, Upon this, the orthodox Kumarila grows very wroth, and says: These Sakyas, Vaiseshikas, and other heretics who have been frightened out of their wits by the faithful Mimansakas, prattle away with our own words as if trying in lay hold of a shadow.

They say that their sacred works are eternal; but they are of empty minds, and only out of hatred they wish to deny that the Veda is the most ancient book. And these would-be logicians declare even, that some of their precepts (which they have stolen from us,) like that of universal benevolence, are not derived from the Veda, because most of Buddha's other sayings are altogether against the Veda. Wishing, therefore, to keep true on this point also, and seeing that no merely human precept could have any authority on moral and supernatural subjects, they try to veil their difficulty by aping our own argument for the eternal existence of the Veda. They know that the Mimansakas have proved that no sayings of men can have any authority on supernatural subjects; they know also that the authority of the Veda cannot be contradicted, because they can bring forward nothing against the proofs adduced for its divine origin, by which all supposition of a human source have been removed.

Therefore, their hearts being gnawed by their own words, which are like the smattering of children, and having themselves nothing to answer, because the deception of their illogical arguments has been destroyed, they begin to speak like a foolish suitor who came to ask for a bride, saying, 'My family is as good as your family'.

In the same manner they now maintain the eternal existence of their books, aping the speeches of others. And if they are challenged and told that this is our argument, they brawl, and say that we, the Mimansakas have heard and stolen it from them. For a man who has lost all scheme, who can talk away without any sense, and tries to cheat his opponent, will never get tired, and will never be put down! "Towards the end of this harangue, Kumarila adds, what is more to the point, that the Buddhas, who ascribe to everything a merely temporary existence, have no business to talk of an eternal revelation."

From the foregoing discussion it will be seen that Caste is born in religion which has consecrated it and made it Sacred so that it can be rightly and truly said that Religion is the Rock on which the Hindus have built their social structure. Does this not show that Caste is a very peculiar institution not to be compared with other forms of social grouping? I venture to say that any one who maintains that there is nothing strange in caste simply does not know what Caste is. I repeat that Caste is Sacred, which is its distinguishing feature. Caste is Sacred, which is what makes it abiding.

Prof. Max Muller makes some very instructive observations on the effects of Religion with Sacred books on the progress of Society. Says Max Muller: History, however, teaches us another lesson, namely that codes of law are apt to become a kind of fetish, requiring an implicit and unquestioning submission, that their historical or natural origin is often completely forgotten, and that the old ideas of what is right and just are almost absorbed, nay, almost annihilated, in the one idea of what is written and legal. The study of Eastern religions teaches us the same lesson.

Sacred books often become a kind of fetish, requiring an implicit and unquestioning faith; their historical or natural origin is often completely forgotten, and the old ideas of what is true and divine are almost absorbed in the one idea of what is written and orthodox. And there is a third lesson which history teaches us.

The sense of responsibility of every citizen for the law under which he lives is in great danger of becoming deadened, when law becomes a profession and is administered with mechanical exactness rather than with a strong human perception of what is right and what is wrong. Nor can it be denied that the responsibility of every believer for the religion under which he lives is in the same danger of becoming deadened, when religion becomes a profession, and is administered with ceremonial exactness rather than with a strong human perception of what is true and what is false.

My object, however, is not to show the dangers which arise from sacred books, but rather to protest against the prejudice which prevails so widely against religions which have no sacred books. There is great difference between book-religions and bookless religions, and the difference offers, from an historical point of view, a very true ground of division. But because the book-religions have certain advantages, we must not imagine that the bookless religions are mere outcasts. They have their disadvantages, no doubt; but they have a few advantages also.

A Blackfoot Indian, when arguing with a Christian missionary, described the difference between his own religion and that of the white man in the following words: 'There were two religions given by the Great Spirit, one in a book for the guidance of the white men who, by following its teachings, will reach the white man's heaven; the other is in the hands of the Indians, in the sky, rocks, rivers, and mountains. And the red men who listen to God in nature will hear his voice, and find at last the heaven beyond.'

"Now that religion which is in the head and in the heart, and in the sky, the rocks, the rivers and the mountains is what we call Natural Religion. It has its roots in nature, in human nature, and in that external nature which to us is at the same time the veil and the revelation of the Divine.

It is free, it grows with the growth of the human mind, and adapts itself to the requirements of every age. It does not say, 'Thou shall, but rather, 'I will'. These natural or bookless religions are not entirely without settled doctrines and established customs. They generally have some kind of priesthood to exercise authority in matters of faith, morality, and ceremonial.

But there is nothing hard and unchangeable in them, nothing to fetter permanently the growth of thought. Errors when discovered, can be surrendered, a new truth, if clearly seen and vigorously defended, can be accepted.

If, however, there is once a book, something black on white, the temptation is great, is almost irresistible, to invest it with a more than human authority in order to appeal to it as infallible, and as beyond the reach of human reasoning. We can well understand what the ancient poets of the Veda meant by calling their hymns God-given, or by speaking of them as what they had seen or heard, not what they had elaborated themselves. But a new generation gave a new meaning to these expressions, and ended by representing every thought and word and letter of the Veda as 'God-given,' or revealed. This was the deathblow given to the Vedic religion, for whatever cannot grow and change must die. From this danger the bookless religion are exempt." Similar observations are made by Sir William Muir. Speaking of Islam he has given powerful expression to the dangers arising from Sacred Codes of Religion. Sir William Muir says: "From the stiff and rigid shroud in which it is thus swathed, the religion of Mahomed cannot emerge. It has no plastic power beyond that exercised in its earliest days. Hardened now and inelastic, it can neither adapt itself, nor yet shape its votaries, nor even suffer them to shape themselves, to the varying circumstances, the wants and developments of mankind". (Quoted by E de Bunsen in an article in the Asiatic Quarterly Review, April, 1889, Mahomed's Place in the Church, p. 287.) Every one who is interested in the progress of humanity cannot fail to echo these sentiments regarding the social consequences of Sacred Codes of Religion.

But it seems to me that a further distinction is possible within the Class of Religion with Sacred Codes. It is a pity that Prof. Max Muller did not pursue the matter further. But it is worth pursuing because it discloses a difference which is very real which marks off the Hindus as a people with a Sacred Code of Religion from other people also possessing a Sacred Code of Religion. The difference will be clear if one begins to examine the different religions to find out what are the objects which religions have sought to consecrate. Such an examination will show that there are instances where Society has consecrated inanimate things and inculcated on the minds of its members the religious belief that they are sacred. There are cases where stones, rivers, trees are made gods and goddesses. There are instances where Society has consecrated living things and inculcated on the minds of its members the religious belief that they are sacred. There are cases of animals which have become clan totems. There are instances where Society has consecrated human beings and inculcated the religious beliefs that they are sacred.

Religion and Made Sacred

But there are no instances where a particular Social Order has been consecrated by Religion and made Sacred. The primitive world had its clan order and its tribal order. But the clan or the tribal order was only a social order and was never consecrated by religion and made sacred and inviolate. The ancient world countries like Egypt, Persia, Rome, Greece etc., each had its social order in which some were free and some were slaves, some were citizens, some were aliens, some of one race, some of another. This class order again was only a social order and was never consecrated by religion and made sacred and inviolate. The modern world has its order, in some it is Democracy, in some Fascism, in some Nazism and in some Bolshevism. But here again the order is only Social order. It is not consecrated by religion and made sacred and inviolate.

Nowhere has Society consecrated its occupations, the ways of getting a living. Economic activity has always remained outside the sanctity of religion. Hunting society was not without religion. But hunting as an occupation was not consecrated by religion and made sacred. Pastrol Society was not without religion. But pasturage was not consecrated by religion and made sacred. Farming as an occupation did not become consecrated by religion and made sacred. Feudalism with its gradations, with its Lords, villains and serfs was a purely social in character. There was nothing sacred about it. The Hindus are the only people in the world whose Social order the relation of man to man is consecrated by religion and made sacred eternal and inviolate.

The Hindus are the only people in the world whose economic order the relation of workman to workman is consecrated by religion and made sacred, eternal and inviolate. It is not therefore enough to say that the Hindus are a people with a sacred code of Religion. So are the Zoroastrians, Israelites, Christians and Muslims. All these have sacred codes. They consecrate beliefs and rites and make them sacred. They do not prescribe, nor do they consecrate a particular form of social structure the relationship between man and man in a concrete form and make it sacred inviolate. The Hindus are singular in this respect. This is what has given caste its abiding strength to defy the ravages of time and the onslaughts of time. There is one other respect in which Hindus differ from other folk possessing codified religions similar to that of the Hindus.

The Hindu Code of Religion is a revelation from God. That is why the Vedas are called Shruti (what is heard). So are the Codes of Religions accepted by the Zoroastrians, Jews, Christians and Muslims. Ask to whom this God's word sent to the Zoroastrian, Jews, Christians, and Muslims was revealed, who heard this word of God? The Zoroastrian will say that the word of God contained in their Religious Code was heard by Zoroaster. The Jews will say it was heard by Moses, Christians will say it was heard by Jesus and Muslims will say it was heard by Muhammad. Now ask the Hindu who heard the word of God contained in the Vedas, to whom was it revealed. The Hindu has no answer.

He cannot name the person who heard this word of God. Now the Mantras contained in the Vedas have their authors mentioned in the Vedas themselves. But the Hindus will not say that these are the persons who heard the word of God, which is contained in the Vedas. This difference goes a great way to protect the sacred character of the Vedas. For the Bible as a Sacred Book can be attacked by attacking the character of Moses or Jesus. Similarly, the Quran as a Sacred Book can be attacked by attacking the character of Mahommed. But the Veda cannot be attacked by attacking the character of the messenger or the founder. For the simple reason that there is none. As I have said Religion is the Rock on which the Hindus have built their house. It will now be seen that it is not an ordinary sort of hard Rock. It is granite.

9 Movements Against Caste within Hinduism

PROMINENT MOVEMENT

The most prominent movement within the framework of Hinduism to fight against casteism was the Bhakti movement. Though started first in Tamil Nadu as early as in 6th century BC by Shaiva saints, it found a powerful expression against caste system when Veerashaiva movement was led by Basavanna in Karnataka in 12th century. The Bhakti movement democratised, broad-based and humanised Hinduism as never before. Even if it may not have succeeded in eliminating caste system, it brought home the important fact that caste distinctions based on birth can have no sanctity in the eyes of god. The movement effectively undermined the authority of texts, which supported caste, though a false impression was also created more by upper castes than by lower castes that Vedas supported caste. As a result, several Bhakti sects declared that they rejected the authority of the Vedas, prominent among them being the Veerashaiva movement and Sikhism. The Bhakti movement cut across not only castes, but even religions and spread all over India.

Kabir in north India, Shishunal Sharif in Karnataka, and Shirdi Sai Baba in Maharashtra were born as Muslims, but were a part of Bhakti movement and highly respected by Hindus. The movement explicitly and powerfully condemned caste system, including untouchability. Basavanna's movement in Karnataka was most aggressively against caste, and included several Dalit Sharanas and Sharanes as pointed out earlier. Basavanna went to the extent of getting a Brahmin disciple's daughter married to an untouchable disciple's son, causing a serious commotion.

Basavanna was far ahead of his time. Since the lower castes were from the working class, he preached dignity of manual labour as an important principle of his philosophy. The Bhakti movement in Maharashtra also was very similar, drawing saint-poets from the lower caste working class, though it included brahmins too.

The movement in Maharashtra was started by an outcaste Brahmin, Sant Jnaneshwar, whose family lost caste because his father, a Sannyasi renounced sannyasa and got married on receiving a message from god to that effect. The movement in Maharashtra too emphasised dignity of manual labour. There is thus quite a lot of evidence to show that Hinduism constantly, deliberately and consciously fought against caste system and untouchability from time to time, even before the modern age and before the influence of western ideas. Apart from the scattered and sporadic attacks on caste system, there were also concerted attempts to lift individual communities of untouchables as a whole and to bring them into the mainstream. These attempts started from the 19th century itself. Two glorious examples may be taken-that of Ezhavas in Kerala and Nadars in Tamil Nadu. Both examples relate to the pre-independence period of late 19th to early 20th century. These examples are of great interest as they involved two Dalit communities elevating their caste status entirely through self-efforts and very much within the framework of Hinduism. They have been much more successful than other efforts involving conversion to other faiths for the purpose of elevation in social status.

Shri Narayan Guru (1854-1928) was the chief force behind elevating the social status of Ezhavas, who is venerated by them as well as by others. He gave three slogans to his followers: "One caste, one religion, and one god for man". "Ask not, say not, think not caste." "Whatever be the religion, let man improve himself." Though a religious leader, his religion was not sectarian and emphasised that all human beings are equal before god. He wanted to totally remove all caste consciousness. When he saw that the caste Hindus did not permit the entry of Ezhavas and other dalits into temples, he first started building new temples for them into which non-dalits too could enter. Then he started vedic schools where Dalit priests could be trained both in rituals and the philosophy of Hinduism. Next, he encouraged general and secular education for all, by starting schools and colleges.

His initial temple building programme was only to mobilise his community, but his later emphasis was more on general education so that all Ezhavas and other dalits could get properly educated and seek good opportunities. He also started credit cooperative societies so that the dependence of dalits on higher castes was avoided. Thus, the guru sought all-round development of dalits. Like Gandhiji, he also tried to change the attitudes of upper castes. He did not preach hatred of upper castes to his followers, as he did not want a rift between them. An example of his success in this regard is the support he received from progressive sections of upper castes, which resulted in a Savarna procession in support of dalits' entry in to the famous Vaikom temple during temple entry satyagraha started by Gandhiji.

Narayana Guru and Gandhiji worked together in temple entry movement. Narayana Guru did not confine himself only to his own community of Ezhavas. There were other communities among untouchables in Kerala, which were even lower in social status than Ezhavas. But the guru involved them too in his attempts to elevate the status of all dalits. Though the Nadars did not seem to have had the advantage of a charismatic and religious leader like Narayana Guru, they also did equally well under their secular leaders. The elevation of caste status came mainly through the spread of education and skills, mutual self-help by making credit available for starting enterprises, by helping caste members secure jobs by functioning as an informal employment exchange and also through Sanskritisation. The members of both these communities- Ezhavas and Nadars are now highly literate and occupy important positions. Nadars have also emerged economically strong, creating a niche for themselves in industry and commerce.

The example of Ezhavas and Nadars offers important lessons for dalits. It is not enough to build their own organisation merely to spread awareness, make demands and protest against in justice, but it is also equally necessary to launch constructive programmes for the welfare of the community. The tendency to rely mainly on making demands on the government to promote social welfare among dalits is not enough. By its very nature, government bureaucracy has limitations in promoting social welfare and social mobility. The communities' own efforts at constructive programmes are also necessary. These programmes may be to induce Dalit parents to send their children to schools, to help them in getting training and skills for jobs outside their traditional vocations, to provide guidance and help to those who wish to migrate from villages to towns and cities and help in getting jobs and houses, preventing addiction to liquor and so on. The community organisations of both Nadars and Ezhavas took care of the members of their communities like parents. Once Dalit organisations take up constructive programmes, help will come to them in a big way from private sources too like voluntary and social service organisations and philanthropic associations.

The successful example of Ezhavas and Nadars also has shown how irrelevant are conversions to other faiths to solve Dalit problem. Another important lesson, particularly from Shri Narayana Guru, is that his movement was not adversarial in character. He broke through upper caste resistance to social change, without making enemies of them. He could even enlist their cooperation and support. He was Gandhian in his approach. In Indian ethos, conciliation seems to have been far more successful in effecting change than confrontation. A difference between Ezhava and Nadar movements, however, is that the former was not concentrated only on one community, but aimed at reaching all untouchables and lower castes which suffered social deprivation. It was a serious attempt to hit out at ritual hierarchy, which existed among dalits themselves. Success in this task, however, perhaps was not as great as in elevating the status of Ezhavas. Both Nadars' and Ezhavas' movements however, were successful in significantly reducing social deprivation among two numerically important untouchable communities, which had also a higher level of social status than others among dalits. There have been more movements in modern Hinduism, which are not caste or community based and have helped to enrich the moral and spiritual life of their followers-such as those led by Ramakrishna Mission, Aurobindo, Brahmakumaris, ISKON, Shri Satya Sai Baba and Mata Amritanandamayi. Their main significance for this paper is that they have shown that Hinduism can very well thrive without caste system. 19

How then did Caste System Emerge and Survive?

If all that is contended above is true and if Hinduism as a religion and philosophy was against caste system based on birth, and even in practice, it opposed the system, how did it emerge and survive for so long? Simply because, the system performed certain functions that were valued by the society. These functions had nothing to do with religion, being entirely in the 'Aihika' (mundane) sphere. The unfortunate part of the story is that caste identities have outlived these functions. These functions may now be enumerated and explained.

A System of Checks and Balances

The varna system was not just a division of labour. It was also a system of checks and balances such that there is no concentration of power in any varna or class. It was more a system to avoid concentration of power than one meant for appropriation of economic surplus. As per the varna system, brahmins were not supposed to seek regal power. Their duty was to seek knowledge and preserve the Vedas and carry on the vedic tradition. They were not supposed to amass wealth and had to depend on other varnas for their sustenance. According to dharmashastras, 'a brahmana (Brahmin) should not hanker after gifts; he may collect them only for his livelihood, a brahmana taking more than what is required for his maintenance incurs degradation' (Kane 1990: Vol II, Part 1, p 531). As Dumont says there was a clear separation of ritual status from material power.

While the duty of Kshatriyas, particularly of kings, was to maintain law and order, protect Dharma and defend people, they too had no absolute power. It was their duty to consult their ministers and listen to people and meet their grievances. The ministry consisted of representatives of all varnas, including shudras. B. R. Ambedkar cites Shantiparva of Mahabharata, in which Bhishma advises Yudhisthira (Dharmaraja) to have four brahmins, eight Kshatriyas, 21 vaishyas and three shudras as ministers to guide him in the affairs of the state (Moon 1990:112). The relatively large allocation to vaishyas may be reflective of their numerical majority as agriculturists then, apart from their being merchants too. It is also possible that vaishyas were the largest source of revenue for the state and hence were given greater representation. If the king was unable to uphold Dharma or protect people and their property, he could even be removed by the ministers with the support of people, according to dharmashastras. A picture of harmony and perfect alliance may not always have been obtained, but it was at least the ideal.

Division of Labour-Easy Acquisition of Skills and Knowledge

Though there was significant social mobility initially, varnas became gradually hereditary and jati system evolved with increasing division of labour and specialisation. It was easier for skills and knowledge to be imparted within family from father to children as there were no trade schools or polytechnics as such. Education in skills and knowledge required in hereditary occupations began quite early right at home from childhood. As families became specialised in arts and crafts, they flourished and sought even distant markets. Kane observes that "professional castes were wealthy and well organised" as seen from dharmashastras and epigraphic records. The organisation had reached such sophistication that there were larger professional associations called as 'gana', and village level associations called as 'sangha'. Kane observes further that 'the Sudra gradually rose in social status so far as occupation was concerned and could follow all occupations except those specially reserved for the brahmana, so much so that Sudra became even kings and Manu (IV. 61) had expressly to enjoin upon brahmanas not to dwell in the kingdom of a Sudra' (ibid:121).

Interestingly, while vaishyas and shudras were so organised in professional associations or guilds, there were no such organisations for brahmins. As Kane says, 'the Brahmanas had no organised corporate body like for Anglican church with its hierarchy of archbishops, bishops and other divines' (ibid:118). It is often argued that being at the top of the caste system brahmins designed the caste system and perpetuated it by giving religious sanctity. But they did not have an organisation to enforce it. The caste system could not have continued because of a small minority, which had neither regal nor monetary power. It continued only because all castes accepted it as in their interest.

Decentralised Democracy-Lobby Group

When the varnas transformed themselves into ethnic endogamous groups based on birth, they developed their own caste/jati panchayats to decide their own affairs, reducing their dependence on the king. The caste panchayats settled disputes within the caste in an inexpensive and prompt way. They also imparted tremendous social stability. Kings came and went, but the society remained stable in spite of all invasions, wars and political instability. The panchayats looked after the welfare of the members of their castes in a decentralised way. The caste system provided a mechanism for decentralised democracy. Though this mechanism provided stability, it also made at least the medieval Hindu society more conservative. The panchayats strictly discouraged inter-caste marriages and severely punished elopement in love affairs, because inter-caste marriages had the potential of weakening caste-panchayats.

The separation of caste from caste was made more rigid. The hold of caste panchayats, though weakened considerably after independence, has not vanished at least in a few cases. We still hear news reports of lovers across castes intending to marry driven to suicide. This is more common in rural India, including the so-called low castes and untouchables. The continued hold of caste panchayats is ensured by continued dependence of families on members of their caste during birth, wedding and death, and excommunication by caste panchayat is still considered a matter of terrible disgrace and shame. Caste panchayats or their more modern avatar-caste lobbies-are simply instruments to preserve caste identities or ethnic identities, to seek concessions from or make demands on the larger society or the state. In this form, they are completely disjointed from the traditional notions of ritual status, purity and pollution.

Ecological Role

There is also an ecological dimension to the caste system, brought out by Madhav Gadgil in 1983. The caste system performed an important function of reducing competition for and avoiding overexploitation of natural resources. Only fishermen caste could go for fishing, and their caste panchayats evolved rules for sustainable exploitation of fisheries. Only hunters' caste could go for hunting wildlife in the forests, except the king who did it occasionally for pleasure and also to kill man-eating tigers, which intruded into villages. Only chamar or cobbler caste had the right to the dead animals and their skin. Caste panchayats evolved rules for restricting hunting in particular seasons, or particular animals so that wild life is protected and not driven to extinction. Certain forest areas known as sacred groves (known as 'devara kadu' in Kannada, or 'dev-ran' in Marathi, or 'pavithra-vana' in Sanskrit) were out of bounds for any hunting or even cutting green trees. The caste system also functioned in a way so as to control the growth of population by creating barriers for marriage. After giving several illustrations, Madhav Gadgil observes: The caste society had thus developed two special mechanisms to regulate the exploitation of natural resources. The occupational specialisation of each caste ensured that any particular resource was primarily if not exclusively utilised by one particular caste. The intra-caste territoriality then spread the exploitation evenly over geographical regions.

Gadgil points out both positive and negative ways 'of viewing this ecological steady state': It may be viewed positively as a desirable state of man living in balance with nature. Alternatively, it may be viewed negatively as a state of stagnation. For if the resources are used in a balanced fashion, there would be no pressures for cultural change and technological innovation. This is no doubt what happened and the Indian society remained largely balanced (or stagnant!) freezing its caste system for perhaps two and half millennia between the time of Buddha when the agricultural colonisation of much of the subcontinent was complete and the beginning of the British rule. But value judgments apart, an important consequence of the Indian caste system was this attainment of ecological approximate steady state.

Security of Livelihood and Employment

An important feature of caste system was its localised system of production based on jatiwise division of labour for meeting local needs, rather than the needs of the larger market. As M N Srinivas explains in a posthumously published article, the base of this localised production was not necessarily a village, but a cluster of neighbouring villages, each cluster having one or more "weekly markets, where villagers and itinerant traders would gather to exchange goods, or buy paying cash. The cluster could claim a large degree of self-sufficiency as far as the production of basic needs was concerned..." In most parts of the India, there developed a system of making annual payments in kind or cash, as soon as harvesting was done, for services rendered by village artisans, barbers, washermen, agricultural labourers and the like.

The system of payment was not on piece-work, but involved the principle that taking care of the artisans and labourers and their basic needs was the responsibility of land owning families. Whenever there were special occasions of urgent need such as marriage, the working class families were given special help. M N Srinivas refers to different names of this system in different parts of India: "jajmani in the north, bara balute in Maharashtra, 'mirasi' in Madras, 'adade' in Mysore. The relationship between the jajman and his kamin is unequal, since the latter is regarded as inferior". The continuing tensions between land owning communities and communities which traditionally were subservient, resulting sometimes into atrocities against the latter owe their origin to this patron-client relationship and its breakdown, rather than to any canonical support to caste system.

This institution in the past at least recognised the right to work and livelihood, and in the process controlled competition. The relationship between patron and client extended beyond generations, and in the traditional system at least, it was not open to a landlord to prefer a new client merely because he charged lower for the services offered. Nor could the client seek alternative employment outside his traditional patron for a higher wage-at least not when his services were needed by his patron. It was the obligation of the patron that the client and his family did not starve. The much maligned 'Apasthambha Dharmasutra' even says that if an unexpected guest comes and there is limited food, the head of the family and his family members have to cut down their own food, but not that of the servants. The latter have to have their proper meal. The guest should not be fed at the expense of servants.

The system was certainly not an ideal one without blemish. All the shortcomings resulting from patron-client relationship, curbing competition and subsistence oriented production followed from the system. In conditions of frequent droughts and high political instability since the medieval age, what mattered most was food security, more than growth. Yet, even under this system, arts and crafts flourished made possible by specialisation and division of labour, especially under political patronage, as happened for example under the Vijayanagara kings and Mughal emperors. It was no wonder that caste system survived under such security. Neither the Muslim rulers nor the British interfered with the system. Many Hindus may have been converted, but the caste system was imbibed into the new religions of Islam and Christianity in India, since the jajmani system and other functions of caste system had nothing to do with religion.

COLLAPSE OF CASTE AS A SYSTEM

A posthumously published paper by M N Srinivas (2003) carries the assertive title-'An Obituary on Caste as a System'. Paradoxically, the system has expired but caste identities remain and show no sign of going. It looks, caste system is dead but its ghost remains. Caste as a system is taken to mean by Srinivas as involving mainly its localised social production base, subsistence economy, and jati (caste) based occupations. Caste as a system, however, covers all the features listed in the beginning of this paper and its functions listed in the preceding Section VIII. Srinivas refers specifically to the last function discussed here. But other functions also were no less significant in determining the structure of the system. Caste as a system has collapsed today because all its functions have collapsed. It has lost whatever relevance, role, utility and justification it may have had. Several factors contributed to the collapse of the system-ethical, political social, economic and technological.

Though the system gave some stability and even security, it lost on the side of humaneness and social justice. All kinds of indignities were imposed on lower castes, their access to learning was barred, and they were pushed to unenviable and inhuman positions. It was thus that the caste system, particularly its extreme form-untouchability, became disgraced and condemned right from Buddha's time, and again from the medieval age, and then again in the modern times. The functional significance of the caste system also vanished, making its collapse all the more inevitable.

A major factor is the emergence of the modern state as a much stronger, much more powerful and pervasive institution than it ever was with its different wings-the executive, judiciary and legislature, able to exercise powers on all. Hinduism has accepted the emergence of the modern state to enact its own laws, including personal laws, and the sphere of dharmic laws regulating the conduct of people in day-to-day life has shrunk very significantly. There is thus no need for either dharmashastras which served as de facto legislation in dharmic matters, nor for caste panchayats which acted as judiciary. To the extent that their role still continues, it is much less powerful and is superceded by the role of the state. For the same reason, the role of the varna system in providing a system of checks and balances also has vanished. The legally enacted constitution, accepted by all, provides now a system of checks and balances to maintain equilibrium and stability.

Since in the bargain, decentralised democracy of the caste system has broken down, a new type of decentralised democracy, which is village based, has taken its place. It does not need any authentication by religion, but is backed by the Constitution and state power, which is more important. For some time, the dominant castes (which are not the same as ritually upper castes) may try to hijack the village panchayats, but it is a losing battle. The system of reservation for backward castes and untouchables and also for women will gradually but definitely reduce the role of dominant castes. The secular and inclusive forces will prevail over the caste forces before long, even if they have not already done so in some areas. The political consensus against caste system and the power of adult franchise in democracy will ensure the success of democratic and secular forces and defeat caste forces. The next factor, which worked against the caste system, was the rise of modern secular education.

Education need not be and is not family-based though family education will supplement outside education. It is in schools and colleges including trade schools, professional colleges and polytechnics that skills and education are provided. Thus the need for hereditary occupation is now redundant, and social mobility will be much more. The need for hereditary principle in occupation is now redundant also because of the rise of new occupations and the extinction of several old occupations. The dynamics of the growth of diversity of occupations is such that the hereditary principle looks totally outdated and nonsensical. The information age has thrown up an opening for new occupations, which cannot be classified into the sphere of the four traditional varnas. It is wrong to interpret that all the intellectual tasks were assigned exclusively to brahmins in the traditional varna system. Brahmins had no monopoly of intellect even if they had some monopoly to study the Vedas and officiate as priests. Even the monopoly as priests has been broken, with different jatis arranging their own priests from outside the caste of brahmins and evolving their own rituals.

The institutions started by Shri Narayana Guru and Mata Amritanandamayi have been training priests from all castes including women. The exclusive role of brahmins in conducting rituals and ceremonies is highly exaggerated. In any case, it could not have been exclusively intellectual, because every task-regal, warfare, agriculture, arts and crafts required the role of intellect. This is even more so in the modern age, particularly the information age, under which every sector demands the role of intellect and information and not one sector alone. The reason why this point is elaborated is because the new intellectual tasks of the information age cannot be mechanically interpreted as brahmanical. Can we say that the study and research in medicine fits into Brahmin varna, but practice of medicine into shudra varna? How can we separate the two?

Just as new professions and occupations emerged, quite a few old occupations have vanished. Some of them have moved right into homes and do not any longer require specialised occupations and caste groups, thanks mainly to technological change. The system of toilets has undergone a revolutionary change during the last 50 years even in rural areas, making it totally unnecessary to handle human waste and carry it on head as in the past. Toilets have moved inside the homes now, and family members themselves clean them. Several tasks which were considered as dirty and polluting need not be done now directly by hand, and can be handled by tools and machines. It is now possible to be clean and hygienic even while handling the so-called dirty tasks. Thus any rationale for separate castes for doing dirty jobs and for isolating them is now totally lost.

Alvin Toffler (1980) in his book, The Third Wave, has pointed out to the recent phenomenon of what he calls the 'prosuming' or 'prosumer', occasioned by the blurring line between producing and consuming. This refers to 'do-it-yourself' kits and self-service, which is becoming more prominent. From furniture pieces to cars to computers, several things are supplied with step-by-step instructions for assembling them at homes. This has reduced the cost to producer and the price to consumers. What is more, the consumer enjoys the thrill of doing it oneself, of creating some thing. This phenomenon is not limited to commodities and has invaded services too. Thus, we do the daily shave ourselves with safety razor, taking over a part of the task of barber. Many of us, with or without washing machines, wash our clothes ourselves and iron them too. The social significance of all this is that the old wall of distinction between artisans and arm-chair consumer is falling apart. The old division of labour separating manual tasks from the intellectual is losing its meaning. In this context, Arvind Sharma's reinterpretation of the purusha sukta in the 10th mandala of Rig Veda is of interest.

According to Sharma, the reference here need not be to social structure as such, but to combining in the same individual different duties one has to perform during one's life,-learning, helping in the management or governance of the community and the country as in a democracy (voter being the king) including offering militancy service when needed, participation in economic or professional activities and service to society including manual labour (for one's own benefit and for the society). In his words: 'The idea is that all varnas are contained in every individual from now on instead of every individual being comprised within one of the varnas'.

M N Srinivas (2003) refers to a combination of new forces in operation, responsible for the destruction of the caste system.

These forces have led to the breakdown of the caste-based mode of social production in turn leading to the collapse of the caste system. The new forces are breakdown of the Jajmani System, emergence of the larger market and decline of the village based subsistence production, urbanisation, and above all the rise of democracy based on adult franchise. Along with these, there is widespread acceptance of new values-equality, self-respect, and human dignity. He cites several instances of how village artisan based production has given place to factory production-mass produced edible oil replacing the oil-seed pressing caste, factory produced plastic and aluminum vessels replacing the village potter caste, urban textiles replacing the village weaver and so on. Srinivas observes significantly: "The moral is that ideological attacks on hierarchy and brahmanical claims to supremacy failed to create an egalitarian social order since at the local level the production of basic needs was intrinsically bound up with jati".

Last, the caste system has also lost its ecological role and relevance, as observed by Madhav Gadgil himself in the same paper in which he pointed out this role of the caste system. The resources under the control of local communities have been depleted significantly, thanks to their take over by the state and their exploitation by the larger market forces. "Thus alienated from their ecological resource base which was depleting rapidly, the Indian caste society was rudely thrown out of the ecological steady state maintained perhaps for more than a hundred generations".

The recent attempts at regeneration of local natural resources through local committees under schemes like Joint Forest Management, are not based on caste but are secular. Moreover, with the breakdown of social base of production, it is doubtful if the caste-based occupations will ever get a new lease of life. It is evident from the above analysis that the emergence as well as survival of the caste system had nothing to do with Hinduism as a religion. The caste system was purely social phenomenon, very much in the mundane sphere. It is Aihika sphere (mundane), and not Paramarthika or Adhyatmika (spiritual). Being in Aihika sphere, rules of conduct and custom are liable to change from time to time, and not eternally fixed, as Hindu texts themselves concede.

The support to it given by dharmashastras including Manusmrti could be only a result of the social significance and role of the caste system of the time, and not the cause of it. Dharmashastras reflected what is already there in the society. They also approved rejection of it like when Manusmrti (IV 176) indicated clearly that any dharmic rule could be rejected if it led to people's unhappiness and indignation. There can be no ground for fear that dharmashastras would give a new lease of life to the caste system inspite of its being redundant and irrelevant in the modern age. Most of the verses in dharmashastras have themselves become irrelevant, at least those parts supporting caste system.

On the other hand, the collapse of the caste system would also pose no threat to the continuation and survival of Hinduism. Hinduism has been thriving with renewed vigour thanks to such leaders as Satya Sai Baba, Mata Amritanandamayi and Sri Sri Ravishankar, and institutions like Ramakrishna Mission, Brahmakumaris and ISKON on an entirely non-caste basis. This is because caste is not intrinsic to basic principles and tenets of Hinduism as enshrined in Hindu canon. Hinduism itself has fought and is still fighting against casteism in a significant way. If caste system were intrinsic to Hinduism, Shri Narayana Guru and Mata Amritanandamayi would not have worked within the framework of Hinduism.

10 The Revolt of the Untouchables

MOVEMENT OF THE UNTOUCHABLES

The movement of the Untouchables against the injustice of the Hindu Social Order has a long history behind it, especially in Maharashtra. This history falls into two stages. The first stage was marked by petitions and protests. The second stage is marked by open revolt in the form of direct action against the Hindu Established Order. This change of attitude was due to two circumstances. In the first place it was due to the realisation that the petitions and protests had failed to move the Hindus. In the second place Governments had declared that all public utilities and public institutions are open to all citizens including the Untouchables. The right to wear any kind of clothes or ornaments are some of the rights which the British Indian Law gives to the Untouchables along with the rest. To these were added the rights to the use of public utilities and institutions, such as wells, schools, buses, trams.

Railways, Public offices, etc., were now put beyond the pale of doubt. But owing to the opposition of the Hindus the Untouchables cannot make any use of them. It is to meet the situation, the Untouchables decided to change the methods and to direct action to redress their wrongs. This change took place about 1920. Of such attempts at direct action only few can be mentioned so as to give an idea of the revolt of the Untouchables against the Hindu Social Order. Of the attempts made to vindicate the right to use the public roads, it is enough to mention one, most noteworthy attempt in this behalf was that made by the Untouchables of Travencore State in 1924 to obtain the use of the roads which skirted the temple *at* Vaikorn. These roads were public roads maintained by the State for the use of everybody, but on account of their proximity to the temple building, the Untouchables were not allowed to use certain sections, which skirted the temple too closely. Ultimately as a result of Satyagraha, the temple compound was enlarged and the road was realigned so that there the Untouchables even if they used it were no longer within the polluting distance of the temple. Of the attempts made to vindicate the right to take water from the public watering places, it is enough to mention the case of the Chawdar Tank.

This Chawdar Tank is situated in the town of Mahad in the Kolaba District of Bombay Presidency. The tank is a vast expanse of water mainly fed by the rains and a few natural springs. The sides of the tank are embanked. Around the tank there are small strips of land on all sides belonging to private individuals. Beyond this strip of land lies the Municipal road which surrounds the tank and beyond the road are houses owned by the Touchables. The tank lies in the heart of the Hindu quarters and is surrounded by Hindu residence. This tank is an old one and no one knows who built it or when it was built. But in 1869 when a Municipality was established by the Government for the town of Mahad, it was handed over to the Municipality by the Government and has since then been treated as a Municipal *i.e.,* public tank. Mahad is a business centre.

It is also the headquarters of a taluk. The Untouchables either for purposes of doing their shopping and also for the purpose of their duty as village servants had to come to Mahad to deliver to the taluka officer either the correspondence sent by village officials or to pay Government revenue collected by village officials. The Chawdar tank was the only public tank from which an outsider could get water. But the Untouchables were not allowed to take water from this tank. The only source of water for the Untouchables was the well in the Untouchables quarters in the town of Mahad. This well was at some distance from the centre of the town. It was quite choked on account of its neglect by the Municipality. The Untouchables therefore were suffering a great hardship in the matter of water. This continued till matters got going. In 1923 the Legislative Council of Bombay passed a resolution to the effect that the Untouchable classes be allowed to use all public watering places, wells, Dharmashalas which are built and maintained out of public funds, or are administered by bodies appointed by Government or created by Statutes as well as public schools, courts, offices and dispensaries. Government accepted the resolution and issued the following orders: "In pursuance of the foregoing Council Resolution the Government of Bombay are pleased to direct that all heads of offices should give effect to the resolution so far as it related to the public places, institutions belonging to and maintained by Government. The Collectors should be requested to advise the local bodies in their jurisdiction to consider the desirability of accepting the recommendations made in the Resolution."

In accordance with this order of the Government, the Collector of Kolaba forwarded a copy thereof to the Mahad Municipality for consideration. The Mahad Municipality passed a resolution on 5th January 1924 to the effect that the Municipality had no objection to allow the Untouchables to use the tank. Soon after this resolution was passed there was held at Mahad, a Conference of Untouchables of the Kolaba District over which I presided. The Conference met for two days, the 18th and 20th March 1927. This was the first Conference of the Untouchables held in the Kolaba District. Over 2,500 Untouchables attended the Conference and there was great enthusiasm. On the first day of the Conference, I delivered my presidential address, in which I exhorted them to fight for their rights, give up their dirty and vicious habits and rise to full manhood. Thereafter high caste Hindus who were present and, who held out that they were the friends of the Untouchables, addressed the gathering and told the Untouchables to be bold and exercise the right that is given to them by law.

With this, the proceedings of the first day were closed. The subject committee met at night to consider the resolution to be moved in open conference the next day. In the Subject Committee, attention was drawn by some people to the fact that there was great difficulty at Mahad for the Untouchables in the matter of obtaining water for drinking purposes, and that this difficulty was felt particularly by the members of the Reception Committee of the Conference which had to spend Rs. 15 an enormous amount to employ caste Hindus to dole out water in sufficient quantity to satisfy the needs of those who had attended the Conference. Next day on the 20th, the Conference met about 9 in the morning. The resolutions agreed upon in the Subject Committee were moved and passed by the Conference.

It took about three hours in all. In the end one of my co-workers in moving a vote of thanks to the President and others who had helped to make the Conference a success referred to the question of the difficulty in the matter of getting water and exhorted the Untouchables present to go to the tank and exercise their right to take water from Chawdar tank, especially as the Municipality had by resolution declared it open to the Untouchables and that their Hindu friends were ready to help them. The Hindus who had exhorted them to be bold and begin fearlessly to exercise their rights, instantly realised that this was a bombshell and immediately ran away. But the effect upon the Untouchables was very different. They were electrified by this call to arms. To a man they rose and the body of 2,500 Untouchables led by me and my co-workers marched in a procession through the main streets. The news spread like wild fire while crowds thronged the streets to witness it. The Hindu inhabitants of the town saw the scene.

They were taken by storm. They stood aghast witnessing this scene which they had never seen before. For the moment they seemed to be stunned and paralysed. The procession in form of fours marched past and went to the Chawdar tank, and the Untouchables for the first time drank the water. Soon the Hindus, realising what had happened, went into frenzy and committed all sorts of atrocities upon the Untouchables who had dared to pollute the water. These atrocities will be narrated in their proper places. The assault committed by the Hindus on the Untouchables at Mahad when they entered the Chawdar tank was undoubtedly a challenge to the Untouchables. The Untouchables on the other hand were determined not to be satisfied with merely exercising their right but to see it established. They naturally felt that they must take up the challenge thrown at them by the Hindus.

Accordingly a second Conference of the Untouchables was called. The Untouchables were told that they must come fully prepared for all eventualities for Satyagraha (*i.e.*, for civil disobedience and even for going to gaol). The Hindus, when they came to know of this, applied to the District Magistrate of Kolaba for issuing an order under Section 144 of the Criminal Procedure Code against the Untouchables, prohibiting them from entering the Chawdar Tank and polluting its water. The District Magistrate refused and said that the tank was a public tank open to all citizens and he could not by law prevent the Untouchables from taking water therefrom. He advised them to go to a Court of law and get their right of exclusive user established. The dates fixed for the Conference were 25th, 26th, 27th of December 1927.

As these dates drew near, and as they heard that the Untouchables were quite in earnest, and knowing that the District Magistrate had refused to come to their rescue, they did the only thing that was open to them, namely, to get their right to exclude the Untouchables from a public tank established by law. Accordingly, nine Hindus drawn from different castes joined as Plaintiffs in filing on 12th December 1927 a suit No. 405 of 1927 as representatives of the Hindus, in the Court of Sub-Judge of Mahad. I and four others were made defendants as representing the Untouchables. The suit was for obtaining a declaration 'that the said Chawdar tank is of the nature of private property of the Touchable classes only and that the Untouchable classes have no right to go to that tank nor take water therefrom and also for obtaining a perpetual injunction restraining the defendants from doing any of those acts.' On the same day on which the suit was filed, the plaintiffs applied to the Court for a temporary injunction against the defendants restraining them from going to the tank and taking water therefrom pending the decision of the suit. The judge holding that it was a fit case, granted a temporary injunction against me and the other defendants on the 14th December 1927.

The temporary injunction issued by the Judge was sent to Bombay and was served upon me two or three days before the Conferences actually met. There was no time to have consultation and no time to postpone the Conference either. I decided to leave the matter to the Conference to decide. The Conference was called with the specific object of establishing the right to take water from the tank, which was challenged by the Hindus last time. The District Magistrate had left the way open. But here was a Judge who had issued an order banning such action. Naturally, when the Conference met, the first question it was called on to consider was whether to disobey the order of injunction issued by the Court and enter the tank. The District Magistrate who had been favourable to the Untouchables now took a different view.

He explained his view very clearly to the Conference, which he came and addressed personally. He said that if the Civil Court had not issued an injunction, he would have helped the Untouchables in their attempt to enter the tank as against the caste Hindus, but that as the Sub-Judge had issued his order, his position had become different. He could not allow the Untouchables to go to the tank because such an act would amount indirectly to help them to break the order of His Majesty's Court with impunity. He therefore felt bound to issue an order prohibiting the Untouchables, should they insist on going to the tank notwithstanding the injunction not because he wanted to favour the Hindus but because he was bound to maintain the dignity of the Civil Court by seeing to it that its order was respected. The Conference took what the Collector had said into its consideration and also the reaction of the Hindus to the attempt of the Untouchables going to the tank in defiance of the order of the Court, which they had obtained. In the end, the Conference came to the conclusion that it was better and safer for them to follow law and see how far it helped them to secure their rights. It was therefore decided to suspend civil disobedience of the order of the Judge till the final decision of the suit.

The occasion for civil disobedience never came because the Untouchables won the suit and the Hindus lost it. One of the principal reasons which led the Untouchables to follow law and suspend civil disobedience was that they wanted to have a judicial pronouncement on the issue whether the custom of untouchability can be recognised by the Court of law as valid. The rule of law is that a custom to be valid must be immemorial, must be certain and must not be opposed to morality or public policy. The Untouchables' view is that it is a custom which is opposed to morality and public policy. But it is no use unless it is declared to be so by a judicial tribunal. Such a decision declaring the invalidity of the custom of untouchability would be of great value to the Untouchables in their fight for civil rights because it would seem illegal to import untouchability in civic matters. The victory of the Untouchables in the Chawdar tank dispute was very great. But it was disappointing in one way that the Bombay High Court did not decide the issue whether the custom of untouchability was valid or not. They decided the case against the Hindus on the ground that they failed to prove that the custom alleged by them in respect of the tank was not immemorial. They held that the custom itself was not proved. The tank became open to the Untouchables. But the Untouchables cannot be said to have gained their point. The main issue was whether the custom of untouchability was a legal custom. Unfortunately the High Court avoided to give judgement on that issue. The Untouchables had to continue their struggle. The next item in this history of direct action which is worthy of mention relates to the entry in the famous Hindu Temple at Nasik known as the Kala Ram Temple. These are instances of direct action aimed to achieve specific objects. The movement includes two cases of direct action aimed at the demolition of the Hindu Social Order by applying dynamite to its very foundations. One is the burning of the Manusmriti and the second is the mass refusal by the Untouchables to lift the dead cattles belonging to the Hindus and to skin them.

The Burning of Manusmriti took place at Mahad on the 20th of December 1927. The function was a part of the campaign for establishing the right to take water from the Chawdar tank. The Burning of the Manusmriti took place publicly and openly in a Conference of Untouchables. Before burning the Manusmriti, the Conference passed certain resolutions. As these resolutions form a land mark in the history of the movement of the Untouchables they are given below:

Resolution No. 1

Declaration of the Rights of a Hindu: This conference is firmly of opinion that the present deplorable condition of the Hindu Community is only an illustration of how a community becomes fallen by reason of its tolerating social injustice, following erroneous religious beliefs and supporting economic wrongs. The fall of the Hindu community is due entirely to the fact that the masses have not cared to know what are the birth-rights of a human being and much less have they cared to see that they are recognised and not set at naught the base acts and deeds of selfish people. To know what are these birth-rights of man and to endeavour to see that they are not trampled upon in the struggle between man and man and class and class, are the sacred duties of every person. In order that every Hindu may not know what are in the opinion of the Conference the inalienable birthrights of man, this Conference resolves to issue the following proclamation containing a list thereof:

(i) All Hindus have the same social status from birth. This equality of social status is an attribute, which they retain till death. There may be distinctions and differences between them in point of their functions in society. But that must not cause differences in their social status. This Conference is therefore opposed to any action—whether in the political, economic or social field of life— which would result in producing a difference in social status.

(ii) The ultimate aim of all political, economic or social changes should be to maintain intact the equal status of all Hindus. That being the view of the Conference, the Conference strongly disapproves of all literature of the Hindus, whether ancient or modern, which supports in any way the pernicious doctrine of inequality underlying the Hindu social system.

(iii) All power is derived from the people. The privileges claimed by any class or individual have no validity if they are not granted by the people. This Conference therefore repudiates the social and religious privileges enjoyed by some classes of Hindus in as much as they are founded upon the Vedas, Smritis and Puranas and not upon the free consent of the people.

(iv) Every person is entitled as his birthright to liberty of action and speech. This liberty could be limited only for the purpose of saving the right of another person to his liberty and for no other purposes. Further this limitation can be imposed only with the sanction of the people and not by any injunction of the Hindu Shastras. This Conference therefore repudiates all restraints on religious, social and economic freedom imposed upon the thought and action of the Hindus in as much as they are impcsed by the Shastras and not by the people.

(v) Hindus can be deprived of their rights other than their birthrights only by law. What is not prohibited by law, a Hindu must be free to do and what is not obligatory by law, a Hindu must not be forced to do. For this reason there must be no obstruction to persons using public roads, public wells and tanks, public temples and all other public utilities. Persons, causing obstruction in matters where law has laid down no prohibition, are in the opinion of this Conference enemies of the public.

(vi) Law is not a command of an individual or a body of individuals. Law is the peoples prescription for change. That being so, law to be respected, must be made with the consent of ail and must have equal application to all without any distinction. Social divisions if they are necessary for the ends of society can only be made on the basis of worth and not of birth. This Conference repudiates the Hindu caste-system firstly as being detrimental to society, secondly as being based on birth and thirdly as being without any sanction from the people." The Second Resolution passed by the Conference was worked as follows:

Resolution No. 2

Taking into consideration the fact that the laws which are proclaimed in the name of Manu, the Hindu lawgiver, and which are contained in the Manusmriti and which are recognised as the Code for the Hindus are insulting to persons of low caste, are calculated to deprive them of the rights of a human being and crush their personality. Comparing them in the light of the rights of men recognised all over the civilised world, this conference is of opinion that this Manusmriti is not entitled to any respect and is undcserving of being called a sacred book to show its deep and profound contempt for it, the Conference resolves to burn a copy thereof, at the end of the proceedings, as a protest against the system of social inequality it embodies in the guise of religion."

A cursory reading of these resolutions will show the line which the-Conference adopted.

Although the Conference met to redress a particular wrong, it showed that it was not going to be satisfied with the redress of petty wrongs. The Conference felt that the time had arrived for laying down the goal of the Untouchables. The goal laid down by it was far-reaching. The Conference proclaimed that the Untouchables wanted a complete overhauling of the Hindu social system. It proclaimed that this reconstruction must not be on the old foundation of Shastras. It proclaimed that whatever character of the new foundations, they must be consonant with justice and equity between Hindu and Hindu and to leave no doubt that in the matter of this reconstruction, they would not consent to the Hindu shastras being drawn upon. The Conference not only repudiated them but actually went to the length of burning them to ashes.

It was an echo of Voltare's denunciation of the Catholic Church of his time. For the first time a cry was raised against the Hindu Social Order *"Ecraze la Infame"*. It is also clear that these resolutions were absolutely revolutionary in character.

The rock on which the Hindu Social Order has been built is the Manusmriti. It is a part of the Hindu Scriptures and is therefore sacred to all Hindus. Being sacred it is infallible. Every Hindu believes in its sanctity and obeys its injunctions. Manu not only upholds caste and untouchability but gives them a legal sanction. The burning of the Manusmriti was a deed of great daring. It was an attack on the very citadel of Hinduism. The Manusmriti embodied the spirit of inequality which is at the base of Hindu life and thought just as the Bastille was the embodiment of the spirit of the Ancient regime in I France. The burning of the Manusmriti by the Untouchables at Mahad in 1927 is an event which has the same significance and importance in the history of the emancipation of the Untouchables which the Fall of Bastille had in the liberation of the masses in France and Europe. The second instance of direct action against the frame of the Hindu Social Order itself is the refusal to skin the dead animals belonging to the Hindus and carrying them. One often hears the Untouchables being condemned for having brought upon themselves the curse of untouchability. The main ground on which this accusation rests is the adoption by the Untouchables as their occupation, the carrying of the dead animals of the Hindus and skinning them and eating the carrion.

Even so great a friend of the downtrodden as the Abe Dubois writing about the *Pariahs* of the Madras Presidency said: "What chiefly disgusts other natives is the revolting nature of the food which the Pariahs eat. Attracted by the smell, they will collect in crowds round any carrion and contend for the spoil with the dogs, jackals, crows and other carnivorous animals. They then divide the semi-putrid flesh and carry it away to their huts, where they devour it, often without rice or anything else to disguise the flavour. That the animal should have died of disease is of no consequence to them, and they sometimes secretly poison cows or buffaloes so that they may subsequently feast on the foul, putrefying remains. The carcasses of animal's that die in a village belong by right to the *thoti* or scavenger, who sells the flesh at a very low price to the other Pariahs in the neighbourhood. When it is impossible to consume in one day the stock of meat thus obtained, they dry the remainder in the sun, and keep it in their huts until they run short of their food. There are few Pariah houses where one does not see festoons of these horrible fragments hanging up; and though the Pariahs themselves do not seem to be affected by the smell, travellers passing near their village quickly perceive it and can tell at once the caste of the people living there.... Is it to be wondered at, after what has been just stated that other castes should hold this in abhorrence? Can they be blamed for refusing to hold any communication with such savages, or for I obliging them to keep themselves aloof and to live in the separate hamlets?...."

It is true that this occupation has created a feeling of repugnance against the Untouchables in the mind of the Hindus. But the Abe or those who adopt his reasoning forget to raise two very important questions. First is why do the Untouchables eat carrion? Will the Hindus allow the Untouchables the freedom to give up skinning and carrying their dead animals? The answer to the question why the Untouchables eat carrion has already been given in this books. No one would prefer carrion to flesh meat if it is available. If the

Untouchables have been living on carrion it is not because they like it. They eat carrion, because there is nothing else on which they can live. This will be clear to anyone who realises that on account of untouchability they have no way left to earn a living. All professions have been closed to them. There is no land on the produce of which they can live. There is no trade, which they can engage in. Their main stay is therefore the food they collect from the villagers and the carrion, which is left to them. Without carrion they would literally die of starvation. It is therefore clear that the fault does not lie with the Untouchables. If the Untouchables eat carrion it is because the Hindus have left no honourable way of earning a living open to them.

To the second question the answer is equally clear. If the Untouchables skin and carry the dead animals of the Hindus, it is because the Untouchables have no choice. They are forced to do it. They would be penalised if they refused to do it. The penalty is legal. In some provinces the refusal to do this dirty work is a breach of contract. In other provinces it is a criminal offence involving fines. In Provinces like Bombay the Untouchables are village servants. In their capacity as village servants they have to serve the Government as well as the Hindu public. In return for this service they are given lands which they cultivate and on the produce of which they maintain themselves. One of the duties of the Untouchables is to skin and carry the dead animals of the Hindus in the villages. If the Untouchables refuse to perform these duties to the Hindu public, the land which they live on is liable to be confiscated. They have to choose between doing the dirty work or facing starvation.

In Provinces like the United Provinces, refusal to do scavenging by sweeper is made an offence. The United Provinces Municipalities Act II of 1916 contains the following provisions:

Section 201(1).—" Should a sweeper who has a customary right to do the house-scavenging of a house of building (hereinafter called the customary sweeper) fail to perform such scavenging in a proper way, the occupier of the house or building or the board may complain to a Magistrate." (2) "The Magistrate receiving such complaint shall hold an inquiry and should it appear to him that the customary sweeper has failed to perform the house-scavenging of the house or building in a proper way or at a reasonable intervals, he may impose upon such a sweeper a fine which may extend to ten rupees, and upon a second or any later conviction in regard to the same house or building, may also direct, the right of the customary sweeper to do the house scavenging the house or building to be forfeited and thereupon such right shall be forfeited."

Exactly similar provision is to be found in Section 165 of the Punjab Municipalities Act of 1911. The Punjab Act is an advance over the U. P. Act, in as much as it provides for punishment of a sweeper who is not customary sweeper but a contract-sweeper. The Punjab Act adds: "(3) Should any sweeper (other than a customary sweeper), who is under a contract to do house-scavenging of a house or a building, discontinue to do such house-scavenging without fourteen days' notice to his employer or without reasonable cause, he shall on conviction be punishable with a fine which may extend to Rs. ten."

"227. Every order of forfeiture under Section 165 shall be subject to an appeal to the next superior court, but shall not be otherwise open to appeal."

People may be shocked to read that there exists legal provision which sanctions forced labour. Beyond doubt, this is slavery. The difference between slavery and free labour lies in this. Under slavery a breach of contract of service is an offence which is punishable with fine or imprisonment. Under free labour a breach of contract of service is only a civil wrong for which the labourer is liable only for damages. Judged in the light of this criterion, scavenging is a legal obligation imposed upon the Untouchables which they cannot escape. Given these conditions, how can the Untouchables be accused of doing these dirty work voluntarily?

The question whether the Untouchables can be accused of having invited the curse of untouchability upon themselves for doing the dirty work of the Hindus is really beside the point. What is important to note is that the Conference of the Untouchables which met in Mahad resolved that no Untouchable shall skin the dead animals of the Hindus, shall carry it or eat the carrion. The object of these resolutions was two-fold. The one object was to foster among the Untouchables self-respect and self-esteem. This was a minor object. The major object was to strike a blow at the Hindu Social Order. The Hindu Social Order is based upon a division of labour which reserves for the Hindus clean and respectable jobs and assigns to the Untouchables dirty and mean jobs and thereby clothes the Hindus with dignity and heaps ignominy upon the Untouchables. The resolution was a revolt against this part of the Hindu Social Order. It aimed at making the Hindus do their dirty jobs themselves. This is a brief summery of the history of the revolt of the Untouchables against the established order of the Hindu. It originated in Bombay. But it has spread to all parts of India.

A WARNING TO THE UNTOUCHABLES

Revolt and rebellion against the Established order is a natural part of the history of the poor in all countries of the world. A student of their history cannot but be struck by the thought entertained by them, of the way victory would come. In the theological age, the poor lived by the hope that spiritual forces would ultimately make the meek inherit the earth. In the secular age, otherwise called modern times, the poor live by the hope that the forces of historical materialism will automatically rob the strong of their strength and make the weak take their place. In the light of this psychology, when one begins to think of the Untouchables in their role of rebels against the Hindu Social Order one feels like congratulating them on their realization that neither spiritual forces nor historical forces are going to bring the millennium. They know full well that if the Hindu Social Order is to fall to the ground, it can happen only under two conditions. Firstly, the social order must be subjected to constant fire. Secondly, they can't subject it to constant fire unless they are independent of the Hindus in thought and in action. That is why the Untouchables are insistent upon separate electorates and separate settlements.

The Hindus on the other hand are telling the Untouchables to depend upon the Hindus for their emancipation. The Untouchables are told that the general spread of education will make the Hindus act in a rational manner. The Untouchables are told that the constant preaching of reformers against Untouchability is bound to bring about a moral transformation of the Hindus and the quickening of his conscience. The Untouchables should therefore rely on the good will and sense of duty of the Hindus. No Untouchable believes in this facile proposition. If there are any who do, they are hypocrites who are prepared to agree to whatever the Hindus have to say in order that by their grace they may be put in places reserved for the Untouchables.

They are a predatory band of Untouchables who are out to feather their nests by any means open to them. The Untouchables are not deceived by such false propaganda and false hopes. It is therefore unnecessary to comment on it. At the same time, the propaganda is so alluring that it may mislead the unwary Untouchables into being ensnared by it. A warning to the Untouchables is therefore necessary. Two agencies are generally relied upon by the social idealists for producing social justice. One is reason, the other is religion.The rationalist who uphold the mission of reason believe that injustice could be eliminated by the increasing power of intelligence. In the mediaeval age social injustice and superstition were intimately related to each other.

It was natural for the rationalists to believe that the elimination of superstition must result in the abolition of injustice. This belief was encouraged by the results. Today it has become the creed of the educationists, philosophers, psychologists and social scientists who believe that universal education and the development of printing and press would result in an ideal society, in which every individual would be so enlightened that there would be no place for social injustice. History, whether Indian or European, gives no unqualified support to this dogma. In Europe, the old traditions and superstitions which seemed to the eighteenth century to be the very root of injustice, have been eliminated.

Yet social injustice has been rampant and has been growing ever and anon. In India itself, the whole Brahmin community is educated, man, woman and child. How many Brahmins are free from their belief in untouchability? How many have come forward to undertake a crusade against untouchability? How many are prepared to stand by the side of the Untouchables in their fight against injustice? In short, how many are prepared to make the cause of the Untouchables their own cause? The number will be appallingly small. Why does reason fail to bring about social justice? The answer is that reason works so long as it does not come into conflict with one's vested interest. Where it comes into conflict with vested interests, it fails. Many Hindus have a vested interest in untouchability. That, vested interest may take the shape of feeling of social superiority or it may take the shape of economic exploitation such as forced labour or cheap labour, the fact remains that Hindus have a vested interest in untouchability. It is only natural that vested interest should not yield to the dictates of reason. The Untouchables should therefore know that there are limits to what reason can do. The religious moralists who believe in the efficacy of religion urge that the moral insight which religion plants in man whereby it makes him conscious of the sinfulness of his preoccupation with self and thereby of the duty to do justice to his fellows. Nobody can deny that this is the function of religion and to some extent religion may succeed in this mission.

But here again there are limits to what religion can do. Religion can help to produce justice within a community. Religion cannot produce justice between communities. At any rate, religion has failed to produce justice between Negroes and Whites, in the United States. It has failed to produce justice between Germans and French and between them and the other nations. The call of nation and the call of community has proved more powerful than the call of religion for justice.

The Untouchables should bear in mind two things. Firstly, that it is futile to expect the Hindu religion to perform the mission of bringing about social justice. Such a task may be performed by Islam, Christianity, or Buddhism.

The Hindu religion is itself the embodiment of inequity and injustice to the Untouchables. For it, to preach the gospel of justice is to go against its own being. To hope for this is to hope for a miracle. Secondly, assuming that this was a task which Hinduism was fitted to perform, it would be impossible for it to perform. The social barrier between them and the Hindus is much greater than the barrier between the Hindus and their men. Religion, however efficacious it may be within a community or a nation, is quite powerless to break these barriers and (make) them one whole.

Apart from these agencies of reason and religion the Untouchables are asked to trust the enlightened self-interests of the Hindu privileged classes and the fraternity of the Hindu proletarian. As to the privileged classes it be wrong to depend upon for anything more than their agreeing to be benevolent despots. They have their own class interests and they cannot be expected to sacrifice them for general interests or universal values. On the other hand, their constant endeavour is to identify their class interests with general interests and to assume that their privileges are the just payments with which society rewards specially useful and meritorious functions.

They are a poor company to the Untouchables as the Untouchables have found in their conflict with the Hindus. For Untouchables to expect to gain help from the Hindu proletariat is also a vain hope. The appeal of the Indian Communists to the Untouchables for solidarity with the Hindu proletariat is no doubt based on the assumption that the proletarian does not desire advantages for himself which he is not willing to share with others. Is this true? Even in Europe the proletarian are not a uniform class. It is marked by class composition, the higher and the lower. This is reflected in their attitudes towards social change, the higher are reformist and the lower are revolutionary. The assumption therefore is riot true. So far as India is concerned it is positively false. There is very little for a common front. Socially, there is bound to be antagonism between them. Economically, there cannot be much room for alliance. What must the Untouchables strive for?

Two things they must strive for is education and spread of knowledge. The power of the privileged classes rests upon lies which are sedulously propagated among the masses. No resistance to power is possible while the sanctioning lies, which justify that power are accepted as valid. While the lie which is the first and the chief line of defence remains unbroken there can be no revolt. Before any injustice, any abuse or oppression can be resisted, the lie upon which it is founded must be unmasked, must be clearly recognized for what it is. This can happen only with education. The second thing they must strive for is power. It must not be forgotten that there is a real conflict of interests between the

Hindus and the Untouchables and that while reason may mitigate the conflict it can never obviate the necessity of such a conflict. What makes one interest dominant over another is power. That being so, power is needed to destroy power. There may be the problem of how to make the use of power ethical, but there can be no question that without power on one side it is not possible to destroy power on the other side. Power is either economic or political. Military power is no power today. Because it is not free power. The economic power of the working class is the power inherent in the strike. The Untouchables as a part of the working class can have no other economic power. As it is, this power is not adequate for the defence of the interests of the working class. It is maimed by legislation and made subject to injunctions, arbitrations, martial law and use of troops. Much more inadequate is the Untouchables' power to strike.

The Untouchable is therefore under an absolute necessity of acquiring political power as much as possible. Having regard to his increasingly inadequate power in social and economic terms the Untouchable can never acquire too much political power. Whatever degree of political power he acquires, it will always be too little having regard to the vast amount of social, economic and political power of the Hindus. The Untouchable must remember that his political power, no matter how large, will be of no use if he depends for representation in the Legislature on Hindus whose political life is rested in economic and social interests which are directly opposed to those of the Untouchables.

UNTOUCHABILITY AMONG HINDUS

In the matter of pollution there is nothing to distinguish the Hindus from the Primitive or Ancient peoples. That they recognised pollution is abundantly clear from the Manusmriti. Manu recognises physical defilement and also notional defilement. Manu treated birth, death and menstruation as sources of impurity. With regard to death, defilement was very extensive in its range. It followed the rule of consanguinity. Death caused defilement to members of the family of the dead person technically called *Sapindas* and *Samanodakas* It not only included maternal relatives such as maternal uncle but also remote relatives It extended even to nonrelatives such as (1) teacher, (2) teacher's son, (3) teacher's wife, (4) pupi (5) fellow student, (6) Shrotriya, (7) king, (8) friend, (9) members of the household, (10) those who carried the corpse and (11) those who touched the corpse. Anyone within the range of defilement could not escape it. There were only certain persons who were exempt. In the following verses Manu names them and specifies the reasons why he exempts them:

"V.93. The taint of impurity does not fall on kings and those engaged in the performance of a vow, or of a Sattra; for the first are seated on the throne of India, and the (last two are) ever pure like Brahman.

94. For a king, on the throne of magnanimity, immediate purification is prescribed, and the reason for that is that he is seated (there) for the protection of (his) subjects.

95. (The same rule applies to the kinsmen) of those who have fallen in a riot or a battle, (of those who have been killed) by lightning or by the king, and for cows and Brahmins, and to those whom the king wishes to be pure (in spite of impurity).

96. A king is an incarnation of the eight guardian deities of the world, the Moon, the Fire, the Sun, the Wind, Indra, the Lords of wealth and water (Kubera and Varuna) and Yama.

Because the king is pervaded by those lords of the world, no impurity is ordained for him for purity and impurity of mortals is caused and removed by those lords of the world." From this it is clear that the king, the kinsmen of those who have fallen in a noble cause as defined by Manu and those whom the king chose to exempt were not affected by the normal rules of defilement. Manu's statement that the Brahmin was 'ever pure' must be understood in its usual sense of exalting the Brahmin above everything. It must not be understood to mean that the Brahmin was free from defilement. For he was not. Indeed besides being defiled by births and deaths the Brahmin also suffered defilement on grounds which did not affect the Non-Brahmins. The Manusmriti is full of tabus and don'ts which affect only the Brahmins and which he must observe and failure to observe which makes him impure.

The idea of defilement in Manu is real and not merely notional. For he makes the food offered by the polluted person unacceptable. Manu also prescribes the period of defilement. It varies. For the death of a Sapinda it is ten days. For children three days. For fellow students one day. Defilement does not vanish by the mere lapse of the prescribed period. At the end of the period there must be performed a purificatory ceremony appropriate to the occasion.

For the purposes of purification Manu treats the subject of defilement from three aspects:(l) Physical defilement, (2) notional or psychological defilement, and (3) ethical defilement The rule for the purification of ethical defilement which occurs when a person entertains evil thoughts are more admonitions and exhortations. But the rites for the removal of notional and physical defilement are the same. They include the use of water earth cows urine, the kusa grass and ashes Earth, cow's urine, Kusa grass and ashes are prescribed as purificatory agents for removing physical impurities caused by the touch of inanimate objects. Water is the chief agent for the removal of notional defilement. It is used in three ways (1) sipping, (2) bath, and (3) abludon Later on *panchagavya* became the most important agency for removing notional defilement. It consists of a mixture of the five products of the cow, namely, milk, urine, dung, curds and butter.

In Manu there is also provision for getting rid of defilement by transmission through a scapegoat namely by touching the cow or looking at the sun after sipping water. Besides the individual pollution the Hindus believe also in territorial and communal pollution and purification very much like the system that prevailed among the early Romans. Every village has an annual *jatra*. An animal, generally a he buffalo, is purchased on behalf of the village. The animal is taken round the village and is sacrificed, the blood is sprinkled round the village and towards the end toe meat is distributed among the villagers. Every Hindu, every Brahmin even though he may not be a beef eater is bound to accept his share of the meat. This is not mentioned in any of the Smritis but it has the sanction of custom which among the Hindus is so strong that it always overrides law.

If one could stop here, one could well say that the notion of defilement prevalent among the Hindus is not different from that which obtained in Primitive and in Ancient Societies. But one cannot stop here. For there is another form of Untouchability observed by the Hindus which has not yet been set out. It is the hereditary Untouchability of certain communities. So vast is the list of such communities that it would be difficult for an individual with his unaided effort to compile an exhaustive list. Fortunately such a list was prepared by the Government of India in 1935 and is attached to the Orders-in-Council issued under the Government of India Act of 1935. To this Order-in-Council there is attached a Schedule.

The Schedule is divided into nine parts. One part refers to one province and enumerates the castes, races or tribes or parts of or groups within steps which are deemed to be Untouchables in that province either in the whole of that province or part thereof. The list may be taken to be both exhaustive and authentic. To give an idea of the vast number of communities which are regarded as hereditary Untouchables by the Hindus. I reproduce below the list given in the Order-in-Council.

Bibliography

Agarawal, S.: *Dr. B.R. Ambedkar: The Man and his Message: A Commemorative Volume*, Prentice-Hall of India, New Delhi, 1991.

Ainapur, L. S.: *Dynamics of Caste Relations in Rural India*, Rawat Publications, Jaipur, 1986.

Anand, Mulk Raj; and Zelliot: *An Anthology of Dalit Literature*, Gyan Publishing House, New Delhi, 1992.

Anant, S. S.: *Changing Caste Hindu Attitudes Towards Harijans: A Follow Up After Four Years*, Vikas, New Delhi, 1979.

Benjamin, Joseph: *Scheduled Castes in Indian Politics and Society*, Ess Ess Publications, New Delhi, 1989.

Beteille, A.: *The Backward Classes and the New Social Order*, OUP, New Delhi, 1981.

Bhatt, V.: *The Harijans of Maharashtra*, All India Harijan Sevak Sangh, Delhi, 1941.

Bondurant, Joan V.: *Conquest of Violence; The Gandhian Philosophy of Conflict*, University of California Press, Berkeley, 1965.

Chaudhary, S.N.: *Changing Status of Depressed Castes in Contemporary India: Essays in Honour of Professor S.C. Dube*, Daya, Delhi, 1988.

Dietrich, Gabriele: *Dalit Movements and Women's Movement*, Horizons India Books, New Delhi, 1992.

Dubois, Abbe: *Hindu Manners, Customs and Ceremonies*, AES, New Delhi, 1983.

Fisher, F.B.: *Touching the Untouchables, India's Silent Revolution*, MacMillan, New York, 1920.

Forrester, D.: *Caste and Christianity: Attitudes and Policies on Caste of Anglo-Protestant Missions in India*, Curzon, London, 1980.

Ghurye, G. S.: *Caste and Class in India*, Popular Books, Bombay, 1950.

Gore, M.S.: *The Social Context of an Ideology: Ambedkar's Political and Social Thought*, Sage, New Delhi, 1993.

Guru, G.: *Dalit Cultural Movement and the Dialectics of Dalit Politics in Maharashtra*, Vikas Adhyayan Kendra, Mumbai, 1997.

Jadhav, N.: *Dr. Ambedkar's Economic Thought and Philosophy*, Popular Prakashan, Bombay, 1993.

Jatav, D.R.: *Dr. Ambedkar's Role in National Movement*, Boudha Sahitya Samelan, New Delhi, 1979.

Kadam, K.N.: *Dr. B.R. Ambedkar: The Emancipator of the Oppressed*, BR Publishing, Delhi, 1994.

Karve, Irawati: *Hindu Society: An Interpretation*, Sangam Press, Poona, 1961.

Kaul, Rekha: *Caste, Class and Education: Politics of the Capitation Fee Phenomenon in Karnataka*, Sage Publications, New Delhi, 1993.

Keer, D.: *Dr. Ambedkar. Life and Mission*, Popular Prakashan, Bombay, 1954.

Khairmode, C.B.: *Dr. Bhimrao Ramji Ambedkar*, Pratap, Bombay, 1978.

Kuber, W.N.: *Dr. Ambedkar: A Critical Study*, People's Publishing House, New Delhi, 1973.

Lokhande, G.S.: *Bhimrao Ramji Ambedkar: a Study in Social Democracy*, Intellectual Publishing House, New Delhi, 1977.

Marriott, Mckim: *Village India: Studies in the Little Community*, The University of Chicago Press, Chicago, 1955.

Mitter, Sara S.: *Dharma's Daughters: Contemporary Indian Women and Hindu Culture*, Rutgers University Press, NJ, 1991.

Nagaraj, D. R.: *The Flaming Feet: A Study of the Dalit Movement*, South Forum Press, Bangalore, 1993.

Narain, A.K. & Ahir, D.C.: *Dr. Ambedkar, Buddhism and Social Change*, BR Publishing, Delhi, 1993.

Nim, H.L.: *Thoughts on Dr. Ambedkar*, Siddhartha Educational and Cultural Society, Agra, 1969.

Omvedt, G.: *Dalits and the Democratic Revolution: Dr Ambedkar and the Dalit Movement in Colonial India*, Sage, New Delhi, 1994.

Pardeshi, Pratima: *Dr. Babasaheb Ambedkar and the Question of Women's Liberation in India*, University of Pune, Pune, 1998.

Patnaik, Nitayananda: *Caste and Social Change: An Anthropological Study of Three Orissa Villages*, National Institute of Community Development, Hyderabad, 1969.

Prabhavathi, M.: *Dalit Women in Contemporary Indian Situation*, Gyan Publishing House, New Delhi, 1995.

Punekar, S.M.: *Harijan Contribution to Medieval Thought*, Prasaranga, Bangalore University, Bangalore, 1991.

Raju, G.G.: *The Life of B.R. Ambedkar*, Babasaheb Dr. Ambedkar Memorial Society, Hyderabad, 1979.

Rao, Hanumantha G.: *Caste and Poverty: A Case Study of Scheduled Castes in a Delta Village*, Savithri Publication, Mulikipuram, 1977.

Robbin, J.: *Dr. Ambedkar and His Movement*, Dr. Ambedkar Publishing Society, Hyderabad, 1964.

Shabbir, M.: *B.R. Ambedkar. Study in Law & Society*, Rawat, Jaipur, 1997.

Silverberg, James: *Social Mobility in the Caste System in India*, Mouton Publishers, The Hague, 1968.

Singh, S. N.: *Reservation: Problems and Prospects*, Uppal Publishing House, New Delhi, 1987.

Sinha, Archana: *The Social and Political Philosophy of Sarvodaya*, Janaki Prakashan, Patna, 1978.

Suman, R.D.: *Dr. Ambedkar: Pioneer of Human Rights*, Bodhisattva Publications, New Delhi, 1977.

Tope, T.K.: *Dr. B.R. Ambedkar, A Symbol of Social Revolt*, Maharashtra Information Centre, New Delhi, 1964.

Varale, B.H.: *Dr. Babasaheb Ambedkarrancha Sangaki*, Shrividya Prakashan, Pune, 1988.

Viswanadhaam and Reddy, Narashima: *Scheduled Castes: A Study in Educational Achievement*, Scientific Services, Hyderabad, 1985.

Zelliot, Eleanor: *From Untouchable to Dalit: Essays on the Ambedkar Movement*, Manohar, New Delhi, 1992.

Index

♦♦♦